Ending the Seven-Year Itch

The Story of Liverpool's 1972-73 League Championship and UEFA Cup Winning Season

Steven Horton

VERTICAL EDITIONS
www.verticaleditions.com

First published in the United Kingdom in 2012 by Vertical Editions, Unit 4a, Snaygill Industrial Estate, Skipton, North Yorkshire BD23 2QR

www.verticaleditions.com

ISBN 978-1-904091-68-4

A CIP catalogue record for this book is available from the British Library

Cover design by HBA, York

Printed and bound by MPG, Bodmin

Contents

Acknowledgements

This book came about somewhat by accident as it had first been planned to write about the 50th anniversary of the 1961-62 promoiton season. Due to another project I was contracted to and publishing deadlines, it was soon apparent that it would not be possible to release it during the anniversary of the season, so a secondary idea was sought. A 40th anniversary commemoration of 1972-73, when Liverpool FC became the first English club to win the League Championship and a European trophy seemed a logical choice. I have been fascinated by the history of the club since Father Christmas gave me the annual on 25th December 1979, a book which contained the background of all previous title wins. How I didn't go on to wear the tape out on the BBC's *Official History of Liverpool* video, released in 1988 I'll never know, I can still recite it almost word for word. It has been a pleasure researching and writing this book, but it would not have been possible without the following, who I acknowledge in no particular order of importance.

The management and players of Liverpool Football Club for making the 1972-73 season such a year to remember for those fans who were lucky enough to have witnessed it.

The staff of Liverpool Central Library who have preserved the newspapers on microfilm so I have been able to research it and to the reporters of the *Liverpool Echo* and *Daily Post* who recorded the information at the time, as well as those who have posted goals from games on youtube.

Arnie Baldursson and Gudmundur Magnusson for their painstaking work in making a detailed record of every game Liverpool have ever played available online at www.lfchistory.net, which has been an invaluable resource in filling in some gaps.

Fans Peter Etherington, Phil Rimmer and Chris Wood for sharing their experiences of the season with me, with additional thanks to Chris Wood for the meticulous stats checking he has carried out, even to the degree of making sure I got the age of Eintracht Frankfurt's manager right as well as his photographs from the second leg of the UEFA Cup final.

Phil Thompson for sparing a couple of hours to have a chat regarding his memories of the season.

Rob Gowers from the Liverpool Programme Club and Hyder Jawad for providing me with scans of memorabilia from the season.

Anfield stadium announcer George Sephton for providing me with his memories regarding this season.

Karl Waddicor from Vertical Editions for believing in this book and publishing it.

Karen Gill for writing the foreword.

Mark Platt whose own books regarding other memorable seasons have provided an inspiration for this one and for his support and encouragement to me regarding this project.

Finally to my wife Lynne and son Luke for supporting me during the writing of the book and my long departed nan Hilda for making sure I supported Liverpool FC and taking me to my first games.

Steven Horton

Foreword

In 1972-73 my granddad was named Manager of the Year. It was a great accolade. It's an award any manager would be proud of and he was. As he said, 'It's the manager who gets the kicks when things are going wrong, it is perhaps acceptable to collect the bouquets when things go well'. However, this was not what would make that season so memorable for him. What was much more important, in fact something he would never forget, was the success of his young team, young men who in his words 'played like veterans'. It really had been worth the wait and seven year drought of trophies. This was a real affirmation of his abilities as a manager. This was worth much more than any award.

My own memories of my granddad begin to come alive at this time too. I was eight years old in 1973. This was a time when wherever we went he would be followed and then swallowed up in a crowd of adoring supporters. It was impossible for an eight year old to understand, but something I have come to comprehend over the years. My granddad made great sacrifices for Liverpool Football Club, but his achievements were also great. That 1972-73 season was the epitome of those achievements and a year later he was to retire. It is of some consolation to me that he had the best of memories to cheer him in his retirement and an incredible legacy to leave behind.

Karen Gill (Granddaughter of Bill Shankly)

1

The Decline and Break-up of the Great 1960s Side

On 30th April 1966 Liverpool beat Chelsea 2-1 at Anfield to become champions of the Football League. It was their second title in just three years with an FA Cup sandwiched in between and coming just four years after promotion from the Second Division. Kopites could be forgiven for thinking the trophies would never end.

With Bill Shankly in charge there seemed no limit to what could be achieved as the Reds had also gone agonisingly close in Europe twice, losing the 1965 European Cup semi-final 4-3 on aggregate to Inter Milan in hugely controversial circumstances and then going down 2-1 in the 1966 Cup Winners Cup final against Borussia Dortmund. However, as the decade went on there was frustration for Reds fans as they failed to capitalise on promising starts and fell off the pace in the title race, suffered some disappointing exits in Europe and big name signings failed to live up to expectations.

In 1966-67 it looked to be business as usual for the first two-thirds of the season as Liverpool were well in the running to secure their first back-to-back titles since 1922 and 1923. A 1-0 win at Anfield over Aston Villa kept the Reds a point clear of Manchester United on 11th February, although United did have a game in hand. Two weeks later, the Reds dropped to second on goal average after a 2-2 draw at Fulham but on 4th March they returned top with a 2-1 home win over Stoke as United were held 1-1 at Arsenal. The only disappointment so far had come in Europe where the Reds were hammered 5-1 by Ajax in foggy Amsterdam. The result was dismissed as a fluke by Shankly and 53,846 packed into Anfield for the return leg to see if the Reds could overturn the deficit. Had Peter Thompson's first minute effort gone in and not hit the bar things may have been different but a classy Ajax side, with a young Johann Cruyff being in excellent form, returned home with a 2-2 draw.

The turning point of 1966-67 came on 11th March 1967 at Goodison Park when Liverpool faced Everton in an FA Cup fifth round tie. The game captivated the imagination of the Merseyside public and eight giant screens were erected at Anfield for fans who couldn't get a ticket to watch it on closed circuit television there. The *Liverpool Echo* reported that ground tickets with a face value of five shillings were fetching as much as £5 on the black market and the Liverpool City Police were conducting the biggest traffic control operation the city had ever seen. 40,149 watched on giant screens at Anfield in addition to the 64,851 inside Goodison but the game, which was ruined by a gale, failed to live up to expectations. The Reds barely managed a shot on goal as Alan Ball's effort was enough to take Everton into the sixth round.

Following on from the cup defeat the next five league games saw three draws and two defeats, including a 0-0 stalemate with United at Anfield, as the Reds slipped to third in the table. On 1st April they were five points behind United with six games to go, and with only two points on offer for a win only the most optimistic of Kopites were predicting title success by now. By the time United sealed the championship with a 6-1 win at West Ham in their penultimate game the Reds lingering hopes had long gone as they stumbled over the finishing line, losing three of their last five games. The nadir came on the last day of the season when already relegated Blackpool won 3-1 at Anfield, leaving the Reds to finish in fifth place. The attendance was just 28,773, only the second time the crowd had dipped below 40,000 all season (the previous being 39,883) as fans voted with their feet.

The summer of 1967 saw only one major incoming transfer, as Tony Hateley was signed from Chelsea for a club record £96,000. A tall and powerful centre forward, Hateley took over the number 9 shirt with Ian St John moving to a deeper role and Willie Stevenson losing his place in the side. Emlyn Hughes, who had forced his way into the team midway through 1966-67 after signing from Blackpool, kept his place with Gordon Milne continuing to miss out. Otherwise the other nine players who Shankly saw as his best line up had all played in the 1965 FA Cup final.

The Reds began the season well, Hateley hitting a hat trick in a 6-0 home win over Newcastle United in the third game. Apart from one week in early October, they led the league table until 11th November, when Manchester United won 2-1 at Anfield to go above them. Liverpool and Leeds United clung to Manchester United's coat tails for three months but two successive defeats in early February against Everton and Chelsea saw them fall five points behind the leaders. These had come just after a major blow was suffered when Gerry Byrne was seriously injured in an FA Cup tie at Bournemouth.

The Reds rallied and went five games unbeaten, a 2-1 win at Old Trafford on 6th April lifting them to within two points of new leaders Leeds in what was developing into a thrilling four horse race, Manchester City having also forced themselves into the mix. However this good work was undone the following week when relegation threatened Sheffield United won 2-1 at Anfield on Good Friday. On 20th April an exhausted side lost 1-0 at West Ham, a defeat that looked to have ended their title hopes completely. It was their fifth game in nine days, coming less than 48 hours after an FA Cup sixth round second replay defeat against West Bromwich Albion at Maine Road.

This left Liverpool fourth in the table, six points behind Manchester United and although the Reds had games in hand on all the teams above them, it wasn't enough to overhaul them and they also had inferior goal average.

On 29th April Manchester United were surprisingly beaten 6-3 by West Bromwich Albion but Liverpool failed to take advantage as they could only draw 1-1 with Tottenham Hotspur at Anfield. On that night Manchester City hit the top for only the second time that season and although the two Manchester clubs were neck and neck on 54 points with two games to play, Leeds were the new title favourites. They were a point behind with a game in hand, with the Reds a further two adrift also with a game in hand. However the following Saturday Liverpool beat Leeds 2-1 at Elland Road to hand the initiative back to the Manchester clubs and give themselves an outside chance.

Going into the final day of the regular season on 11th May the Reds knew that if they beat Nottingham Forest and both Manchester clubs lost, then they could pinch the title with a win in their final game at Stoke four days later – providing Leeds also dropped points in one of their last two games. It's hard to imagine how the media today would build up an end to the season where four teams all had a chance of winning the title on the last day but Liverpool's fans weren't showing any false optimism. Just 38,850 (8,000 lower than the average for the season) turned up to see them do their bit by thrashing Forest 6-1 but it was all in vain as Manchester City won 4-3 at Newcastle to clinch the title. A 2-1 defeat for Manchester United by Sunderland on the last day had given the Reds a chance of finishing second but they lost their last game 2-1 at Stoke and had to settle for third. It was enough for another crack at European competition though, 1967-68 having ended in disappointment again as Ferencvaros won both legs of a third round Fairs Cup tie 1-0, becoming the first continental side to win at Anfield.

Going into 1968-69 Shankly kept faith in the side that had gone close the previous season but before the end of September he decided change was necessary. The day after Liverpool were eliminated from the Fairs Cup at the first hurdle to Athletic Bilbao on the toss of a coin, out went Tony Hateley to Coventry for £80,000 while in came teenager Alun Evans from Wolverhampton Wanderers. At £100,000 Evans was the most expensive teenager in English football and he made an instant impact, scoring on his debut in a 4-0 win at Anfield over Leicester City, a game where all four goals came in the first twelve minutes. A week later he returned to haunt his old team mates at Molineux, scoring twice in a 6-0 win that took Liverpool into second place, a point behind Arsenal. Hateley's departure was no real surprise and to recoup 80% of what had been paid for him was good business. On his day he was very good, but too often this was against weaker opposition and on many occasions against stronger teams, or when the chips were down, he was found to be lacking.

On the whole Liverpool had a very good season in 1968-69. Their total of 61 points was more than they had amassed during their title winning years of 1922, 1923, 1947 and 1964 and the same as they had gained in 1966. Unfortunately for them, Don Revie's Leeds United lost just twice all season as they won the title with a record points total of 67, their first ever title being confirmed at Anfield on 29th April when they earned a 0-0 draw.

Evans, though, was a disappointment. After his stunning start he managed just four more goals in his next 31 games. The season also saw the beginning of the end of Roger Hunt's glorious Reds career, the marksman being furious when he was substituted in an FA Cup fifth round replay with Leicester, throwing his shirt at the dugout before storming down the tunnel in the days when tactical changes were unheard of. Hunt was still the Reds leading scorer in the league with thirteen goals, but it was his lowest total since he forced his way into the team shortly before Bill Shankly arrived in 1959-60. Another player who had played for Liverpool in the second Division, Gerry Byrne, called time on his career due to injury, making the last of just three appearances all season against Wolves at Anfield on 5th April.

Again no major signings were made prior to the start of the 1969-70 season. Shankly kept faith in Roger Hunt and Bobby Graham, only ever a bit part player since joining from Motherwell in 1964, was finally given an extended run in the side in as the Reds won seven and drew two of their opening nine league games. A 1-0 defeat at Manchester United on 13th September saw the Reds knocked off the top of the table but they bounced back with a record 10-0 win over Dundalk in the Fairs Cup and then beat Stoke City 3-1 to stay third in the table, a point behind leaders Everton. The Reds then went five league games without a win and, although they ended this sequence by beating Southampton 4-1 a week later, they went down 4-0 at Derby County. This defeat left them eight points adrift of Everton and there was further disappointment in the Fairs Cup when Portuguese side Vitoria Setubal won a secondround tie on away goals.

However, on 6th December 1969 Liverpool went to Goodison Park and inflicted a stunning 3-0 defeat on an Everton side that had won their opening ten home league games. The match was a tight affair in the first half with both midfields cancelling each other out and Ian Ross doing a man-marking job on Alan Ball. It exploded into life in the second half, which was most famous for Sandy Brown's own goal. This came in the 54th minute, seven minutes after Emlyn Hughes had made it 1-0. Bobby Graham completed the scoring in the 74th minute to give the Reds their first win at Goodison Park since winning promotion in 1962. The derby win brought the Reds to within five points of Everton but the euphoria was over the following Saturday when Manchester United, themselves struggling in mid-table, cruised to a 4-1 win at Anfield. Roger Hunt came on as a substitute for Ian Ross against United and by the time of the next game against Burnley on Boxing Day the

Reds leading scorer of the time had left for Bolton Wanderers. Liverpool won 5-1 that day, Ross netting his first goal for the Reds but it was clear that the title was turning into a two-horse race between Everton and Leeds. By the end of February Liverpool were down in ninth, albeit with enough games in hand to lift them into fourth but still well adrift of the top two. Even Anfield wasn't a fortress anymore, with only seven wins coming from the sixteen home games so far.

The FA Cup did offer some hope of silverware and when bogey side Leicester City were overcome in the fifth round, the Reds winning a replay 2-0 at Filbert Street, hopes were high especially given the quarter final draw had handed them a trip to Watford, struggling near the Second Division relegation zone. Liverpool had already won 2-1 at Vicarage Road in the League Cup earlier in the season but this time they were humbled by a late header from ex Everton apprentice Barry Endean.

Shankly decided enough was enough and that he'd need to break the team up and start again. On the whole Shankly had remained loyal to the players that had served him so well in the mid-60s. There had been some shipped out already, such as Willie Stevenson and Gordon Milne, while Gerry Byrne's career was ended by injury, but now he was brutal in the way he ripped the team apart. For the next game against Derby County at Anfield, keeper Tommy Lawrence was dropped to make way for Ray Clemence, signed from Scunthorpe in the summer of 1967. Also out of the team were the two signings that had been the basis of the sixties revolution, Ron Yeats and Ian St John. The versatile Geoff Strong went centre half against Derby and Doug Livermore was given a chance in attack. The Reds lost that game 2-0 and for the rest of the season the side had a very much experimental look about it each week as Shankly tried out various youngsters such as Roy Evans at left back, Larry Lloyd at centre half and Alec Lindsay in midfield. The experience of Yeats earned him a recall either at centre half or left back, but St John made just one more appearance in the Anfield derby against Everton. The Reds went on to finish fifth in the table, reasonable given the circumstances and enough to earn a place in the following season's Fairs Cup.

2

The Rebuilding and Near Misses of 1971 and 1972

At the end of 1969-70 Steve Heighway arrived from Skelmersdale United. Heighway had a university degree, as had Brian Hall who was also promoted to the first team set-up. At the time it was seen as extremely unusual for two players with university degrees to pursue football careers, given the fact wages in the game weren't astronomical then.

For the opening game of 1970-71, Shankly paired Bobby Graham and Alun Evans up front, while youngster John McLaughlin was given a chance in midfield and Ian Ross tried out at left back. The side remained the same for the first six games, with the exception of left back, where Roy Evans came into the side for the fourth game against West Bromwich Albion. By the end of the season Alec Lindsay had managed to make that position his own after Ron Yeats had also filled in there.

The side started the season steadily and weren't beaten until the ninth game. However, five of the opening eight games were draws and although the Reds were now much tighter at the back, there was a clear lack of firepower. Changes were enforced in October when Bobby Graham broke his leg against Chelsea, leading to Shankly going out and paying Cardiff City £110,000 for John Toshack. An injury to Ian Callaghan gave Brian Hall his chance while Shankly also decided to give Heighway an opportunity at left wing, replacing Peter Thompson. Against champions Everton on 21st November everything fell into place as Liverpool came from 2-0 down to win 3-2, all the Reds' goals coming in the last 21 minutes. Heighway got the first with a mazy run and low shot that beat the keeper at the near post and then four minutes later he crossed for Toshack to head the equaliser. But it was an old stalwart, Chris Lawler, who ghosted in to score the winner with six minutes to go. That win put the Reds sixth, although any hopes of a title charge were firmly dashed the following week when they lost 2-0 against Arsenal at Highbury.

From a league perspective the rest of the season would be a frustrating one for Liverpool. The Everton game was the last time that the Reds scored three league goals in a game that season as they finished fifth, fourteen points behind Champions Arsenal. However there were positives to be taken from the fact no games were lost at Anfield and they also set a record for the least goals conceded, letting in just 24 from 42 games.

In the cups, though, it was a different story as the Reds went close to double glory. For the first time since 1966 they reached the semi-finals of European competition in the Fairs Cup. Tricky ties against eastern European opposition in the shape of Ferencvaros and Dinamo Bucharest were overcome in the first two rounds, before Hibernian were beaten 4-0 on aggregate in an all-British third round clash. It was in the quarter-finals that the potential of the side was shown, as Bayern Munich were beaten 3-0 at Anfield, Alun Evans hitting a hat-trick. In the second leg Ian Ross came in to do a magnificent man-marking job on Franz Beckenbauer and then scored himself for good measure as the Reds earned a 1-1 draw to set up a semi-final with old foes Leeds United, which Shankly dubbed the 'tie of the century'.[1] A Billy Bremner goal in the first leg at Anfield, where the Reds rued a series of missed chances, turned out to be the only goal of the tie.

Despite the Fairs Cup disappointment, the Reds still had an FA Cup final against Arsenal to look forward to. Liverpool had beaten Aldershot, Swansea City and Southampton on their way to a tricky home tie with Tottenham Hotspur in the quarter-final. A 0-0 draw at Anfield looked to have ended the Wembley dream but Steve Heighway scored the only goal of the replay at White Hart Lane. The opponents for the semi-final were Everton, who took a 1-0 lead at Old Trafford before second half goals from Alun Evans and Brian Hall put the Reds in the final.

League champions Arsenal awaited the Reds at Wembley. On a baking hot day Steve Heighway looked to have won the cup in extra time only for a scrambled goal from Eddie Kelly following a defensive mix-up and screamer by Charlie George to clinch the Double for Arsenal. Bill Shankly bemoaned Arsenal's fortunate equaliser afterwards, the 10th May's *Daily Post* quoting him as saying:

'The cup was there for the taking, we got a boost from the goal and you could see Arsenal sag. Only a tragic mistake could bring them back into the game, this was their chance and they got it, what a foolish goal to give away. They got their equaliser just when it mattered'.

Despite the defeat, 100,000 fans turned out in Liverpool the next day, lining a nine mile route from Allerton station to St George's Hall. Bill Shankly told the crowds gathered on St George's Plateau 'Yesterday at Wembley we lost the cup. But you the people have won everything. You won over the policemen in London, you won over the London public'.

As Liverpool went into 1971-72, it was clear that the back line was solid but improvements were needed in attack, where Evans was failing to provide any consistency. Kevin Keegan was signed from Scunthorpe for £35,000 and looked to be starting the season in the reserves, failing to make the line-up for the Charity Shield against Leicester City at Filbert Street on 7th August

(Arsenal had declined to take part). However, he was given a chance for the opening league game against Nottingham Forest at Anfield and took just twelve minutes to get off the mark in a 3-1 win.

The Reds were inconsistent during the first half of 1971-72. Although they remained unbeaten at Anfield until New Year, away form was disappointing, meaning that until the end of January they weren't able to string together three successive wins. The Christmas period was extremely disappointing, with three defeats and a draw from their four games. The FA Cup looked to be the best hope of success but, after Oxford United were beaten 3-0 away from home, Leeds United drew a 4th round tie 0-0 at Anfield before winning the replay 2-0 at Elland Road. The European campaign had come to an early end, Bayern Munich winning 3-1 on aggregate in the second round of the Cup Winners Cup to gain revenge for the previous season's Fairs Cup defeat, while the League Cup was also forgotten by Christmas, the Reds going down 2-1 at West Ham in the fourth round.

With fifteen games to go the Reds were tenth in the league table, seven points behind leaders Manchester City. However, with no cup distractions they clicked into gear and on 19th February a 2-0 win over Sheffield United at Anfield meant they had managed three straight wins for the first time of the season. The following week they beat Manchester City 3-0 to go within four points of the leaders and followed this up with a 4-0 derby win over Everton at Anfield. By the time Newcastle United came to Anfield on 18th March the 'This is Anfield' sign was up over the tunnel as the new main stand neared completion. Newcastle striker Malcolm Macdonald quipped to his boss Joe Harvey that they had come to the right place. Shankly told them they'd soon find out and the Reds ran riot, winning 5-0. That scoreline, though, didn't tell the full story. Newcastle played extremely well but the Reds' defence and Ray Clemence in particular were exceptional. This was the Reds' sixth successive clean sheet as the mean streak of 1970-71 returned, only this time it was being coupled with a potent forward line as five different players scored the goals.

The Reds' incredible surge saw them record thirteen victories in fourteen games, the last ten with an unchanged side, to set up what is arguably the most exciting finish to an English league season ever. A 2-0 victory over Ipswich Town on 22nd April, the last Saturday of the season, lifted them into second place with two games in hand remaining. On that last Saturday, Manchester City had completed their fixtures by beating Derby 2-0 to leave them top of the table by one point from Liverpool and Derby. Agonisingly for City, though, their inferior goal average and the fact Derby and Liverpool were still to play each other, meant it was impossible for them not to be overhauled. Also in the equation were Leeds, a further point behind with two games to play. Shankly maintained that Derby were the team he respected more than any other and that whoever finished above them would be champions.

On 1st May Liverpool travelled to the Baseball Ground knowing that if they won and Leeds lost at home to Chelsea they would be champions. However, in a contentious game their unbeaten run came to an end, Derby's 1-0 victory courtesy of a second half John McGovern goal taking them to the top of the table one point ahead of the Reds with their fixtures now completed. The game was ruined as a spectacle by referee Clive Thomas, who hardly allowed it to flow, awarding 62 free-kicks yet still only finding the need to book just four players. The Reds had a strong penalty appeal turned down when Kevin Keegan was felled by Colin Boulton and Steve Heighway was a passenger for most of the game after being concussed by a challenge early on. Shankly, though, didn't want to risk making his only substitution so early and Heighway struggled on until midway through the second half when he was replaced by John McLaughlin. A miserable day for Keegan was completed when he got back to Liverpool in the early hours to find that his Ford Capri had been stolen from the car park of the Crest hotel on the East Lancashire Road, where it had been parked up since the Sunday.

A victory for Leeds over Chelsea on the same night that the Reds lost at Derby left the title out of Liverpool's hands. It meant that on 8th May, when the Reds travelled to Arsenal and Leeds went to Wolverhampton Wanderers, just a point for Leeds would be enough to make them champions on goal average. The Reds knew that only a win would do and that had to be coupled with a Leeds defeat. In fact, it was so close at the top that defeat for the Reds would mean they wouldn't even qualify for Europe the following season. They did have the advantage of having had a week's rest since their last game, while Leeds had faced Arsenal in the FA Cup final on 6th May, winning 1-0 to deny the Gunners a second successive success.

Despite having nothing to play for and being deflated by the cup final defeat Arsenal did not roll over as Alan Ball and Ray Kennedy were inspirational in midfield and up front, and Frank McLintock solid at the back. The Reds gave everything they had, Emlyn Hughes hitting the bar and Ian Callaghan, John Toshack, Larry Lloyd, Kevin Keegan and Brian Hall all going close. With news coming through that Wolves were beating Leeds 2-1 the Reds pounded the Arsenal goal late on and with three minutes remaining thought they had clinched the title. Keegan's mis-cued shot was turned into the net by Toshack to send the travelling Reds massed on the Clock End into raptures – only for the goal to be ruled out for offside. The referee at Highbury was Roger Kirkpatrick, who had already attracted criticism from Bill Shankly for ruling out a Reds' goal in the 2-0 defeat to Leeds at Anfield on New Year's Day with the score 0-0. Shankly went into the Highbury dressing room to make his feelings to Kirkpatrick known after the game, something that would lead him to being censured and warned over his future conduct by an FA disciplinary panel during the summer.

The results of 8th May meant that Brian Clough's Derby, who were on an end-of-season break in Majorca, were champions for the first time. Two days after the Arsenal match the squad, minus Larry Lloyd and Emlyn Hughes who had been called up by England for a European Championship qualifier against West Germany, and Chris Lawler, who had family commitments, flew to Spain for their own holiday, a nine-day break that included three friendly matches. Kevin Keegan kept fans up to date with goings on in his weekly *Echo* column, stating that the tin trophy they got for beating Benidorm 3-0 was rusting within a couple of days, all the team were sunburnt, that he had learned how to say 'bacon and eggs in bed' to hotel staff and the players' favourite bar was run by an Evertonian called Ronnie Marr!

When it came to the controversy surrounding refereeing incidents in the final two games, Shankly refused to blame them for the Reds failure to secure the title. He told the *Liverpool Echo* the next day:

> 'We didn't lose it last night at Highbury. We lost it three or four months ago when we lost at West Bromwich and Leicester. Just one point in either of those matches would have been enough to win us the title'.

Shankly also said it was some consolation that Derby, the best side the Reds had faced all season, were the champions and that the form shown in the second half of the season bode well for 1972-73. Kevin Keegan prophetically told fans via his *Liverpool Echo* column on 12th May:

> 'I feel disappointed that we should go so close and yet miss out after such a good run and yet I look back on the season with a lot of satisfaction. We'll win something next year, I'm certain of that and so are the rest of the lads. We can only get better now, time is on our side. I see great things in store over the next five years or so'.

Shankly was right with his verdict, Liverpool did win something the next year and the rest of this book reveals how...

3

Summer of 72, a Big Mack but no Worthington

After returning from Spain on 19th May most of the players went off on their summer holidays. Some were on international duty in the Home International Championships, while Kevin Keegan was called up by England for an Under-23 tour of East Germany, Poland and USSR. Keegan was sent off for retaliation in the first game, a 2-2 draw against East Germany in Magdeburg on 1st June. This raised fears that he may face a four-game ban in the new season, two for the sending-off and two more as he was already under a suspended ban for three bookings. Shankly called for common sense to be applied as the sending-off occurred in a friendly and also because two of the bookings involved in the suspended ban had occurred during 1970-71 when he was a Scunthorpe United player. Fortunately for Keegan, after England manager Sir Alf Ramsey had offered his support, the FA decided, as they had generally done in previous cases, that being sent off in an England shirt was punishment enough.

There was no movement on the transfer front for the first month after the season had ended. The only playing news reported at all was on 22nd May when the club announced that veteran winger Peter Thompson, who had featured in only ten league games in 1971-72, would require a knee operation due to cartilage trouble. Although it was unknown at the time, Thompson, signed in the summer of 1963, would make no further first-team appearances for the Reds and would eventually join Bolton Wanderers in December 1973.

The refereeing decisions that had played a part in denying Liverpool the title still appeared to be rankling somewhat. On 30th May Bob Paisley suggested that things may improve if the same trio of linesmen and referees worked in teams week-in week-out, rather than officials being selected on an ad hoc basis so they weren't familiar with each other.

There was some tragic news on 2nd June when former reserve keeper Trevor Roberts, who had left the club for Southend United in 1965 and was now at Cambridge United, died of a brain tumour at the age of 30. Bill Shankly paid tribute to him in that evening's *Liverpool Echo*, describing him as quiet and inoffensive, while Tommy Smith said 'we were good friends when Trevor was at Anfield and he was an exceptionally nice lad'.

On 9th June, a month after the last game, the *Liverpool Echo* stunned fans with the headline SHANKLY: MINE'S A WORTHINGTON. The Reds had moved in cloak-and-dagger fashion to sign one of the most exciting young strikers in the game, Frank Worthington, for a club record £150,000 from relegated Huddersfield Town subject to a medical. Worthington had been in negotiations with Leicester City prior to joining the England Under-23 tour where he played in two of the three matches. Knowing that Worthington had not yet agreed personal terms with Leicester despite the club agreeing a fee with Huddersfield, Shankly moved fast to agree a price with Huddersfield and,along with Liverpool chairman Eric Roberts, met him off the England plane at Heathrow airport on 8th June. Worthington was whisked off to a hotel where terms were thrashed out and all three men then flew to Liverpool the next morning, to the disbelief of Leicester manager Jimmy Bloomfield who had also been at Heathrow but was refused permission by Huddersfield officials to speak to Worthington until Shankly had done.

At Anfield Shankly spoke of his joy at the capture, telling reporters: 'We want to play Frank alongside Kevin Keegan. If he makes us a better team than last season we'll be a hell of a side and don't forget we nearly won the Championship then'. Worthington spoke of his joy at signing for the Reds and linking up with his international strike partner: 'I teamed up well with Kevin on the Under 23 tour and I'm sure we'll be looking for goals together. Kevin and Larry told me what a great club Liverpool is and here I am signing for then. I'm over the moon about it'.

Liverpool's bid for Worthington meant the end of the road at Anfield for Alun Evans. On the same day that Liverpool agreed their price with Huddersfield, they accepted an £80,000 bid from Aston Villa, newly promoted to the 2nd Division. Evans had been making no secret of hisdesire to leave Anfield, having made just six league appearances during 1971-72 and,with his parents still living in nearby Wolverhampton, Villa was an ideal move for him. The player who had made such a promising start to his Reds career three and a half years earlier never lived up to expectations, as he suffered a series of injuries including a facial injury sustained in a Midlands nightclub attack that left him scarred and short of confidence.

As Evans left, the Worthington deal was suddenly put on ice after the medical showed that he had abnormally high blood pressure. The *Daily Post* reported the next day that the specialist had put it down to the travelling involved in the Under-23 tour, the dash to Merseyside and the stress of changing clubs and told him to take a pre-planned fortnight's holiday then hopefully the situation could be re-assessed on his return. Shankly himself did not seem too perturbed about the delay, commenting 'He is dog weary and when your spirits are low it affects your physical fitness. He is basically fit, he just needs a rest'. Huddersfield's chairman Frank Drabble wasn't overly concerned either, saying:

'It is not a serious matter but you have to appreciate that Worthington has been racing around in the last five days and has had very little rest. It is quite understandable that Liverpool would prefer to complete the transfer after Worthington has rested. We think Liverpool have done the right thing, it is what we would have done under similar circumstances'.

Worthington himself explained that he had been up the previous day at 5am to catch a flight from Kiev to London, not getting to bed until 1.30am. He had then risen at 7am to fly to Liverpool and was understandably very tired.

It meant a tense wait for Liverpool and their supporters while Worthington was in Majorca but the *Liverpool Echo* moved to re-assure them on 27th June, reporting that Worthington's mother had told them he was now resting at home in Halifax and she was sure the holiday had done him good. Astonishingly, the next day the paper dropped the bombshell that the deal was off following a medical by the club's doctor, Dr J.J. Reid, that afternoon. As Worthington left Anfield to be driven home by his brother a brief statement read out by chairman Eric Roberts said:'Liverpool Football Club have decided not to continue with the negotiations to sign Frank Worthington. Any further comment must come from Huddersfield Town. No questions'.

Nobody from Huddersfield was available for comment on the day that Worthington failed the medical, leaving fans in the dark, but the next day their chairman Frank Drabble did shed further light on the situation. He announced that Worthington would go into hospital for further tests regarding his high blood pressure, but they were of the opinion that the condition was not serious or permanent. Drabble also confirmed that Huddersfield would have acted in exactly the same way as Liverpool had done if they were in the same situation. Worthington himself bore no ill feeling to Liverpool and was instead looking forward, telling the *Liverpool Echo* on 29th June:

'I've had a setback in my career but I'm not blaming Liverpool for their attitude and I am quite happy with the action Huddersfield are taking. They are doing all they can to help me. I'm pretty confident that my condition is only temporary. Over the last few months I've been under a lot of strain which would probably account for it'.

In his autobiography *One Hump Or Two*, published in 1994 by ACL & Polar, Worthington shed some further light on the reason for his high blood pressure. He stated that after first taking 1971's Miss Great Britain Carolyn Moore, who once had a fling with George Best, to his brother's wedding, he did go on holiday to Majorca. However, it was hardly about relaxing as he set about burning the candle at both ends as soon as he was seated on the plane, managing to persuade the lady sitting next to him to spend the night with him on arrival. On one memorable day he enjoyed a day-time threesome with two Swedish women before bedding a Belgian girl that night. She was from a town called Knokke, leading to an inevitable joke about knockers!

Worthington did go on to say, though, that despite a career that saw him play on into his 40s, the breakdown of the Liverpool move was his one regret and that he may have done things differently:

'Huddersfield booked me straight into the local Nuffield Hospital for tests. Five days later, though, I was discharged with a clean bill of health. The Nuffield specialists could find nothing wrong with me. Five days. Five days (sic).When all I needed was a good rest. People ask if I have regrets in life. If I have one, it is that the Liverpool move did not go through. I have no doubt that Anfield would have been my making on the world and European stage, just as it was for Kevin Keegan. Instead of the eight caps I won for England it might have been 58 and who knows, maybe more. I suppose it was a little warning from the man upstairs to slow down or else I was going to burn myself out. I've thought about it often since and given my time again I would have heeded the warning and got my feet up in Majorca with a good book, lots of early nights, no threesomes and definitely no knokkers. Well, I might!'

Bill Shankly was naturally extremely disappointed at the deal falling through as he felt Worthington was the only player available who was capable of improving the team. He told the *Liverpool Echo* the day after the second failed medical:

'Nobody is more disappointed than me at what has happened. In fact disappointment isn't the word for it, it's an empty feeling. He was a player I thought would be an asset to us. We finished last season as the best team in the country and I thought he would have made us even stronger'.

Shankly confirmed that the Reds were looking at other players but at that time they were remote interests, although something could come out of one of them. Reds fan Peter Etherington, recalling the episode in his book *One Boy and His Kop*, published by Countyvise in 2001, called the failure to sign him a great pity. Another fan, Chris Wood, remembers how disappointed he was that the deal didn't happen but has enjoyed hearing since of the circumstances surrounding it:

'He later proved what a class player he was, but he could have been as inspired a signing for us as Eric Cantona was for Manchester United two decades later. I loved the story of how he failed the medical because of high blood pressure and being told to go away and rest for a few weeks, with Frank's idea of rest being to jet off somewhere hot and live *La Dolce Vita*. Then when he returned to have his blood pressure checked again it was even higher than the first reading'.

In a strange twist to the tale, Worthington's second wife, Carol Dwyer, was the daughter of Noel Dwyer, who kept goal for Swansea Town against the Reds in the 1963-64 FA Cup sixth round, pulling off a series of remarkable saves in a shock 2-1 win.

With the Worthington deal off and Evans gone, the Reds were desperately in need of more striking options in case of injury or loss of form to Steve Heighway, Kevin Keegan or John Toshack. Peter Thompson was not the player he once was and youngsters Jack Whitham and Phil Boersma were both struggling with recurring knee and ankle injuries respectively. In the *Liverpool Echo* on 30th June, correspondent Chris James pointed out the lack of experience in the Reds squad, with only fifteen players having played more than ten league games. He suggested that three signings were needed, a forward, midfielder and a centre back.

In preparation for the season, which was to start on 12th August, the players reported back to Anfield on 10th July to be weighed and kitted out. The *Liverpool Echo* reported that evening that goalkeeper Ray Clemence appeared to have the best tan and a big cheer was given to Emlyn Hughes when he appeared, in recognition of his marriage at the beginning of the month. On the whole it was said that the mood amongst the squad was good, as if they felt that something great was going to happen that season. Training proper started at Melwood the next day, with all the squad looking in decent shape and those with injuries – Boersma, Thompson and Whitham – expected to be fit for the start of the season. Even though Thompson had undergone a serious operation, Shankly predicted that he still had another few seasons left in him yet.[2]

As the Reds got kitted out Bill Shankly revealed to the press that he had tried to sign two players within days of the season ending but one had gone elsewhere from a lower division club and the other hadn't moved. If these deals had been completed then that would have been it for the summer but Shankly reiterated it was now a case of waiting for the right player capable of strengthening the squad to become available before making a move. Shankly would not elaborate further on his earlier targets but the following day's *Daily Post* speculated that the lower division player was Alf Wood, who had joined 2nd Division Millwall from Shrewsbury Town for £50,000 and the other was either Southampton's Mick Channon or Manchester United's Brian Kidd. Shankly also stated that he expected the players to put the previous year behind them and draw on the experience to get better, and that they were bursting to win for the number one professional crowd in England.[3]

The big name player who would come in was Scot Peter Cormack, who, like Worthington, had suffered relegation in 1971-72, in his case with Nottingham Forest. Cormack made it clear he did not want to play in the 2nd Division but Forest initially resisted any offers for him, their manager Matt Gillies flatly refusing to discuss the possibility of him moving when the previous season ended. But on 14th July he became a Liverpool player two days after Forest had decided that he could leave. On hearing of Forest's decision to sell, the Reds had no hesitation in meeting Forest's asking price of £115,000, which made him a club record signing, beating the £110,000 paid for John Toshack in 1970. Cormack took no chances regarding his medical after being told on arrival at training for Forest that a fee had been agreed with Liverpool. Knowing of the problems Frank Worthington faced, rather than drive himself Cormack took a train to Crewe. From there he was met by a Liverpool official and driven to Anfield where he passed a medical with flying colours.

Capped nine times by Scotland, Cormack had joined Forest from Hibernian in 1970 and could play anywhere across the midfield or in attack. Shankly was quoted in the *Liverpool Echo* on 15th July as saying 'Peter is a footballer of the class we are looking for and should blend well with men like Keegan, Heighway and Callaghan'. Cormack himself was delighted with the move, telling reporters 'Now I hope I am beginning my success story, Forest was just a stepping stone although I never expected to end up at a club as big as Liverpool'. The *Daily Post* reported on 20th July that he had set himself a target of eighteen goals for the coming season, more than he had managed in two whole seasons at Forest, but he believed it was achievable due to the quality of the players around him.

After the disappointment of not signing Worthington, it was a deal that pleased Chris Wood, He remembers:

'I rarely took much notice of opposition players unless they were an already-established big name. But I remember being very impressed by Cormack when he played at Anfield for Forest in the very early Seventies and it was no surprise that he settled down so quickly into our squad and added an extra dimension as an attacking midfield player.'

However, despite the arrival of Cormack and the optimism among players, manager and fans, the bookmakers only made Liverpool second favourites for the title, offering odds of 5/1 against the Reds, with Leeds favourites at 7/2.[4] Cormack's first training session was on 17th July, the hottest day of the year so far. This pleased Shankly as he knew it meant any excess pounds could be shed quicker.

Cormack was joined at Melwood by another Scot, twenty-year-old Dunfermline Athletic defender David McNicoll who was at the club on trial. However, McNicoll didn't make the grade with Liverpool and returned to Scotland where he now owns a golf shop in Carnoustie. With no deal going ahead for McNicoll, the Reds ended up signing a defender from far closer to home. On 28th July Trevor Storton was signed from Tranmere Rovers, now managed by Ron Yeats, for £25,000 as cover for Larry Lloyd. It was good business for Rovers who were able to balance their books by getting a fee for a player who had joined them from school seven years earlier. The arrival of Cormack and Storton, as well as the departure of Alun Evans and aborted signing of Frank Worthington, marked the end of Liverpool's activity in the transfer market that summer. Worthington received complete medical clearance after a spell in hospital in the same week that Cormack arrived, leading to a call from Bill Shankly wishing him the best of luck for the future.

Off the pitch, Liverpool's finances were in a reasonable shape as they prepared for the season ahead, with a profit of £107,079 being reported at the Annual General Meeting on 21st July. However caution was expressed that further ground improvements may be necessary in the wake of the Wheatley Report that had followed the Ibrox Disaster of 1971. The club's finance officer Eric Sawyer advised that if this became law, the capacity of the Kop could be cut to 15,000 and the cost of improvements would be 'tremendous'. The club had already spent £500,000 on the new main stand that was nearing completion but Sawyer said it would be rash to assume this was the end of spending on ground improvements. It was also estimated that a rise in VAT to 10% would cost the club up to £70,000 a year but there was no danger that money would be diverted from team-building. Sawyer, who had persuaded a notoriously prudent board to part with the money for Ian St John and Ron Yeats eleven years earlier, insisting that the club could not afford not to sign them – knew that despite a potential rise in outgoings the only way to ensure further income was to invest in a winning team. He told shareholders: 'We must be on our guard to ensure that the game at Anfield which is so attractive today will continue to be so and that we will enjoy the marvellous support that is essential to our survival.[5]

The Reds opened their pre-season with a behind closed doors 2-0 win over Chester at Sealand Road on 25th July, in which Peter Comack made his first appearance in a red shirt and the goals were scored by Brian Hall and Steve Heighway. A few days later they played another behind-closed-doors game, this time against Tranmere and lost 1-0. The next two games in West Germany and Holland, which would be played against top flight opposition in front of spectators, were sure to provide a far sterner test.

4

A Pre-season Injury Blow

Friendly: Bochum 0 Liverpool 2
Wednesday 2nd August 1972

On 1st August Liverpool's players flew to Dusseldorf in West Germany in readiness for the next day's friendly against Bundesliga side Bochum, who had just finished a creditable ninth in their first season after gaining promotion. It was the second year running that the Reds had faced West German opposition, having played SV Hamburg a year earlier. Shankly believed a tough test like this was needed to fine-tune the side after the three weeks of hard preparation at Melwood.

The party consisted of the eleven players who had formed the side towards the end of 1971-72, as well as the two new signings and reserve full back John Webb. Webb was drafted in to replace the injured Phil Thompson, who had initially been selected having been a star performer in the side that reached the FA Youth Cup final the previous season as well as making one substitute appearance for the first team.

With air fares being prohibitive for many, only a handful of fans made it over to Bochum, with two intrepid Reds hitching most of the way. Trevor O'Neill from Whiston and James Beattie from Knotty Ash spent just £8 each on fares, £7 of this on crossing the English Channel by ferry. The rest of the journey, save from a train journey from Essen to Bochum, was made by hitchhiking and the two lads were lucky enough to run into the Bochum directors who gave them match tickets near the directors' box after hearing of their journey. With much being made of rising admission prices at English grounds, any fans travelling to West Germany would have been in for a shock to find covered seats cost £2.25 and ground admission was 75p. This was much higher than it cost to watch games at Anfield, where admission to the Kop was being increased from 30p to 40p for the new season.

Chris Wood was one of a number of fans who managed to secure a free ticket from Reds players who came out of the ground before the game to hand out tickets to any fans present. Having grown up in Upton near Chester, his first memory of the Reds was screaming so loud when they scored in the 1965 FA Cup final that his mum thought he'd injured himself. Having first attended a Liverpool game away to Chelsea on Christmas Eve 1966, this was his first time following them on the continent. He'd managed to get over to West Germany cheaply, too, as being employed by British Rail allowed him to apply for a continental travel card which gave him huge travel concessions. He recalls how many Reds fans were able to save money over there by buying as much food as possible from vending machines. With a one shilling/5p piece being exactly the same size as the German mark, which was worth about 25p, it worked in the machines which was great for those in the know but must have been frustrating for those who came to empty the machines. The Reds who had made the trip were joined by a number of British soldiers from nearby army bases, although Wood remembers this additional support wasn't necessarily welcomed: 'Quite a few of the soldiers only came along to rile the locals, it was only 27 years since the end of World War 2 and this was still fresh in the minds of many'.

The night before the game the *Liverpool Echo* speculated that if Peter Cormack was given a place in the starting eleven it would be Steve Heighway, John Toshack or Brian Hall who would make way. However, Shankly sprung a surprise in his line-up when he left both Cormack and Toshack on the bench and played Trevor Storton as a centre forward. Despite having been signed as a centre half, Storton had played in attack while at Tranmere and, after an outstanding performance against Witton Albion in a reserve friendly the previous weekend, Shankly decided to give him a chance.

The game was played in a high tempo, Bochum employing a rigorous man-marking system and not shying away from tackles despite the game's status as a friendly. Cormack came off the bench in the second half to score one of the Reds' goals in a 2-0 victory, the other coming from Tommy Smith. However, he was forced to leave the field after being on it only half-an-hour when he twisted and damaged his knee. Cormack was impressive during his brief time on the pitch, getting forward from a midfield position to score, something Shankly said had been lacking in the side the previous season.

The following day Cormack flew home to receive treatment from reserve trainer Ronnie Moran at Melwood and Phil Boersma was called up as a replacement for the next game at Utrecht. Emlyn Hughes and Tommy Smith also picked up minor knocks although they weren't expected to be ruled out of the game in Holland, which was three days away.

Storton had performed well, as had John Webb who didn't look out of place when he came on during the second half. Shankly explained of the decision to give Storton a role in the starting eleven:

'This boy ran the friendly match we had at Witton last week. I was sorry to let Ian Ross go but this boy is better than Ross will ever be. He was the best utility player available, he has the right temperament and although he has only been with us six days I was able to throw him in at the deep end. I was very pleased with the way he played. There is still time for anyone to earn himself a place in the side'.[6]

A few days later Shankly also explained why Cormack had started on the bench, saying that it was to show him that no matter how much the transfer fee, nobody was guaranteed a place in the starting line-up.[7] Now, though, it was doubtful that Cormack would even be ready at all for the first game of the season, which was little more than a week away.

Liverpool: Clemence, Lawler, Lindsay, Smith, Lloyd, Hughes, Storton, Callaghan, Heighway, Hall, Keegan. Used Subs: Cormack, Toshack, Webb

Friendly: Utrecht 0 Liverpool 1
Saturday 5th August 1972

On 4th August the Reds party flew from Dusseldorf to Amsterdam and transferred to their hotel in Utrecht in preparation for the final pre-season match, which would take place on a Saturday evening. Despite the squad now being threadbare due to injuries to other fringe players such as Peter Thompson, Phil Thompson and Jack Whitham, there was no question of the Reds taking it easy in their final friendly. With the season proper just seven days away Shankly wanted the players to fight for every ball, believing that pulling out of tackles was more likely to increase injuries. Holding court in the hotel bar, the Reds boss confirmed that Peter Cormack was part of his envisaged first eleven for the season ahead, playing in the midfield role that Brian Hall had been fulfilling. He also predicted that Cormack was capable of getting ten goals a season from that position, whereas Hall had managed only one league goal in the previous campaign. On a lighter-hearted note he also had journalists in stitches when the miniature train that delivered drinks around the horseshoe shaped bar arrived, telling the barman that it was late[8].

Fan Chris Wood arrived in Utrecht on 4th August too, having taken in a friendly between Borussia Mönchengladbach and Feyenoord the night before. On the morning of the Utrecht match he went to watch Liverpool train on the pitch at the Stadion Galgenwaard. With this game being played on a Saturday and being somewhere slightly more accessible, a lot more fans made it to Utrecht than had done so to Bochum, although numbers were still small enough for most of them to be provided with complimentary tickets by players and officials.

Liverpool beat Utrecht 1-0, thanks to a fine goalkeeping performance on his 24th birthday by Ray Clemence who made five great saves in the second half, including one where he bravely dived at the feet of Leo Van Veen. Steve Heighway got the Reds goal in the first half, accepting a Brian Hall pass before going on a mazy forty-yard run and hitting a shot from the edge of the area that was in the net before Danish international keeper Jorgen Henriksen had even dived. Another run by Heighway, in which he beat three players, resulted in him being tripped by Piet Van Oudenallen who was booked. Kevin Keegan forced a good save by the keeper and John Toshack hit the post as the Reds threatened to put the game out of sight before half-time. After the break the Reds lost control of the midfield and Utrecht were a good bet for an equaliser, but Tommy Smith marshalled the defence well and with Clemence outstanding in goal, the Reds held on for victory.

After the game many Reds fans took full advantage of the fact Dutch bars stayed open well into the early hours, whether it was in Utrecht or Amsterdam. Chris Wood remembers not booking any accommodation due to this, knowing there was a dormitory establishment near the station where a bed for a few hours could be secured for around £1. One fan, whom it's best not to name, didn't even want to pay this amount and went into a derelict house opposite the station to get his head down, only to fall through rotten floorboards and end up in the cellar with a badly sprained ankle.

Utrecht had been a far better side than Bochum, the Reds having deliberately chosen to make their hardest match of the pre-season their last one. Bill Shankly was extremely pleased with the workout they had given his side, saying after the game:

> 'We will be properly fit by the end of the week and it will be a case of maintaining that fitness throughout the season. We will be very difficult to beat, we finished last season as the form team, losing only one of our last seventeen games. We only conceded four goals during that run and teams are going to have a very hard job scoring against us'.[9]

Shankly was also boosted by the fact there were no further injuries sustained during the Utrecht game, but acknowledged Cormack was unlikely to be fit in time for the next game, the start of the season proper against Manchester City.

Liverpool: Clemence, Lawler, Lindsay, Smith, Lloyd, Hughes, Heighway, Hall, Toshack, Callaghan, Keegan. Attendance: 13,000

5

Out of the Starting Blocks, a Manchester Double and Capital Gains

Football League Division One: Liverpool 2 Manchester City 0
Saturday 12th August 1972

After flying back from Holland on the Sunday, the players were given the Monday off before reporting for duty on Tuesday 8th August as the final preparations for the new season began. That evening's *Liverpool Echo* reported Shankly describing it as 'the final pepping up and quickening up to improve our reflexes'. All the injured players were back in training, although it didn't look like Peter Cormack would be risked for the opening game.

Liverpool were looking to maintain an outstanding record on the opening day of the season. Not since their first game back in the 1st Division after promotion in 1962, when they lost 2-1 at home to Blackpool, had they suffered defeat in the first game. Eight of nine since had been won, the only draw coming against Manchester City at Maine Road in 1967. Two days before the big kick off, Shankly told the *Echo*:

> 'Let's hope we can keep up the record, we are nearly ready, most of the hard work is done now and we hope the next two days will bring us to our peak. The injuries we have are nothing serious, they are niggling and will slow people down'.

In a special edition of the *Echo* to mark the start of the season Reds correspondent Chris James pinpointed six factors the team possessed that he believed could make them champions come May – consistency, the lessons learned from the last two seasons, a settled team, defensive stability, strength in reserve, and finally a determination to succeed.

There was a late scare when Alec Lindsay had a back problem but he overcame a fitness test the day before the game. Shankly named the same side that ended the previous season, with Trevor Storton as substitute. It would be a real test of Liverpool's title credentials, as City were also being tipped by many as contenders having come close the previous season. They had an exciting forward line of Wyn Davies, Francis Lee and Rodney Marsh, while in midfield there were the creative qualities of Colin Bell and Mike

Summerbee, meaning the Reds defence needed to be at their best. If there was a question mark over City's abilities for the coming season, it was the fact that over the summer, manager Joe Mercer had left following a boardroom power struggle that saw him and his assistant Malcolm Allison supporting different factions. Mercer ended up resigning and taking over at Coventry and it remained to be seen how Allison would do in the hotseat.

Anfield was in splendid condition for the start of the season. The rebuilding of the main stand was completed over the summer, with the original 4,500 seats from the old structure being renewed. A set of elegant gates and wrought iron fencing was now in place by the main stand car park instead of the old wooden red painted structure. The gates were similar to the W.G. Grace Memorial Gates at Lord's cricket ground and Horace Yates in the *Daily Post* suggested that they should be named the W. Shankly Gates in recognition of Shankly pulling Liverpool out of the doldrums into the finest phase of their history.[10] The pitch, overseen by 68-year-old head groundsman Arthur Riley, the Reds keeper during the 1930s, was in great shape. In welcoming fans to Anfield for the opening game, chairman Eric Roberts wrote in his programme column:

> 'My colleagues and I are delighted to see, not to mention hear, you supporting our team again. Over the whole of last season we had the highest average attendance of any club in Great Britain at home league matches. We thank you for this wonderful support and we look forward hopefully to a continuation of this tremendous encouragement'.

In front of a full house, the gates being shut 25 minutes before kick-off, the Reds made the best possible start and it was Brian Hall, the player most threatened by Cormack's arrival, who got the opening goal after just three minutes. Steve Heighway got the ball on the left and cut into the box and as defenders were drawn towards him he laid a square ball to the unmarked Hall, who waited for keeper Joe Corrigan to commit himself before firing his shot into the corner of the goal. It was a blistering start by Liverpool, who were kicking into the Anfield Road end for the first half despite losing the toss. In the first minute Kevin Keegan, who was presented with the Young Player of the Season award before kick-off by Eric Roberts and Football League Secretary Alan Hardaker, had glanced a header from a corner that drew a good save from Corrigan.

For the next twenty minutes or so both sides looked capable of adding to the single goal scored so far. Keegan's dipping volley from a John Toshack flick on was well caught by Corrigan and Francis Lee hit a hard low shot which Ray Clemence got down to save. Rodney Marsh missed a golden chance when he sliced his shot after Wyn Davies had teed him up. All of Liverpool's players were getting involved in attacks, Chris Lawler getting forward to have a header which was tipped over by Corrigan and Tommy Smith breaking up opposition play and then advancing to set up a chance for Heighway. As the half wore on the Reds took full control of the game, Toshack going close with two headers as Heighway, switching between wings, put in crosses with pinpoint accuracy. However, despite the game having been played in sporting fashion, in the 42nd minute both sides were reduced to ten men when Larry Lloyd and Wyn Davies were sent off. They had swapped punches after a City corner and the dismissals meant both would be banned for three games under the FA's new disciplinary code.

In the second half it was mainly one-way traffic as Liverpool attacked the Kop. City's danger man Davies was off and with Keegan dropping into midfield the Reds totally dominated the middle of the park allowing them to create chance after chance. Corrigan made a double save from Hall and Toshack during a goalmouth scramble, Heighway ran Tony Book ragged all the time and had a shot just wide of the post, Smith forced a fingertip save from a 25 yard effort and Toshack headed just over the bar from a Hall cross. City didn't threaten until fourteen minutes from time when Lee got into the box but Emlyn Hughes, who had dropped back into defence due to Lloyd's sending off, made a perfectly-timed tackle. The totally deserved second goal finally came after 84 minutes when Hall's shot was saved by Corrigan but only into the path of Ian Callaghan who swept the ball home.

It was the perfect start for the Reds, who had beaten one of their main rivals for the title with the 2-0 scoreline flattering City. Heighway, Keegan and Toshack had been outstanding and worked extremely well together, Tommy Smith was a rock at the back and Brian Hall made it clear he wasn't going to give up his place to Peter Cormack that easily. The only cloud over the victory was the sending off of Lloyd for violent conduct and the impending three-match ban. The centre half maintained that he had done nothing wrong, having seen a free kick awarded in his favour for pushing following a corner and then being punched in the nose. The incident had been captured by BBC's *Match of the Day* cameras and the Reds were likely to request footage to use as evidence in any appeal. Bill Shankly was angry at anybody who felt it was a dirty game, being quoted in the *Liverpool Echo* on 14th August as saying 'I've seen far, far, rougher matches than that. None of our players committed a nasty foul and only one or two City players committed bad tackles. What do people expect, the players to go around kissing each other'.

Liverpool: Clemence, Lawler, Lindsay, Smith, Lloyd, Hughes, Keegan, Hall, Heighway, Toshack, Callaghan. Sub: Storton.

Manchester City: Corrigan, Book, Donnachie, Doyle, Booth, Bell, Summerbee, Lee, Davies, Marsh, Towers. Sub: Jeffries.

Referee: Mr G. C. Kew (Buckinghamshire).

Attendance: 55,383.

Division One: Liverpool 2 Manchester United 0
Tuesday 15th August 1972

Liverpool immediately turned their thoughts to the next game, which was at home against Manchester United the following Tuesday 15th August. There may have been some rivalry between the two sides, stemming from the title battles in the 1960s and envy that United had become the first English side to win the European Cup in 1968, but it was nowhere near like it is today.

Despite it being only four years since their European triumph, United were now no longer considered contenders and had finished eighth three seasons running. The previous season they had slipped away in alarming fashion after being top on New Year's Day and now an opening day defeat at home to Ipswich only served to heap the pressure on Frank O'Farrell. The former Leicester City boss had been in the job a year and like his predecessor Wilf McGuiness was struggling to live up to the expectations set by Sir Matt Busby who had retired in 1969. However, despite finishing well below Liverpool in the league for the last three seasons, United had been unbeaten at Anfield during that time, winning 4-1 in 1969-70 and drawing the next two encounters 1-1 and 2-2.

With Larry Lloyd's ban not due to come into effect for another week and no injuries reported from the City game, the Reds were set to remain unchanged. There was a setback for Peter Cormack who had hoped to be involved in a reserve fixture away to Blackpool the same evening, but it was deemed too early for him. United also had injury problems, with Denis Law suffering from an ankle injury that O'Farrell decided not to risk aggravating any further.

Anfield was again packed, the crowd falling not too far short of capacity as the Reds again recorded a 2-0 victory. John Toshack played arguably his best game in a Liverpool shirt to date, causing havoc in the penalty area but also dropping back into midfield to win the ball and distribute it to others. He put the Reds ahead after just twelve minutes, latching on to a perfectly weighted pass from Ian Callaghan and firing past Alex Stepney from just outside the box. After seventeen minutes Toshack set up the second goal, beating Martin Buchan on the right near the half-way line before homing in on goal. As Stepney advanced, he laid the ball off for Steve Heighway who gleefully slid the ball into an empty net.

After cruising to a two-goal lead the rest of the game was played at a much slower pace but there was never any danger of the Reds letting the lead slip. George Best and Bobby Charlton showed some good vision for passes but the rest of United's team didn't have the quality to make any use of them and Ray Clemence never made a meaningful save all night. The following evening's *Liverpool Echo* commented that even if Peter Cormack didn't kick a ball all season, the £115,000 was still money well spent given the impact his arrival was having on those players whose place was now under threat.

Liverpool: Clemence, Lawler, Lindsay, Smith, Lloyd, Hughes, Keegan, Hall, Heighway, Toshack, Callaghan. Sub: Boersma.

Manchester United: Stepney, O'Neill, Dunne, Young, James, Buchan, Morgan, Kidd (McIlroy), Charlton, Best, Moore.

Referee: Mr V. James (York).

Attendance: 54,779.

Football League Division One: Crystal Palace 1 Liverpool 1
Saturday 19th August 1972

Following the United game, the Reds had to prepare for two trips to London in five days to face Crystal Palace and then Chelsea. Larry Lloyd's three game suspension for the sending-off against Manchester City was due to start against Chelsea but he confirmed that he intended to appeal the decision, having obtained film of the incident from the BBC. With no date having been fixed for a hearing, it meant he was free to carry on playing in the meantime.

The day before the Palace match, Bill Shankly announced that the Reds side would remain unchanged, with Peter Cormack staying behind to play for the reserves against Derby County at Anfield. Palace had drawn and lost their opening two matches without scoring a goal and the *Liverpool Echo* predicted that if the Reds repeated the displays against the Manchester clubs then they should maintain their 100% start.

Fan Chris Wood remembers the sight outside London's Euston Station on the morning of the game as proof that despite having won no trophies since 1966, the Reds supporters were still second to none:

'I came up the escalator from the Underground that led to the concourse. Today's covered concourse has much the same area now as it had then but in 1972 there were very few retail outlets cluttering it up and it used to be a meeting-point for different groups of football supporters from London clubs travelling to away matches and of provincial clubs travelling to their games. At the south end of the covered concourse was a large concrete area on which there are now some high-rise office blocks but in 1972 it was just a big open space with a slightly raised area at its southernmost point and people would often sit there waiting for their trains or just eating and drinking or reading. On this day the covered concourse was as busy as it usually was with individuals and groups all over it. But it was that outside open area that caught my attention. It was only mid-morning but dozens, maybe as many as two or three hundred Liverpool supporters were sitting out in the sun. There were no replica shirts in those days and because of the heat many were not wearing scarves but they were unmistakably Reds and it was an extraordinary sight and probably quite intimidating for the travelling London supporters who were about to take trains to watch their own clubs. We had been six years without a major trophy whereas the big London clubs had picked up cups a-plenty in the early Seventies. This show of strength in the heart of enemy territory was not confrontational. It was just as if to say "Look at what real support is like"'.

Despite having hit the ground running by winning their first two games, at Selhurst Park Liverpool needed a 75th minute equaliser from Emlyn Hughes to save them from defeat. They started brightly enough, dominating the opening twenty minutes in which John Toshack fired over and Steve Heighway had a header cleared off the line. But Palace came out of their shell and started closing down the Reds better, causing problems for the Reds in the remainder of the first half, Ray Clemence saving well from Ross Jenkins and Bobby Kellard. Palace got their reward four minutes before half-time when Tony Taylor dispossessed Steve Heighway and fought off a challenge from Tommy Smith before hitting a low shot that went in off the post.

The second half got off to a bad start when ex-Reds defender Peter Wall went off after a challenge by Smith, an injury which turned out to be a leg break which would keep him out for a year. The Reds tightened up in midfield and created more opportunities, Chris Lawler and Brian Hall going close but it was Hughes who levelled the scores, hitting home from close range after Smith's 25 yard effort was parried by John Jackson.

Liverpool: Clemence, Lawler, Lindsay, Lloyd, Hughes, Keegan, Hall, Heighway, Toshack. Sub: McLaughlin.

Crystal Palace: Jackson, Payne, Wall (Queen), Kellard, McCormick, Blyth, Craven, Pinkney, Jenkins, Wallace, Taylor.

Referee: Mr J. Taylor (Wolverhampton).

Attendance: 30,054.

Football League Division One: Chelsea 1 Liverpool 2
Wednesday 23rd August 1972

The following Monday during a team meeting Bill Shankly laid into Steve Heighway for his part in conceding the goal at Palace, leading to an unexpected show of petulance by the Reds winger as Tommy Smith recalls in his autobiography *Anfield Iron*, published by Bantam Press in 2008:

'He laid into Steve, admonishing him for having dwelt on the ball. "it was you Steve Heighway who cost us two points" said Shanks, "you dawdled on the ball, lost it and never chased back. Have you no pride son? Have you got no legs? The guy played a one-two and Alec was sold down the river". "I'm not a defender" said Steve, which for such a cerebral guy was not the most intelligent thing to say to Shanks. "No son but you belong to a team. I'll tell you what, if you saw your next door neighbour's house on fire, would you go and get a bucket of water?" "What does that mean" asked Steve. Shanks was taken aback. He was very much aware of Steve's intellectual credentials but he wasn't going to let him denigrate his homespun philosophy. "I'm asking you to provide an answer to my question" said Shanks. "I'll provide a sensible answer when you ask me a sensible question" retorted Steve. That did it, Shanks bristled. His face went puce and the veins on his temples turned as thick as biros. "Get him out now. Take him out now before I...Tommy, Chris!" In what had suddenly turned into a very tense and uncomfortable atmosphere, Chris and I went across to Steve and gently guided him out into the corridor. "He's blaming me for costing us a point. I'm not accepting that. And what have I said?" pleaded Steve. "Listen", I told him, "just take it. If he blames you, say nothing. Accept it and he'll accept it. By taking issue with him you do yourself no favours. You just inflame the situation. Now get in there and say you're sorry. No one is bigger than Liverpool Football Club. He built this"'.

Despite Heighway's run-in with Shankly, there was never any danger of him losing his place for the forthcoming trip back to London to play Chelsea. Smith went on to say that if Shankly singled you out for criticism it meant you were very much in his plans, the time to worry was when he ignored you. Emlyn Hughes, who had continued playing against Palace despite hurting his shoulder when he fell awkwardly, was a doubt for the game and Trevor Storton travelled as cover while Peter Cormack was again left behind to build up his match fitness in a reserve game against Bolton Wanderers. One player who didn't look like he'd be playing for a while was Jack Whitham, who Bill Shankly announced needed a cartilage operation, having been plagued by knee and back problems since January.

Chelsea were seen as dark horses in the title race and had begun the season with two wins and a draw like Liverpool. Their danger man was Chris Garland, scorer of three goals in their opening three matches but they were without John Demspey who had damaged his Achilles tendon. Their ground was three sided as construction of the 12,000 seat East Stand was commencing, the beginning of a £5 million project which aimed to raise the ground's capacity to 60,000 but would ultimately be shelved due to escalating costs with just the first phase complete and the club facing financial ruin. Chelsea had faced crowd disorder in their opening home game against Leeds United, with the pitch being invaded on three separate occasions, mainly by boys, and the match programme for the Liverpool game contained a stark warning: 'If there is any further encroachment onto the playing area juveniles will be charged full admission for the remainder of the season'.

Just as they had in their first three games, the Reds went on the offensive from the start and it paid off as they raced into a 2-0 lead up within the first quarter of an hour. John Toshack headed the first after just two minutes from a cross by Steve Heighway, then on fourteen minutes Ian Callaghan struck a speculative long range effort that keeper John Phillips failed to hold. Now in control, the Reds passed the ball around with confidence and created more opportunities, Phillips saving well from a Chris Lawler volley. Chelsea seemed to run out of belief, knowing Liverpool had only conceded four goals in their previous eighteen league games.

Although Peter Osgood and Chris Garland showed some nice touches, they were seriously lacking in the final third, where Tommy Smith and Larry Lloyd dealt with everything effortlessly. However, Chelsea were thrown a lifeline in the 38th minute when Garland met Steve Kember's cross with a diving header that deceived Ray Clemence. In the second half the Reds held on for victory with comparative ease, with Callaghan, Brian Hall and Emlyn Hughes dominating the midfield. Garland was Chelsea's only threatening player but he was given pitiful support and if another goal was going to come it would have been a Reds one. John Toshack had another outstanding game, tormenting Micky Droy so much that he was substituted, Kevin Keegan hit the bar and Heighway was a constant menace down the flanks.

The win took Liverpool to the top of the table on goal average as Arsenal, the only side with a 100% record after three games, had been held to a 1-1 draw by Coventry City the night before. Bill Shankly was delighted and told the *Liverpool Echo* the next day:

> 'It's a great feeling to be top of the 1st Division, even though there's more pressure when you're there it's better than being a few places lower. There's no other place where we would sooner be. There are not many teams who will win at Chelsea this season, they are a good side and difficult to beat'.

Liverpool: Clemence, Lawler, Lindsay, Smith, Lloyd, Hughes, Keegan, Hall, Heighway, Toshack, Callaghan. Sub: Boersma.

Chelsea: Phillips, Harris, McCreadie, Hollins, Droy (Houseman), Webb, Garland, Kember, Osgood, Hudson, Cooke.

Referee: Mr N. Burtenshaw (Great Yarmouth)

Attendance: 35,375

Football League Division One: Liverpool 3 West Ham United 2
Saturday 26th August 1972

Shankly's big problem going into the next game was what to do with Peter Cormack, who had demonstrated both his ability and return to fitness with three goals in the two reserve games he had played at Anfield while the first team were playing in London.

For the following Saturday's home game against West Ham United, he decided not to change a winning formula, naming an unchanged side with Cormack again in the reserves who were playing Manchester City at Maine Road. Shankly also took time out to take a swipe at the fixture computer which had given some teams, Manchester United included, three successive home fixtures in August and had all the top teams playing each other in the opening weeks of the season. He told the *Liverpool Echo* on 25th August:

> 'It is an unfair system and whoever organised the computer is to blame. It's amazing too that all of the top clubs play each other at the start of the season. We have already played Manchester City, United and Chelsea and in the next few weeks play Arsenal and Derby. Leeds and Chelsea have played each other, so have Manchester City and Derby, and tomorrow Chelsea play City, United play Arsenal and Spurs play Leeds. It's an amazing thing how all these top games have come right at the start of the season'.

One consequence of the top teams playing each other, though, was it gave Liverpool a chance to move clear at the top against a West Ham side with a dismal record at Anfield, having lost their last six visits managing just one goal. West Ham's side included World Cup winning captain Bobby Moore, England Under 23 internationals Billy Bonds and Frank Lampard, as well as Clyde Best, one of the first black players in English football. On the evening before the game the *Echo's* Reds correspondent Chris James predicted that West Ham would not come to Anfield to defend like so many other sides but would instead attack, although Liverpool should have too much strength in depth for them and be able to win the game.

Fan Peter Etherington remembers how distraught he was at the prospect of missing this match. 'Evo' would have done absolutely anything to watch a home match then, such was his love of the team and appreciation shown by the players for the fans' support. At the time he was a young father to a ten-month-old boy and money was tight, and this particular week he had nothing to spare after spending the rest of what he had on baby food. In his book *One Boy and His Kop*, published by Countyvise in 2001, he recalls how he stood by the Kop asking passers-by for spare change and although some coppers came his way he still didn't have enough. Plan A was to be up front and tell the gateman he was 10p short, which was rebuffed. Plan B was to tell the gateman to keep the money he had and he'd jump the turnstile, but this was again given short shrift. He then reverted to Plan C, which was trying to bunk in over the wall but after three failed attempts and the threat of arrest he moved on to Plan D, trying to pass himself off as a fifteen year old to get in the boy's pen. Despite being a married father and four days short of his nineteenth birthday he gave it a go but got nowhere. As he contemplated a long walk home to Bootle, though, fate was smiling as a man thrust a season ticket voucher in his hand telling him to take if for nothing, having seen him trying his best to get in.

When it came to the match James's prediction in the *Echo* wasn't wrong. West Ham became the first team to score two goals at Anfield since Leeds United on New Year's Day in a game that saw the Reds come from behind twice to win 3-2. Both sides played some slick passing football and there were chances at both ends in the first half, John Toshack going close with a header and Chris Lawler almost putting into his own net when he intercepted a Trevor Brooking cross that looped over Ray Clemence but the Reds keeper managed to tip the ball over the bar. West Ham's style of football was earning appreciative applause from the Anfield crowd who, on occasions, got restless with their own side as they struggled to come to grips with the visitors' five-man midfield. In the 38th minute Bryan 'Pop' Robson headed West Ham in front from a free-kick, but the Reds were level six minutes later when Toshack headed in a Kevin Keegan cross. However, there was further drama to come before the half-time whistle as West Ham regained their lead, Liverpool's defence failing to deal with a cross and Robson having the simple task of side-footing the ball home.

The second half began with the visitors maintaining their upper hand, 31-year-old Bobby Moore building play from the back, Robson controlling the midfield and Best being menacing in attack. However, in the 62nd minute the Reds got the most fortunate of equalisers, keeper Bobby Ferguson dropping the ball over the line after he failed to hold an Ian Callaghan cross. Buoyed by this bit of luck Liverpool attacked again and were in front for the first time in the game just two minutes later after a 25 yard effort from Emlyn Hughes that left Ferguson rooted to the spot and the Reds remained in control to keep hold of the two points. Etherington recalls Hughes' wild celebration and jokes that he was on Priory Road before his teammates got hold of him. As for going to the match for the rest of the season, there was no more hanging about outside asking for change as Etherington was fortunate enough to win first prize in a national football quiz competition – a season ticket for the club of his choice.

The victory and Arsenal's 0-0 draw at Old Trafford meant that Liverpool were now a point clear of the Gunners at the top of the table with nine points from a possible ten. Chelsea, Everton, Ipswich and Tottenham were all on seven points while down at the bottom, Liverpool's next two opponents Leicester City and Derby County were both in the bottom eight and there was every reason to believe their unbeaten start to the season would continue.

Liverpool: Clemence, Lawler, Lindsay, Smith, Lloyd, Hughes, Keegan, Hall, Heighway, Toshack, Callaghan. Sub: Boersma.

West Ham: Ferguson, McDowell, Lampard, Bonds, Taylor, Moore, Tyles, Best, Holland, Brooking, Robson. Sub: Lock.

Referee: Mr J. H. Yates (Redditch).

Attendance: 50,491.

Top of the Division One Table

		Pl	W	D	L	F	A	GA	Pt
1	Liverpool	5	4	1	0	10	4	2.5	9
2	Arsenal	5	3	2	0	9	3	3	8
3	Chelsea	5	3	1	1	10	5	2	7

6

Trouble in the East Midlands

Despite the confidence of being unbeaten in the opening five games, Liverpool had historically come unstuck at the next two opponents plenty of times before. Derby had only been back in the 1st Division for three seasons after a sixteen-year absence and the Reds had lost two and drawn one of those subsequent visits to the Baseball Ground without scoring a goal. This included the pivotal 1-0 defeat on 1st May that had ultimately decided the destination of the league championship. Back in the 2nd Division days, Derby had beaten the Reds 3-2 in 1954-55, a season when Derby were relegated to the 3rd Division, while in the promotion season of 1961-62 the Reds had still gone down 2-0 at the Baseball Ground. As for Leicester City, just the name was enough to send shivers down the spine of Reds fans. They had defeated the Reds in the FA Cup semi-final in 1963 and the fifth round in 1969, and also won eight of the sixteen league games in which the sides had faced each other since Liverpool's return to the 1st Division in 1962.

Football League Division One: Leicester City 3 Liverpool 2
Wednesday 30th August 1972

The first of two trips to the East Midlands in four days came on 30th August with a midweek visit to Filbert Street to take on Leicester City. The Foxes had failed to win any of their opening three home games and had been beaten 5-2 at Upton Park by West Ham, who had given the Reds a scare at Anfield the previous Saturday. However, their squad had been bolstered by the signing of Frank Worthington, whose blood pressure had now stabilised causing Leicester to renew their interest. The striker had scored on his debut, a 1-1 draw at Manchester United on the same day Liverpool beat West Ham. But Liverpool had a big new addition to their squad, too, as Peter Cormack was included for the first time in the party of thirteen that travelled, Shankly refusing to give any indication beforehand as to where or whether he would play.

On the evening of the game Chris James in the *Liverpool Echo* speculated that Cormack would start on the bench, his presence being a spur to others. His guess was right and Cormack looked on as one of the players threatened by his arrival, John Toshack, hit two in the opening sixteen minutes to put the Reds 2-0 up. The first came in the eighth minute when Toshack started a move that finished with Keegan hitting a drive that Peter Shilton could only block into the path of the Welsh striker who headed the ball into an empty net. In the sixteenth minute Keegan was again the provider, hitting a pass behind the defence that Toshack controlled well and fired home.

A rout looked on the cards but some uncharacteristic complacency set in and Liverpool's defence wasn't its usual commanding self. They failed to deal with the dangerous crosses of winger Len Glover, whose centre in the 25th minute was knocked down by Worthington for Keith Weller to score. Five minutes later it was 2-2 when Chris Lawler lost possession and Weller hit an unstoppable shot that gave Ray Clemence no chance. In the fifth minute of the second half Weller completed his hat trick, seizing on a loose ball in the area to the delight of the home side whose supporters chanted 'Weller for England'.

The Reds never stopped trying to get back into a game that they should have had sewn up in the first half, with Keegan and Emlyn Hughes working tirelessly. A Hughes effort was well saved by Shilton and with just three minutes left Toshack hit the post. However the Reds could have fallen even further behind, a Glover shot hitting the post and bouncing along the line while Larry Lloyd had to tread carefully after being booked for a foul on Worthington.

Liverpool: Clemence, Lawler, Lindsay, Smith, Lloyd, Hughes, Keegan, Hall, Heighway, Toshack, Callaghan. Sub: Cormack.

Leicester: Shilton, Whitworth, Rofe, Cross, Woollett, Sammels, Farrington, Stringfellow, Weller, Worthington, Glover. Sub: Manley.

Referee: Mr T. Reynolds (Swansea).

Attendance: 28,694.

Football League Division One: Derby County 2 Liverpool 1
Saturday 2nd September 1972

Liverpool's next opponents were champions Derby County. Under Brian Clough, the club had been a struggling 2nd Division outfit when he took over in 1967 at the age of 32, having spent the previous two years at Hartlepools United following a career-ending injury. He got promotion within two years and finished 4th and 9th in the 1st Division before the title success of 1972. However, they had started the 1972-73 season slowly, winning only two of their opening six fixtures and they were 18th in the table, just two points off the bottom place which was surprisingly occupied by Manchester City.

If Liverpool were to win at the Baseball Ground, they would have to do so without keeper Ray Clemence, who was suffering a niggling thigh injury that had been troubling him all season and left him struggling to kick the ball during the Leicester game. This meant a debut for former train driver

Frank Lane, signed a year earlier from Tranmere Rovers for £20,000. Another debutant was Peter Cormack, who was finally given his first competitive start, but Shankly sprung a surprise when revealing who was to make way. Instead of one of the regular midfielders or forwards as was expected, Alec Lindsay was dropped and Emlyn Hughes slotted into the left back role.

For Shankly though, it was a 59th birthday to forget as the Reds again took the lead only to end up on the losing side. John Toshack put Liverpool ahead after sixteen minutes, breaking away from his marker Roy McFarland to latch on to a Kevin Keegan pass and fire the ball home. This was Toshack's sixth league goal from just seven games, something Tommy Smith put down to him playing tennis over the summer, which he believed had quickened him up and removed any signs of the sluggishness that he had previously been associated with.[11] Derby had the better of the rest of the half, but Larry Lloyd and Smith were in control at the back and Lane made a couple of good saves from Alan Hinton. Liverpool started the second half better and in the 52nd minute Toshack rose to meet a Steve Heighway cross but Colin Boulton somehow managed to fling himself across the goal to make a save.

Just before the hour Derby were level after a bizarre own goal by Lane. Hinton put in a dipping cross from the left which appeared to pose no danger as no Derby players were there to meet it but after Lane rose to catch the ball he was adjudged to have stepped over his line as he landed. Despite his and the rest of the Reds' players vehement protests a goal was awarded. Lane atoned for his error with some fine saves from Archie Gemmill and Terry Hennessey, while at the other end Ian Callaghan hit a shot just wide and Cormack, who had a steady debut, headed wide of the post. The Reds were the far more dangerous team for the final half-hour but with three minutes remaining a rare Derby foray into the opposition half caught the defence napping and John O'Hare tucked the ball past the oncoming Lane after being set up by David Nish. For the first time in the game, the Derby fans' voices could be heard, leading to a post-match outburst from Clough who labelled them disgraceful. 'Champions should have the blind support of their fans' he commented, leading to an apology from chairman Sam Longson.[12]

Despite the harsh reality of a second defeat in a week that left the Reds sixth in the table, Chris James wrote in the *Liverpool Echo* the following Monday that there were still plenty of positives to take. He pointed out how Lane had proved a confident deputy to Clemence and that his own goal was highly debatable. The defence was also calm and stable, with Hughes outstanding at left back, the position he occupied for England. In attack, Cormack had fitted in well and a real understanding was now developing between Keegan and Toshack, while Steve Heighway was now back in form. In previous seasons the Reds had a mean defence but had found goals hard to come by, but this had now been resolved and if the defensive blips of the last few games could be ironed out, Liverpool could face the rest of the season with confidence.

Steve Heighway, too, made it clear that the players were not worried about the two defeats. He said after the Derby game:

'When you let a victory slip from your grasp you are not pleased. At the same time I can tell you that our mood of confidence has not disappeared with those defeats. On both occasions the team played well and that's the main thing. At Derby we carried the game to our opponents more or less throughout the ninety minutes and I would imagine that Brian Clough, as confident as he sounds, was somewhat relieved at the final scoreline'.[13]

Liverpool: Lane, Lawler, Hughes, Smith, Lloyd, Cormack, Keegan, Hall, Heighway, Toshack, Callaghan. Sub: Lindsay.

Derby: Boulton, Powell, Nish, Hennessey, McFarland, Todd, McGovern, Gemmill, O'Hare, Hector, Hinton. Sub: Durban.

Referee: Mr J. W. Gow (Swansea).

Attendance: 32,524.

Top of the Division One Table

		Pl	W	D	L	F	A	GA	Pt
1	Arsenal	7	4	3	0	11	4	2.75	11
2	Everton	7	4	3	0	8	3	2.67	11
6	Liverpool	7	4	1	2	13	9	1.44	9

7

Frankfurters and Sun

By finishing third in the league in 1971-72 Liverpool gained entry into the UEFA Cup, now in its second season and re-named from the Fairs Cup, although it was often also referred to as the EUFA Cup. During the course of the season Liverpool's match programmes said 'EUFA', the local press referred to it under both names, whileTottenham called it 'UEFA'.

The first winners of the competition were Tottenham Hotspur, who won an all-English final against Wolverhampton Wanderers, winning 2-1 at Molineux before drawing 1-1 at White Hart Lane. Liverpool were one of four English entrants for 1972-73, the others being Tottenham as holders, fourth placed Manchester City and League Cup winners Stoke City. Although the least important in terms of the status of the three European competitions, the UEFA Cup was arguably the hardest to win. It contained one more round than the European Cup and European Cup Winners Cup and whereas those competitions had just one entrant per country the UEFA Cup had three or four teams from the strongest European countries.

UEFA Cup 1st Round 1st Leg Liverpool 2 Eintracht Frankfurt 0
Tuesday 12th September 1972

The first round draw paired Liverpool with Eintracht Frankfurt, meaning that they would be facing West German opposition for the sixth time in just nine years of European competition. Granted there could have been easier draws, but from a logistical point of view Liverpool were more than happy, given there were few travel or language problems associated with it. The Reds had also triumphed in four of the six previous ties against West German opposition and their stock was high in the country following the impressive 4-1 aggregate win over Bayern Munich in the Fairs Cup two seasons earlier.

Emlyn Hughes was particularly keen to get one over a West German team. Like the rest of the side he had been disappointed at Liverpool's exit to Bayern Munich in the previous season's Cup Winners Cup but he had also been a member of the England side that lost to West Germany in a European Championship qualifier earlier in the year. Furthermore, he was an unused substitute in the 1970 World Cup quarter-final in Mexico when England were beaten 3-2 by West Germany.

Eintracht were playing in Europe for the first time in four seasons after finishing fifth in the Bundesliga and although a technically good side, they weren't known for their physical nature or stamina, two things where the Reds would have a clear advantage. Another thing in the Reds favour was that due to the Olympic Games in Munich the Bundesliga wasn't due to start until the Saturday after the first leg, meaning Eintracht had been restricted to a series of practice games against local junior sides. However two of their players, Bernd Nickel and Jurgen Kalb, had been involved in competitive matches in the Olympics for West Germany.

Their danger man was right winger Jurgen Grabowski, who had come off the bench to provide the cross for Gerd Muller to score the winner for West Germany against England in Mexico two years earlier. Other internationals in their side were Austrian Tomas Parits and Turkish left winger Ender Konca. They were managed by Erik Ribbeck, who, despite being only 35, had been in charge for four years having previously been assistant boss at Borussia Mönchengladbach.

After watching Liverpool v Wolves on the Saturday before the 1st leg, Ribbeck returned to Frankfurt and then flew into Speke Airport with his players the following Monday, the day before the game. Having seen the Reds win 4-2, Ribbeck knew the size of his team's task, saying 'It will be very hard for us, we will just have to try and limit Liverpool to a one goal lead in the first leg. If we could get a draw it would be a very good result for us'.[14] A delay of ninety minutes caused by faulty baggage compartment doors put their training schedule into disarray, a planned afternoon session at Southport FC having to be cancelled. With the Sandgrounders having a league game with Bradford City in the evening, Eintracht were limited to a brief workout on the morning of the game.

Before the game Ribbeck re-iterated how difficult it would be for his side, being quoted in the *Liverpool Echo* on the evening of the match:

> 'The first half hour will be vital to us, it is important we do not concede a goal to Liverpool in that time. If we can keep the game goalless for that period it will give my players the confidence they need to contain Liverpool for the rest of the match. A goalless draw would be very good for us and even a one goal defeat would be good'.

Ribbeck also said how Kevin Keegan, Peter Cormack, Emlyn Hughes and Steve Heighway were the players who had impressed him the most but the *Echo* predicted how Bill Shankly was likely to treat any such praise with scepticism. Shankly would have been far more interested in Ribbeck's comments that his team like to play short-passing possession football, similar to the West German national side.

Unfortunately for Ribbeck, his plan was blown apart after twelve minutes when Keegan scored after a pass from Hughes. Keegan had looked yards offside but despite the appeals of the Eintracht players, the linesman didn't raise his flag to the amazement of the crowd and the striker played to the whistle to score past qualified dentist Peter Kunter. Eintracht's response was to pack the defence and they rarely ventured out of their half. When they did they restricted themselves to long-range efforts. Uwe Kliemann was a rock at the back and Thomas Rohrbach did a superb man-marking job on Keegan.

Eventually, after an hour of probing without success, the defence finally gave way as Liverpool's superior fitness showed in the 75th minute. Keegan sent Cormack away down the right and his cross to the far post was headed in by Hughes. The Reds piled on the pressure for the last fifteen minutes, with Toshack and Keegan both missing goods chances. If there had been any doubts about the legality of the opening goal, it was evened out by two strong penalty appeals for fouls on Keegan being waved away.

Although the tie wasn't over and Eintracht were sure to be more adventurous in front of their own supporters, Bill Shankly was satisfied that the Reds had done enough and could finish the job in West Germany. In the following evening's *Liverpool Echo* he was reported as saying:

'I feel we are capable of scoring one or two goals there. We may have to be patient but it doesn't matter if the goal comes in the first few minutes or the last. To have a two goal lead in a European competition if very satisfying and very comforting'.

Despite the 2-0 scoreline Ribbeck didn't write off his team's chances, the *Echo* reporting his comments as:

'The second leg is another game, we will be more positive in Frankfurt and will be coming forward more. I won't say we have a good chance but we have a chance. Liverpool played very much as I expected them to, but I thought their first goal was offside'.

The match had attracted a crowd some 10,000 less than the previous Saturday's game against Wolves, with higher admission prices playing some part in this. Only the stands were ticketed at £1 each, with Paddock admission 55p and Kop/Anfield Road 45p, a rise on the normal league admission prices of 85p, 45p and 40p. Rises for European games were the norm and club secretary Peter Robinson stated that it was necessary due to the extra costs involved such as away travel and also the fact that the home club was responsible for the travel and hotel costs of the match officials, which in this case came to £600. Robinson wasn't disappointed by the gate, pointing out that in the previous eight European campaigns the first round gate had only surpassed 40,000 on three occasions.[15]

There was also high praise from the UEFA delegate at the game, Albert Gudmundsson, who was President of the Icelandic FA. He was impressed by the newly completed main stand, which he believed made Anfield the best stadium in Britain, ahead of Highbury and Ibrox.[16]

Liverpool: Clemence, Lawler, Lindsay, Smith, Lloyd, Hughes, Keegan, Cormack, Heighway, Toshack, Callaghan. Subs: Lane, Thompson, Hall, Storton, Boersma.

Eintracht: Kunter, Kalb, Lutz, Kliemann, Rorhrbach, Heese, Weidle (Reichel), Grabowski, Parits, Nickel, Konca (Krauth).

Referee: Mr C. Lo Bello (Italy).

Attendance: 33,380.

UEFA Cup 1st Round 2nd Leg Eintracht Frankfurt 0 Liverpool 0 Tuesday 26th September 1972.

For the second leg fans could travel with Towns Travel who were charging £29.50 for a one-night trip including flights from Speke Airport and dinner, bed and breakfast. Given seats for the home leg cost £1, such a price shows how match tickets have got more expensive over time and travel cheaper. Today, if a travel company charged 29-and-a-half-times the most expensive Anfield ticket price for a one-night stay in Germany the price would be £1,416.

One group of fans from the Sefton pub near the Anfield ground in Robson Street made a week away of it, travelling by coach and ferry to Frankfurt, taking in Stoke City's game at Kaiserslautern the following night as well. Their arrival back in England was timed perfectly as they were due to dock at Hull on the Saturday morning, an hour's journey from Leeds where Liverpool would be playing in the league that afternoon.

The Reds team flew from Manchester to Frankfurt the day before the game without John Toshack who was sidelined with a knee injury, while reserve goalkeeper Frank Lane was also injured meaning a call up for Grahame Lloyd from the A Team. Young full-back John Webb also travelled as cover for Chris Lawler, although a bruised foot was not expected to rule the experienced right back out of the game.

The first task faced by Bill Shankly on arrival was to have a word with the hotel management about the building work that was going on. The players arrived to the sight and sound of hammering and chiselling as an extension was being built. They had little choice but to accept Shankly's demands that work didn't start until 1030 the next morning, although he did make a concession that the painters would be able to begin on time. The players then underwent a light training session which Lawler came through unscathed and Shankly confirmed that he would be fit to play.

Eintracht's 72,000 capacity Waldstadion was undergoing redevelopment for the 1974 World Cup and as such only 35,000 could be accommodated for the second leg of the tie, none of them under cover, while there were also only three floodlight pylons in use. Tommy Smith was concerned about this. He wrote in his weekly *Liverpool Echo* column on the Saturday before the game that one of the problems faced playing in stadiums with a running track and no roof was that an optical illusion occurred which made the pitch appear bigger and there was a danger of overhitting passes.

Shankly stated beforehand that he would not be sending his side out looking for the early goal that would kill off the tie, rather they would soak up the Eintracht pressure and try to catch them on the break:

> 'We hope they come out in search of an early score, then we might catch them but I fancy they might take a cautious approach. If I was given the chance of switching places with them and playing the second leg at Anfield starting at 2-0 I would say 'no thank you' I would rather be as we are. If we jog along we might just get that goal'.[17]

Since the first leg the Bundesliga season had started with Eintracht winning two of their opening three games. Their star man Jurgen Grabowski was ruled out but after a slow start, it was far from an easy ride for Liverpool as they battled their way to a 0-0 draw. As Shankly predicted Eintracht started slowly so as not to leave themselves vulnerable to the risk of conceding an away goal, but after half-an-hour they stepped things up. Ray Clemence had to be at his best to deny them for the remainder of the first half and whole of the second on the occasions that the Reds well-drilled rearguard was breached. The Reds were dealt a blow in the second half when Tommy Smith was forced off with a pulled calf muscle after turning awkwardly but Trevor Storton put in an excellent performance, soundly guided by Larry Lloyd and Emlyn Hughes who dropped back to help the defence. Bernd Hölzenbein had a goal ruled out for offside and as the game went on and they became more desperate, Eintracht left themselves more open at the back, Peter Cormack and Steve Heighway both going close in the game's latter stages.

Ribbeck was full of praise for Liverpool afterwards. Refusing to use the absence of four players through injury as an excuse, he said the Reds were one of the best teams in Europe and worthy winners of the tie:

> 'They are top of the league and their league is rated one of the best in the world. At least we can say this was our best display so far. Without four players we played magnificently. Against different opposition it would have been enough, against Liverpool it just wasn't. On balance Liverpool deserved to win, they scored twice and we didn't score at all'.[18]

The team and the bulk of Liverpool's fans stayed in Frankfurt overnight and headed home on charter flights the next day. However one fan, Chris Wood, who worked in London, was conscious of how much leave watching games could cost him and travelled through the night by train to Ostend, taking an early ferry and making it to work the next morning. Given how the rest of the European campaign went it was probably a good job he did.

Liverpool: Clemence, Lawler, Lindsay, Smith (Storton), Lloyd, Hughes, Keegan (Hall), Cormack, Heighway, Boersma, Callaghan. Subs: Lloyd, Webb, Thompson.

Eintracht: Kunter, Reichel, Trinklein, Kliemann, Schamer, Kalb, Hölzenbein, Nickel, Weidle, Heese, Konca.

Referee: Mr G. Muncz (Hungary).

Attendance: 17,500.

UEFA Cup 2nd Round 1st Leg Liverpool 3 AEK Athens 0
Tuesday 24th October 1972

The second round draw handed Liverpool their first trip to Greece in European competition as they were drawn against AEK Athens, the AEK standing for Athlitiki Enosis Konstantinoupoleos. There were immediate problems posed by the fact that Tottenham Hotspur were drawn against Olympiakos as UEFA decreed that two games couldn't be played on the same day within 25 miles of each other. The Spurs game took precedence as it came out of the hat first and as such was scheduled for 8th November, hindering secretary Peter Robinson's attempts to arrange travel and accommodation. AEK took nearly a week to reply to a telegram sent by him confirming that they agreed to his suggestion for the game to be played on 7th November instead.

Although the Reds had never faced a Greek side in Europe before, Bill Shankly was not without other British managers he could call on for advice on AEK and Greece in general. Everton's assistant manager Tommy Eggleston had been with Ethnikos in 1970-71 and Alan Ashman, manager of Shankly's previous club Carlisle, had been in charge of Olympiakos the previous season. Both would provide invaluable assistance ahead of the tie re AEK and the logistics of being in Athens.

This was to be Liverpool's longest European trip so far and one of the costliest to date, with initial estimates of the travel and hotel costs amounting to £7,000. Hence it was no surprise when the club confirmed that prices would again be raised for the home leg, with tickets costing what they had done against Eintracht Frankfurt. Chairman Eric Roberts reminded fans, though, that £1 for seats was still what was being charged for league matches at most other clubs and that the increases had been more in some previous seasons. AEK's Yugoslav manager Branko Stankovic came over to inspect their hotel and training facilities before watching Liverpool draw 1-1 at Southampton and said afterwards 'Liverpool are a great side, they are so well drilled technically. They have a variety of clever attacking moves and look very dangerous. A 2-1 or 3-1 defeat will suit me, with such scores we will have a chance in Athens'. [19]

Such words were unlikely to lull Shankly into a false sense of security and he saw them as part of the general kidology often employed in these situations. Liverpool didn't have as good an opportunity to scout AEK as they hoped, the only chance being a cup match against 2nd Division side Korinthos, which Reuben Bennett watched them win 2-0 but still get jeered off the field. However, Liverpool were aware that they had been unbeaten in their first four league games, winning two and drawing two without conceding a goal. Their side contained four Greek internationals as well as Argentine international goalkeeper Nestor Errea who won the Copa Libertadores, South America's version of the European Cup, with Estudiantes in 1969 and 1970.

AEK were reportedly on a £1,000 a man government-sponsored bonus to beat the Reds.[20] They took their preparations very seriously, flying to Heathrow on the Friday before the game and taking a coach to their Southport headquarters. They then had three days of training at Southport FC and on the sand dunes, also taking in Liverpool's game with Stoke on the Saturday. Southport, then in the 4th Division, had been helping Liverpool's European opponents – and Everton's – for the past nine seasons, offering the use of their ground for training and also assisting with accommodation and transportation. Peter Robinson said it was a pity the Reds couldn't be treated the same way when they played abroad:

> 'I only wish we had the same sort of hospitality when we play abroad. The Greeks were only the latest in a long line of clubs who have returned home enthusing over the hospitality they have received and much of the credit must go to Southport for this. We really do appreciate what they do for the clubs we play in European competitions'. [21]

They were going to be backed by the largest away crowd at a European game at Anfield since Ajax visited in 1966. Many fans had booked on special charter packages that took in both Liverpool v AEK and Tottenham v Olympiakos the following night, while several enquiries were also made at the ticket office from Greeks living in the UK. Around 1,000 were expected to be backing AEK, meaning the Kop would have to be in full voice, but they would have to get their pre-match ale in before they entered the ground. For the first time, fans attending the game were unable to buy alcoholic drinks due to new UEFA rules banning the sale of alcohol at grounds. Liverpool protested, arguing that a blanket ban was unnecessary as there had never been any problems at Anfield and drinks were served in plastic containers. The club pointed out that a ban was likely to lead to more fans smuggling in drinks in bottles and cans which could then be used as missiles, but UEFA refused to change the new policy.

Tommy Smith said beforehand that Liverpool needed a three-goal lead to take to Athens.[22] The *Liverpool Echo's* Reds correspondent Chris James agreed with him, although did write on the evening of the game that a two-goal lead would probably do. Everton's assistant Tommy Eggleston predicted that Liverpool should win by three or four goals at Anfield, warning they needed to take a lead to Athens as it would be a different proposition over there and that Dimitris Papaioannou was capable of causing them problems, being good in the air for his height.[23] Papaioannou and his teammates posed another problem too, as Anfield stadium announcer George Sephton recalls:

> 'I took Spanish and Russian at school so I always felt I could cope with Spanish/Italian and east European names. But with the Greeks it was another matter. I had the programme but that only listed 1 to 11 to practice with so I had to wing it when it came to the substitutions'

From the off, the Reds showed their superior quality and took the lead in the ninth minute when Steve Heighway's low cross across the goalmouth was turned in by Phil Boersma. The goal was unbelievable luck for one Irish fan from Limerick, who netted £100 on the Golden Goal on his first visit to Anfield. The Reds bossed the midfield and although AEK applied a man-marking system, players of the quality of Boersma, Heighway and Kevin Keegan were still easily able to make space for themselves. Plenty of chances were created before Peter Cormack added a second after 28 minutes, scoring from the rebound after Keegan's shot was blocked by Errea. Chris Lawler and Alec Lindsay got forward into shooting positions and it would have been no injustice if the Reds were four or five goals up at half time.

As superior as Liverpool were though, they weren't quite as dominant as hospital radio listeners would have been made to believe. George Sephton was sat in the gantry near to their commentators, remembering that they hardly mentioned any Greek names at all and 'it must have seemed to listeners on hospital radio that Liverpool had 99% of the ball'.

The break disrupted the Reds' rhythm and AEK started the second half well, showing some neat moves. Yiannis Dandelis was denied at the near post by Ray Clemence and seven minutes into the half Papaioannou headed against the post. This was a wake-up call to Liverpool and they began to re-assert their authority without creating any clear-cut chances, although they were dealt a blow after an hour when Emlyn Hughes went off with a thigh injury to be replaced by Phil Thompson. With twenty minutes left Brian Hall replaced Boersma and eventually, after 78 minutes, Keegan was brought down in the area and Tommy Smith dispatched the spot-kick to end any Greek resistance. This led to the headline in the next day's *Daily Post* of REDS TIDE SINKS GREEK EMPIRE.

Liverpool: Clemence, Lawler, Lindsay, Smith, Lloyd, Hughes (Thompson), Keegan, Cormack, Heighway, Boersma (Hall), Callaghan. Subs: Lane, McLaughlin, McAuley.

AEK: Errea, Theodoridis, Lelis, Toskas, Tanidis, Lavaridis, Dandelis (Visente) (Mira), Nikoiau, Nikolaidis, Papaioannou, Pomonis.

Referee: Mr F. De Campos (Portugal).

Attendance: 31,906.

UEFA Cup 2nd Round 2nd Leg: AEK Athens 1 Liverpool 3
Tuesday 7th November 1972

Bill Shankly was more than pleased with the result of the first leg, believing it could have been more given the Reds' possession. The following evening's *Liverpool Echo* quoted him as saying after the match 'A 3-0 lead is a big score and we have no worries about the second leg'. His opposite number Stankovic felt aggrieved by the penalty-award but conceded the Reds deserved their win and agreed that the tie was as good as over, saying: 'It will be a miracle if we can pull back three goals in the second leg. Liverpool were the better side playing a higher quality of football'.

Tommy Smith was dismissive of Stankovic's comments, though, believing them to be a psychological ploy as he maintained the Reds had to approach the next leg with the right attitude if they were to confirm progress. Writing in his column in the *Liverpool Echo* the following Saturday he recalled the European Cup semi-final of 1971 when Red Star Belgrade beat Panathainaikos 4-1 in the first leg and the Greek side said the tie was over, only to storm back with a 3-0 second leg win to go through on away goals. Despite the exotic destination, Smith made it clear the away leg would be no holiday for the players, having written on 21st October :'Believe me it's not all sun and sand, we are not allowed to live it up. Usually we are based out of town to ensure peace and quiet. At the most we get a couple of hours off in the day to allow shopping for presents'.

Liverpool had built up a following in Athens in recent years amongst fans of Panathinaikos, who remembered how the Reds helped their club in 1971 by allowing use of facilities at Melwood as they prepared for a European Cup tie with Everton. Panathinaikos were managed by the legendary Ferenc Puskas, with whom Shankly built up a good relationship which was well reported in the Greek press, with the club offering Shankly a holiday in Greece at their expense. With Liverpool also regularly featuring in English matches that were shown on Greek television, there were expected to be plenty of Reds followers in the stadium in addition to the 100 or so who had paid £41 for a charter flight and two nights in a beach resort with Towns Travel. They would also be watched by the Tottenham side, ahead of their game with Olympiakos the following evening. Chris Wood was one of the fans on the organised trip and remembers how excited the locals were about Liverpool's presence. He was asked at the airport by a lady if he had a souvenir for an Australian friend of hers, which led to him taking the person's address and later developing a friendship that exists to this day.

The hot dry climate meant the Reds needed to be wary of a hard pitch that would lead to the ball bouncing around a lot, although Tommy Eggleston had told Shankly it was in good shape by Greek standards. As the squad left Melwood by coach for Manchester Airport the day before the game, Shankly told the *Liverpool Echo* he would be looking to win the game and believed the presence of John Toshack, who hadn't played in the first leg or any of the games AEK's manager had watched, would be a secret weapon for them.

After a refuelling stop in Munich, the Liverpool party were met at Athens Airport at 8pm by a number of enthusiastic autograph hunters, including one young boy in a full replica strip, as well as a fan playing *You'll Never Walk Alone* on a cassette recorder. It was a far different reception than the openly hostile one that Everton had received two seasons earlier when they played Panathinaikos. Also present was AEK's president who presented Reds vice-chairman Jack Cross with a bouquet of red and white carnations. Accompanying the players on their coach journey to the hotel, the president gave a running commentary and pointed out any landmarks they passed, which were limited to the American Embassy and Hilton Hotel, Greece's tallest building.

They stayed at the Aperghi Hotel in the exclusive Kifissia suburb 15 kilometres north of the city centre, where Kevin Keegan revealed to the *Daily Post* that he had received veiled threats in the first leg, in which opposition players had said to him *'Remember. We'll be waiting for you in Athens'*. However he insisted he would not be allowing this to worry him, as that would be exactly the reaction that the AEK players wanted.

The game in the Nea Philadelphia Stadium was played at 3pm local time due to the lack of floodlights, with tickets costing £2. One ticketless Greek Liverpool fan, 18-year-old Christos Tarazis, managed to hitch a ride on the team bus by acting as an interpreter, before blagging his way into the stadium pretending to be a Reds official and taking up position in the press box, borrowing a pen and paper off another reporter. The teams took the field to a noisy reception from the AEK fans, most of them situated on a bank behind one goal waving flags, setting off firecrackers and sounding klaxons. One banner read: 'LIVERPOOL WILL DIE TODAY AEK IS THE YELLOW DEATH'. If this was one of the better pitches in Greece as Eggleston stated, then heaven knows what the worst must have been like. Tommy Smith described it in his *Liverpool Echo* column the following Saturday as 'iron hard, bumpy and with bare patches that made it look like a patchwork quilt', while Shankly claimed you could grow tomatoes on it. Shankly was also unhappy about the referee being Yugoslav, the same nationality as the AEK coach.[24]

Unsurprisingly AEK came quickly out of the starting blocks and almost took the lead in the first few minutes, Clemence failing to gather a Papaioannou cross under pressure but Nikolaidis's shot was blocked on the line by Hughes. Liverpool weathered the early storm and they had the advantage of a strong wind in their favour. As the crowd quietened down a bit they ventured further forward, although there was a curious booking when Peter Cormack had his name taken for kicking the ball away after offside was given.

In the seventeenth minute Hughes struck a crucial away goal, hitting a shot from thirty yards that hit the bar and bounced just over the line, Toshack helping it into the net to make sure. From Hughes arm-waving celebration, though, there was no doubt he saw the goal as his. Liverpool were dominant now and AEK had no answers as they passed the ball around, their defensive incapability being shown by their tendency to concede corners rather than play their way out of trouble. A Smith free-kick was just tipped over the bar but AEK had a lifeline on 35 minutes when the referee awarded a penalty against Hughes who handled the ball when he fell over. Nikolaidis placed the spot kick perfectly into the corner to re-ignite the crowd a little, but it only prompted Liverpool back on the attack, Errea pushing away a Chris Lawler header. A minute before the interval Hughes completed an eventful half for himself when he restored the lead. Picking the ball up near the halfway line he strode forward and swapped passes with Kevin Keegan before placing the ball past the keeper, meaning that AEK now needed to score five to win.

Given the extent of Liverpool's lead it was no surprise that the pace of the game slowed in the second half, although things may have been different if Larry Lloyd hadn't made a last ditch tackle on Nikolaidis after fifty minutes when he weaved his way into the box. The Greeks didn't threaten again until midway through the half, Dandelis firing over from a good position, and when the Reds attacked they didn't commit extra men forward, opting for safety-first instead. Toshack saw a header cleared off the line and then, with three minutes remaining, substitute Phil Boersma, on for Heighway, had the simple task of tapping the ball into the net after Keegan had beaten three men and crossed from the byline.

It had been one of Liverpool's best away performances in Europe to date, in which they absorbed the early pressure and then slowed the game down to quieten the crowd before netting a crucial away goal. Tommy Smith recalled that the crowd was so quiet you could have heard the dust settle.[25] Emlyn Hughes was singled out for special praise afterwards by the Reds captain who, while having little respect for Hughes as a person, saw beyond that and acknowledged his special qualities as a footballer. Refusing to let personal differences get in the way of the progress of Liverpool FC Smith wrote in his *Liverpool Echo* column the following Saturday:

> 'His goals were invaluable, but so too was the moment in the first minute when he kicked that shot off the line. If AEK had have scored, the match might have been very different. Emlyn and Ray Clemence, with some good saves, saved the day for us and after ten minutes we were in no doubt that we'd go through'.

Back in the early 1970s Greece may have sounded like an exotic sunshine destination, but Smith made it clear that it had been no holiday for the Reds players. He used his column to explain that all he saw of Athens was the hotel and the stadium. The team arrived when it was dark the night before the match, went to bed, had a lie-in on matchday, trained, had lunch, played the game and went to the airport. In total they were in Athens for less than 24 hours, their plane home having departed at 7pm, little more than two hours after the match had finished. Smith believed treating the games as business, rather than a short break, was the best way and minimised disruption to the normal routine preparation for league matches. Such a policy of keeping trips as short as practically possible had been adopted by Peter Robinson who was aware of the risk of boredom to the players. Shankly had reacted angrily, too, during a press conference the evening before the game when he was asked a question about sightseeing, replying 'We're not here for a holiday, we're here to do a job of work'.[26]

The party let their guard down on the flight home, though, enjoying a sing-song with champagne and a cake iced in red and white that had been presented to them by British European Airways staff. The fans' trip did engage in some sightseeing, taking a tour of the Acropolis on the morning of the game, but it was back to football before heading home, with many of the group opting to watch Olympiakos v Tottenham prior to taking taxis to the airport to catch their flight.

Liverpool: Clemence, Lawler, Lindsay, Smith, Lloyd, Hughes, Keegan, Cormack, Heighway (Boersma), Toshack, Callaghan. Subs: Lane, Storton, Hall, Thompson.

AEK: Errea, Lelis, Lavaridis, Toskas, Theothoridis, Tsamis, Dandelis, Nikolau (Karafeskos), Nikolaidis, Papaioannou, Pomonis (Psymogiannos).

Referee: Mr P. Kostovski (Yugoslavia).

Attendance: 19,412.

8

Autumn Rising

Football League Division One: Liverpool 4 Wolverhampton Wanderers 2 Saturday 9th September 1972

Liverpool's next league game after the Derby County defeat was at home to Wolverhampton Wanderers. Ray Clemence was welcomed back to the side and Bill Shankly also recalled Alec Lindsay to defence, with Brian Hall making way as Emlyn Hughes returned to strengthen the midfield and Peter Cormack kept his place for his home debut.

Wolves striker Derek Dougan, who had a weekly syndicated column that was published in the *Liverpool Echo* every Friday, wrote the evening before the game that Anfield and Leicester City's Filbert Street were his favourite grounds. Filbert Street was down to the fact it was his former club, but he had special praise for Anfield:

'There is no greater emotional experience, short of a cup final appearance, than playing at Anfield in front of the Kop. The Kop is more than just a section of the ground, it is a soccer institution, a consummation of all the emotion the game inspires and sustains. A great heaving vociferous celebration of what the game is all about. Fundamentally by its nature the Kop is partisan but this does not mean it is bigoted, far from it. The Kop supporters are good judges of football, they can give other players and teams their due. This sporting instinct is deeply embedded and one of the main reasons I enjoy playing at Liverpool'.

It was to be a home debut to remember for Peter Cormack as he got his first competitive goal for the club, which restored Liverpool's lead in the 75th minute after Wolves had equalised. The visitors, who were only behind Liverpool in the table on goal average, weren't scared to attack and Clemence was forced to make saves from Kenny Hibbitt and John Richards in the first fifteen minutes. Steve Kindon, signed during the summer from Burnley, was a constant thorn in the Reds side and always looked like creating goalscoring opportunities, on one occasion missing a glorious chance himself when he failed to connect with a cross when unmarked.

Liverpool needed a bit of luck to take the lead in the 27th minute when Hughes hit a shot that struck the post only to rebound into the net off the head of Phil Parkes. Buoyed by this good fortune the Reds took control and Kevin Keegan was denied by both the post and crossbar before half-time while another effort was cleared off the line. In the second half Wolves managed to re-assert their earlier authority and on 65 minutes Kindon equalised, firing home from a tight angle after Clemence had saved Richards' shot.

Cormack put Liverpool back in front with a diving header after Steve Heighway had knocked down a Keegan cross, then with ten minutes remaining won a penalty when he was bundled over just inside the box by Jim McCalliog, who was sent off for the offence. Tommy Smith converted the penalty at the second attempt after his first effort was ordered to be re-taken but Liverpool still weren't finished, Keegan scoring a fourth with a glancing header from a Heighway free kick in the 85th minute. To their credit, Wolves never gave up and they deserved their 89th minute consolation which came from Richards after a fine pass from the left by Mike Bailey.

Liverpool: Clemence, Lawler, Lindsay, Smith, Lloyd, Hughes, Keegan, Cormack, Heighway, Toshack, Callaghan. Sub: Hall.

Wolverhampton: Parkes, Shaw, Taylor, Bailey, Munro, McCalle, McCalliog, Hibbitt, Richards, Dougan, Kindon. Sub: Daley.

Referee: Mr C. Howell (North Shields).

Attendance: 43,386.

Football League Division One: Arsenal 0 Liverpool 0
Saturday 16th September 1972

Next up for Liverpool was a trip to Highbury, the scene of the previous season's heartbreak, to face Arsenal. Larry Lloyd would be available for the game after the club decided to take his appeal against the sending-off on the opening day to an independent tribunal. A week earlier, the sending-off and ban had been upheld by an FA disciplinary commission, but Lloyd and Bill Shankly decided that the case would be the first to be heard by the newly set up independent panel, football's version of the 'High Court'. Given the league was the club's priority, the easy option may have been to accept the ban immediately as Lloyd would only have missed one league game, the others being a UEFA Cup tie with Eintracht Frankfurt and League Cup game against Carlisle. However, Shankly would not entertain the thought of backing down and told the *Liverpool Echo* on 11th September:

> 'That would be trickery, choosing your matches. That is not the point, he didn't appeal in the first place for nothing. We have a lot of evidence, the incident was on *Match of the Day* and the fact is that we think we have a chance. It doesn't matter which games he misses, there's a matter of principle involved. If you refuse to appeal because you think it is more convenient to miss three matches now rather than later you're throwing the principles out of the window. The players' union fought for this independent tribunal and if you think you've got a case you must use it'.

The previous Saturday Arsenal had been knocked off the top of the table after a 2-1 defeat at Newcastle United, meaning that Everton were the new leaders. Liverpool were just two points behind, though, in addition to being the league's top scorers and Shankly made it plain he would not be going to North London in search of just a point, telling the *Liverpool Echo* on 15th September that the aim was to win every match and never settle for a draw. Two teenagers, midfielder Phil Thompson and defender Dave Rylands, travelled with the party. Thompson had been named the outstanding player of the Ludwigshafen Youth Tournament, in which Liverpool had competed in June, receiving an award from the local Burgomaster and had already tasted first team action, coming on as a late substitute the previous November against Manchester United. Rylands had signed professional forms for the club in March 1970 and been patiently awaiting his chance.

It was Thompson who got the nod for the substitute's jersey as Liverpool had their backs to the wall on some occasions in the first half. Ray Clemence had to be at his best to deny Peter Marinello and George Graham while John Radford and Ray Kennedy both fired over from good positions. That's not to say Liverpool didn't have their chances, John Toshack was causing problems and Emlyn Hughes hit a powerful shot that Geoff Barnett could only parry before Frank McLintock hooked the ball to safety.

In the second half Liverpool's defence was far tighter than the first and contained Arsenal quite well. As the half wore on the Reds got better and came into it more, Toshack hitting the post in the 72nd minute after a Steve Heighway cross. On the whole, though, it was a game in which defences reigned, the last major action coming three minutes from time when Clemence saved well from Alan Ball.

A big talking point in the match came in the first half when there was a ten minute delay to the game after linesman Dennis Drewitt pulled a thigh muscle and, with no fourth officials, there was a danger the game could be abandoned. However, after an announcement was made TV pundit Jimmy Hill, a qualified referee, stepped forward and the game continued with him running the line in a hastily loaned tracksuit. His first job was to flag for offside against Kennedy after he was caught out following a long ball by John Roberts. The incident led to calls for spare officials to be assigned to matches and Shankly said afterwards that Hill was the best linesman he had ever seen, commenting: 'He was always up in position to carry out his duties and nobody knows the game better. It was a pleasure to have him there'.[27]

Liverpool: Clemence, Lawler, Lindsay, Smith, Lloyd, Hughes, Keegan, Cormack, Heighway, Toshack, Callaghan. Sub: Thompson.

Arsenal: Barnett, Rice, McNab, Storey, McLintock, Roberts, Marinello, Ball, Radford,

Kennedy, Graham. Sub: George.
Referee: Mr P.Partidge (Middlesbrough).
Attendance: 47,957.

Football League Division One: Liverpool 5 Sheffield United 0
Saturday 23rd September 1972

While Liverpool were drawing at Highbury, back at Anfield Brian Hall gave a timely reminder of his abilities as he scored twice for the reserves in a 3-1 win over Leeds United. However, it still wasn't enough to earn him a recall to the starting line-up for the following week's home game against Sheffield United. Although John Toshack had sustained a knee injury in a midweek League Cup replay with Carlisle, Phil Boersma, who had come off the bench to score twice in the game, was given the number ten shirt with Hall having to make do with a place on the bench.

The Blades had been unbeaten in their four away league games so far and came to Anfield with the clear aim of frustrating and stifling the Reds with a man-marking system, while the limit of their passing was back to keeper Tom McAllister. One Kopite must have guessed what was in store, for Ray Clemence was tossed a pack of cigarettes as he took up position in goal before the game, in anticipation of him not having much else to do.

For half an hour the visitors tactics worked as Liverpool were restricted to just three attempts on goal, one from Ian Callaghan that was saved and efforts from Chris Lawler and Kevin Keegan, both of which went wide. In the 28th minute the breakthrough finally came when Keegan flicked on a long ball by Larry Lloyd to Boersma, who chested it down and hit an unstoppable volley past McAllister from the edge of the area. Just three minutes later Alec Lindsay struck his first goal of the season, hitting in a low shot off the post from 25 yards after a corner was only partially cleared. With the visitors' game plan in complete disarray Steve Heighway made it 3-0 on 33 minutes, beating two men on the edge of the area before hitting a right foot shot that went in off the angle of post and bar. United were eventually relieved to go into the dressing room at half time just 3-0 down as Liverpool poured forward for the remainder of the half, Keegan having three efforts saved by McAllister.

With United abandoning their man marking system for the second half and employing a 4-3-3 formation, the Reds had plenty of space and were 4-0 up just six minutes after the restart, Peter Cormack firing home from close range after the ball was headed down by Keegan. There was then drama when the Reds were awarded two penalties within the space of two minutes. The first came when Keegan was brought down but Tommy Smith hit the kick wide. Liverpool were rampant and there was still time for Heighway to hit the bar before the second kick was awarded when Emlyn Hughes was felled. This time Smith stood aside and allowed Keegan to take the kick, despite chants from the Kop for the skipper to try again. Keegan made no mistake to make the score 5-0 with still only 54 minutes gone. Liverpool coasted through the rest of the game, mindful of the forthcoming trip to West Germany in the UEFA Cup, but they still had time to test McAllister with a number of long shots, one of which by Hughes struck the post.

Liverpool: Clemence, Lawler, Lindsay, Smith, Lloyd, Hughes, Keegan, Cormack, Heighway, Boersma, Callaghan) Sub: Hall.

Sheffield United: McAllister, Goulding, Hemsley, Flynn, Colquhoun, Hockey, Ogden (Ford), Badger, Dearden, Currie, Warboys.

Referee: Mr W. B. Johnson (Kendal).

Attendance: 42,940.

Football League Division One: Leeds United 1 Liverpool 2
Saturday 30th September 1972

The win took the Reds to the top of the table on goal average from Tottenham Hotspur although it remained extremely tight at the top, just two points separating the top seven teams with a quarter of the season now gone. The Reds' title credentials would really be put to the test in the next two games which were against teams from the leading pack, away to Leeds United on 30th September and home to Everton on 7th October.

In the week of the Leeds game Kevin Keegan and Ray Clemence were rewarded for their excellent early season performances when they were called up to the England squad for the first time for the forthcoming friendly with Yugoslavia at Wembley. There was also newspaper speculation that the Reds would be in the hunt for Manchester United's Brian Kidd, who was seeking a move following the arrival of Wyn Davies and Ted McDougall at Old Trafford. Although Bill Shankly was a known admirer of Kidd, no formal bid was made, especially given the asking price of £200,000. Shankly also made it clear nobody would be leaving Anfield, with clubs keeping an eye on Brian Hall's situation.

For the Elland Road clash John Toshack was still unavailable and he was joined on the treatment table by Tommy Smith, who pulled a calf muscle in the midweek UEFA Cup tie away to Eintracht Frankfurt. Shankly had no hesitation in naming Trevor Storton, who had come off the bench to perform admirably as the Reds secured a 0-0 draw in West Germany, as Smith's replacement. Storton was confident enough in his own ability, saying:

'I feel confident of putting up a good show, it was an awkward time for me to be brought into the game against Frankfurt but after a few minutes I found myself coping all right. The thought that I might get the job against Leeds gives me a tremendous thrill of anticipation. It will not worry me in the least that the opposition will be Leeds. There is nothing like being thrown in at the deep end'.[28]

The evening before the game the *Liverpool Echo* predicted that the Reds still had enough in them to secure both points and that Leeds were not the force they had been, having relied on a relatively easy run of home games to lift them to sixth in the table. Leeds would be buoyed by the return of Jack Charlton and Paul Madeley from injury, but their capture of Scottish defender Gordon McQueen, signed for £45,000 from St Mirren, had come too late for him to be able to play.

Shankly sprung a surprise when he named Emlyn Hughes as captain in Smith's absence rather than Chris Lawler, meaning Hughes's superstition of going onto the pitch last had to be reversed as he was now leading the players out. For much of the first half the Reds missed Smith's leadership and organisation on the pitch as they struggled to impose themselves. It was an ill-tempered game with Kevin Keegan and Johnny Giles booked for fouls and plenty of free kicks being awarded that disrupted the game's flow. Leeds were the better team and aside from a Phil Boersma effort that went narrowly over the bar the Reds rarely threatened.

After half an hour Leeds took the lead when Mick Jones hit a spectacular overhead kick from a Peter Lorimer free-kick. This prompted the Reds into more attacks and Steve Heighway earned a free-kick outside the area when he was felled in full flight by Norman Hunter but it came to nothing. In the 41st minute Larry Lloyd equalised when he rose at the back post to head home a Boersma corner, meaning every Reds outfield player had scored this season. Keegan almost put the Reds ahead before half time with a long range effort that was well held by David Harvey.

The second half flowed much more freely with less fouls taking place and the Reds were taking command. Heighway was especially dangerous and Ian Callaghan did a great job of breaking up any Leeds movement in midfield to keep Liverpool on the attack. When the goal did come, it was down to an error by Jack Charlton who lost his footing while dribbling the ball across the edge of his area, allowing in Boersma to flick the ball past Harvey to the delight of the thousands of Reds fans massed behind Ray Clemence's goal. Leeds inevitably threw everyone forward in search of an equaliser but the Reds defence was solid, Storton gaining more in confidence after his nervy start and Hughes asserting himself far more as captain. Charlton had the ball in the net but it was ruled out for offside, leading to vehement protests from Leeds and a booking for Allan Clarke. It was on the whole a magnificent display from Liverpool, their defence returning to the meanness it was known for after the blips that had occurred a month earlier.

Liverpool: Clemence, Lawler, Lindsay, Storton, Lloyd, Hughes, Keegan, Cormack, Heighway, Boersma, Callaghan. Sub: Thompson.

Leeds: Harvey, Madeley, Cherry, Bremner, Charlton, Hunter, Lorimer, Clarke, Jones, Giles, Bates. Sub: Reaney.

Referee: Mr V. Sinclair (Guildford).

Attendance: 46,468.

Football League Division One: Liverpool 1 Everton 0
Saturday 7th October 1972

The win at Leeds set Liverpool up perfectly for the next week's derby game at Anfield with Everton, who had surprised many so far and lay third in the table. In 1971-72 Liverpool had won the corresponding fixture 4-0 as Everton languished in the bottom half but this was likely to be a far closer game. Tommy Smith, battling to be fit in time, wrote in his *Liverpool Echo* column in the preceding week that Everton were revitalised by new faces but their lack of derby experience could favour the Reds:

> 'They seem to have gained more confidence in midfield, looking a lot more composed than last season and I think the new faces they have got in their team have a lot to do with their reappearance at the top. Everton have made changes and have been revitalised. None of them has experienced a derby atmosphere and it can have a strange effect. For some reason there is no in-between stage. It either inspires you and you have a good game, or it intimidates you and you have a bad one'.

As Liverpool prepared to face Everton in the derby, they were relieved to see no further injuries occur during the midweek League Cup tie at West Bromwich Albion. Both Steve Heighway and Ian Callaghan, who picked up slight knocks at Leeds, came through unscathed and a slight cut to Emlyn Hughes's shin was not considered a problem. Tommy Smith and John Toshack were back in training as Joe Fagan worked hard to get them fit again for the game but on the Friday both were ruled out. Smith only just failed to make the team, but there was more disturbing news for Toshack whose knee was in a splint due to swelling.

In the *Liverpool Echo* the evening before the game, Michael Charters wrote that Liverpool's superior attack and Everton's shaky defence indicated the Reds should win, but form went out of the window in derby games. He pointed to the game two years earlier when Liverpool went to Goodison and won 3-0 against an Everton side with a 100% home record. In the *Daily Post* on the morning of the match, Horace Yates believed there would be no repeat of the Reds' 4-0 triumph the previous season, but their superior mobility in attack should be enough to give them a narrow win. Smith's absence meant Trevor Storton continued to deputise, making his first Anfield start but he didn't feel nervous, with the *Post* quoting him as saying:

> 'I am enjoying my first team games immensely, Everton can't be any

harder than Leeds and that seemed to work out alright. I am learning all the time, I don't think it's been a bad thing to be thrown in at the deep end. That's the way to learn how to swim'.

Fifteen minutes before the game Shankly was presented with two gallons of whisky as he collected the manager of the month awards for September and the previous April, a presentation that had never been made to him. This really stoked up the atmosphere but Liverpool suffered a blow when Everton captain Howard Kendall won the toss, forcing the Reds to kick into the Kop for the first half.

Everton had the first big chance after four minutes when Larry Lloyd slipped allowing Joe Royle a clear shot at goal, but Lloyd recovered in time to block it. Royle had another 25 yard curling shot saved by Ray Clemence in a half that rarely flowed due to a number of fouls and free-kicks. Liverpool came into the game more in the closing stages of the first half and forced a succession of corners, but their shooting was woeful and Blues keeper David Lawson didn't have a save to make. The closest the Reds came to taking the lead was in the 44th minute when Phil Boersma had a shot from a corner that beat Lawson but John Hurst was covering to clear.

Everton started the better side in the second half, David Johnson forcing a fingertip save from Clemence and Tommy Wright's dangerous centre being cut out by the Reds keeper. Liverpool rallied and had a strong penalty appeal waved away when Kevin Keegan went down after a challenge by Wright, then Chris Lawler shot wide from a great position. Kendall should have given Everton the lead midway through the second half when he caught Clemence off his line but hit his shot over the bar. During the last quarter of the game Liverpool gained the upper hand and after 77 minutes their pressure paid off when Heighway crossed from the left and Peter Cormack flung his body at the ball to head in from eight yards. Everton didn't give up, though, and Mike Bernard shot just over a minute later, while John Connolly was denied by a save from Clemence in the last minute as the Reds held on for victory.

In true Mersey derby spirit, both managers were interviewed together for that night's *Match of the Day*, Shankly dubbing it 'the Merseyside Morecambe and Wise show'. The Reds boss was naturally the happier of the two, saying 'There was tremendous effort from both sides and it was a great game considering the tension was electrifying. But we overcame it, the atmosphere was the best I have known for a long time'. Everton's Harry Catterick felt the referee was inconsistent, booking Keith Newton for an innocuous foul but taking no action against Reds players and that his side deserved a draw given the chances they created. Shankly did have some sympathy, responding 'Just as bad fouls as Newton's were unpunished, possibly Newton was unlucky' but he would never have gone as far as saying Everton deserved a point.

The fans' generosity was shown by the collection of £462.23 for the

Liverpool Sportsmens' Association, who assisted in the provision of sports facilities for boys clubs. Shankly was charitable, too, donating one of his gallon bottles of whisky to the police to raffle off for one of their causes.

Liverpool: Clemence, Lawler, Lindsay, Storton, Lloyd, Hughes, Keegan, Cormack, Heighway, Boersma, Callaghan. Sub: Hall.

Everton: Lawson, Wright, Newton, Kendall, Kenyon, Hurst, Johnson, Bernard, Royle, Harvey, Connolly. Sub: Lyons.

Referee: Mr D. W. Smith (Gloucester).

Attendance: 55,975.

Football League Division One: Southampton 1 Liverpool 1
Saturday 14th October 1972

The derby win took Liverpool two points clear at the top of the table as Arsenal went down 1-0 at Sheffield United on the same day. There is no better time to confirm your worth than by scoring a derby winner and Peter Cormack had done just that. After a frustrating start due to injury he was now firmly settled in the Reds side and justifying his club record fee, ghosting in unnoticed to score goals, exactly what he was bought for. Bill Shankly was delighted with Liverpool's position given the fixtures they had faced. The *Daily Post* quoted him on 10th October:

> 'They have pulled out everything to put Liverpool where they are today and have done a really fantastic job in the most demanding of circumstances. Just look at the opposition they have met away from home, Chelsea, Arsenal, Derby, Leeds, every one of them tough games. Some teams have hardly met any opposition at the top of the table, we have met them all except Tottenham and Ipswich'.

Liverpool were the subject of transfer speculation again, as Motherwell's Tom Forsyth, whom the Reds had enquired about the previous season only to be told was not for sale, was made available for transfer. The *Daily Post* reported on 9th October that Motherwell had decided to consider bids from Dundee and Rangers for their midfielder and out of courtesy were making Liverpool aware of this, should they wish to renew their interest. On this occasion the Reds decided not to make a bid and Forsyth went on to enjoy a successful ten-year career with Rangers.

As Liverpool sought to maintain their two-point advantage over their rivals they were still without Tommy Smith and John Toshack when they made the long trek to The Dell to face tenth-placed Southampton. Trevor Storton and Phil Boersma continued to deputise with Brian Hall on the bench and John Webb was added to the squad as thirteenth man for a game at a venue where the Reds had enjoyed mixed fortune since Saints won promotion in 1966. Each side had won three of the six meetings, all of them being close affairs with only Southampton's 2-0 win in 1968-69 coming by more than one goal. The home side were weakened by the absence in defence of John McGrath and Francis Burns, but they had a potent attack in Mick Channon and Ron Davies. However, the evening before the game the *Liverpool Echo* predicted victory was well within the Reds grasp if they could be contained.

Many Reds fans travelling to the game had a gruelling overnight journey with Crown Coachways, who sold tickets through Barnes Travel in County Road costing £2.20 each, departing from St John's Lane at 1130pm on the Friday. The football special train left Lime Street at 8am, costing £2. The Reds players went down by train the day before and then chartered an aircraft to fly back afterwards.

Liverpool attacked from the off, Steve Heighway going on a goalbound run that resulted in him getting barged off the ball by Jim Steele who was booked. The Reds forced a number of early corners, with Cormack seeing a good effort saved by Eric Martin and Boersma firing over from eight yards. As the half wore on, Southampton got more into the game, Channon being particularly dangerous, heading one chance just over and causing Storton to be booked for a tackle on him. After forty minutes, though, Chris Lawler gave the Reds the lead with a shot from just outside the area after Emlyn Hughes's effort was blocked.

Southampton started the second half better with Channon heading over and Brian O'Neil hitting a shot inches wide. But after absorbing the initial pressure the Reds missed a golden chance on the hour when Steve Heighway took the ball around Martin only to mishit his shot. The Saints' equaliser, which came on seventy minutes, was the result of an error by Peter Cormack, who slipped allowing Terry Paine to take possession near the edge of the area. His shot was tipped over by Ray Clemence but from the corner Channon headed in at the near post. The Reds were paying a price in the latter stages for sitting back on their 1-0 lead as Southampton threatened to turn the game around and earn both points, Clemence making two good saves within three minutes of each other from Channon and Davies. Cormack almost atoned for his earlier error when he had a shot well saved by Martin late on but in the end the Reds had to settle for a draw as their lead at the top was cut to one point.

Liverpool: Clemence, Lawler, Lindsay, Storton, Lloyd, Hughes, Keegan, Cormack, Heighway, Boersma, Callaghan. Sub: Hall.

Southampton: Martin, McCarthy, Kirkup, Fisher, Bennett, Steele, Paine, Channon, Davies, Byrne, O'Neil. Sub: Gilchrist.

Referee: Mr C. Thomas (Rhondda).

Attendance: 24,100.

Football League Division One: Liverpool 2 Stoke City 1
Saturday 21st October 1972

The draw at Southampton extended Liverpool's unbeaten run to twelve games in all competitions and was followed by the team's first free midweek of the season. Bill Shankly used the opportunity to give the players a few days off as they got ready for a hectic period of seven games in 22 days, although there was no rest for Steve Heighway who was away playing for the Republic of Ireland in a World Cup qualifier against the Soviet Union.

There was good news with the return to fitness of both Tommy Smith and John Toshack. Smith was reinstalled for the next game at home to Stoke City as captain, although there was a blow for Toshack when he broke down in training on the Friday after he had been declared fit for inclusion in the reserve side. Another player who had been out for some time was Jack Whitham and he was given a run out for the A team as he began the long road back after his cartilage operation.

Tommy Smith described sitting out the games he missed as 'murder' and after being advised by the specialist not to watch the Leeds game but to rest his leg instead was 'driven around the bend' spending the afternoon watching television and listening on the radio.[29] He watched the Everton game from the press box, having been invited to write some comments for a Sunday newspaper and admitted that despite it supposedly being neutral territory he initially forgot that when the game started.[30]

Shankly believed a week with no game had done the players good. He felt they would be rejuvenated and were likely to be sharper. That was certainly the case as, kicking into the Anfield Road, Liverpool were by far the better team early on, Emlyn Hughes and Phil Boersma shooting just wide, with Gordon Banks saving well from another Hughes effort and a 25 yard low drive by Alec Lindsay. It was all Liverpool, the players revelling in the influence of Smith who was driving them forward while full back Chris Lawler was a regular attacker, seeing a header and lob both saved by Banks. Despite the Reds dominance, though, Stoke had a game plan to pack the penalty area, forcing the Reds into mainly long-range efforts, which Banks was happy to deal with.

In the 33rd minute Stoke took the lead against the run of play from an innocuous looking free-kick that was awarded on the halfway line. John Marsh punted it into the area where Geoff Hurst had a shot that hit the bar. It bounced down to Jimmy Greenhoff who headed it into an empty net with Ray Clemence stranded. Liverpool piled on the pressure for the rest of the half without success and there was one dangerous moment when Stoke counter-attacked and Hurst's half-volley went just wide of a post.

Boersma, who had been quiet in the first half, should have equalised within a minute of the restart but after starting a move that finished with

Steve Heighway crossing into the area he somehow hit the ball over the bar from inside the six yard box. Liverpool continued to dominate possession but were running out of ideas as high balls into the box had no height to meet them and passes were often intercepted by the numbers of Stoke players tracking back. It seemed inevitable that if the Reds were to equalise some good fortune was required and it came when an indirect free-kick was awarded in the 66th minute when Banks took too many steps with the ball. Smith touched the ball to Hughes, who hammered it into the roof of the net to the relief of the Kop.

Liverpool poured forward in search of the winner, Kevin Keegan hitting a shot across the face of goal, Boersma having a dipping volley drop just over the bar and Smith's free-kick bouncing off the wall. Finally, in the last minute Ian Callaghan's shot took a deflection off Eric Skeels and deceived Banks to give the Reds a much-deserved victory.

The Liverpool crowd's reputation for its appreciation and banter with visiting goalkeepers was reinforced in this game. As Banks took up his position in the Kop goal for the second half he was given a tremendous reception by the crowd who chanted 'Clemence for England', with the Stoke keeper blowing a raspberry in return. Clemence had been capped at Under 23 level and called up to senior squads without being involved but World Cup winner Banks was still keeping his place at the age of 34 and had earned over seventy caps. Tragically, though, the Kop's chants came true in the most horrible of circumstances as Banks never played for Stoke again, let alone England. The next day he was involved in a car accident when his Ford Granada collided with a van and he lost the sight of one eye, causing his retirement from football. Writing in the *Daily Post* the day after the accident, Bob Whiting said that if the game at Anfield had turned out to be his last, then there could not have been a more nostalgic setting for it. Banks's misfortune, though, did open the England door for Clemence, who now faced a straight battle with Leicester's Peter Shilton for the national keeper's jersey.

Liverpool: Clemence, Lawler, Lindsay, Smith, Lloyd, Hughes, Keegan, Cormack, Heighway, Boersma, Callaghan Sub: Storton.

Stoke: Banks, Marsh, Pejic, Skeels, Smith, Bloor, Dobing, Greenhoff, Hurst, Mahoney, Conroy (Robertson).

Referee: Mr R. Kirkpatrick (Leicester).

Attendance: 45,604.

Football League Division One: Norwich City 1 Liverpool 1
Saturday 28th October 1972

For the next game the Reds took the unusual step of flying to and from

Norwich at high cost, but the usually prudent Peter Robinson believed it was necessary to eliminate as much tiring travel as possible given the punishing schedule they were undergoing. A coach journey would have been arduous and, if scheduled trains were used, a change at London would have been required involving an underground journey.

The Canaries were flying high in their first season in the 1st Division. They were sixth in the table just four points behind the Reds and unbeaten in their seven home games so far, a sequence that included victories over champions Derby and high-fliers Arsenal. However, their manager Ron Saunders knew they would have to be at their best to take anything from this game, writing in the match programme:

> 'One can always expect any team put together by Bill Shankly to go like bombs and play like prospective champions. I think it goes without saying that any points we are able to get today will have to be very well earned indeed'

Emlyn Hughes was ruled out with a thigh injury sustained in the midweek UEFA Cup game with AEK Athens but there was better news for John Toshack, who had recovered from the previous week's setback and was included in the reserve side to face Sheffield Wednesday at Anfield. The injury to Hughes meant a first start for Phil Thompson, who had patiently been waiting for his chance after making a substitute appearance at Manchester United the previous season and twice being an unused substitute so far in 1972-73. In his autobiography *Stand Up Pinocchio*, published by Trinity Mirror Sport Media in 2005, he recalls of the situation:

> 'This is all part of the learning curve as a young pro. You just have to make sure that when the call does come you are ready in every way. The previous week Emlyn Hughes had scored in a 2-1 home win over Stoke City only to aggravate a thigh injury he had been carrying for weeks. I knew he had a problem but "Crazy Horse" had been intent on playing through the pain barrier with the team playing really well at the start of that season. My chance had finally come, I thought "great I'm going all the way to Norwich with Emlyn left behind for treatment, I must have a chance". Shanks did not name the team until half an hour before kick-off. There were no mobile phones then to relay messages back home to the family. The boss pulled me to one side for yet another surprise. He didn't tell me I was playing. He actually asked me if I wanted to play! I just said "YES YES YES"'.

With Thompson in the starting eleven, a fellow Kirkby youngster, John McLaughlin, was on the bench. With Phil Boersma also starting the game, this meant a quarter of the Reds twelve players were from the overspill town which had begun to be developed in the 1950s. It wasn't just at Liverpool where there was Kirkby talent to be found though. There was also Dennis

Mortimer and Alan Dugdale at Coventry City and Terry McDermott at Newcastle, but Thompson doesn't believe there was any magical secret or remember any one particular sports club where there was a production line. It was just a case that they all loved playing football that led to the area becoming a hotbed of talent.[31]

At Carrow Road Liverpool had to settle for a point as Norwich came from behind to equalise and continue their impressive form. The Reds started by far the better team, forcing four corners in the first five minutes. In the opening quarter of an hour Kevin Keegan and Phil Boersma both had shots saved and Steve Heighway hit a fierce effort just past the post. Thompson was playing in midfield and got stuck in making some good tackles to break up Norwich play, as well as starting moves with some good balls to Heighway.

The Reds took a deserved lead after seventeen minutes when Ian Callaghan played a neat one-two with Heighway before passing the ball to Alec Lindsay, whose cross was headed in at the far post by Peter Cormack. Norwich's only chance during the first half-hour came from a free-kick after Tommy Smith had handled, but Graham Paddon's strike rebounded off the wall. After then normal service resumed as Liverpool dominated, Callaghan having a shot saved by Kevin Keelan and Heighway beating the keeper only for his effort to be cleared off the line. A second Reds goal was ruled out in rather harsh circumstances, the referee blowing for half time as a cross from Heighway was going into the box, meaning Cormack's volley into the net didn't count.

In the second half Norwich went straight at the Reds and only the outstretched leg of Ray Clemence prevented an equaliser from David Cross when he went for placement rather than power as he met a cross from Terry Anderson on the edge of the six-yard box. Liverpool regained control of the game, but went for containment rather than all-out attack, only looking to create chances when Norwich gave them space to do so. Cormack almost added a second on the hour when he headed a Lindsay cross narrowly wide and Thompson, fully justifying Shankly's decision to give him a start ahead of the more experienced John McLaughlin, had a shot blocked.

After 69 minutes Liverpool were left to rue earlier missed chances as Norwich scored after a move begun by former Reds midfielder Doug Livermore. His pass out to the right to Max Briggs led to Clive Payne being released and his cross was met by Anderson. Although Clemence saved his first effort he could do nothing about the rebound. Norwich sensed Liverpool were there for the taking and moments later Clemence was almost embarrassed when he dropped a shot from Cross, but he managed to turn around and gather the ball before it went over the line. He then made saves from Anderson and Paddon as the Reds were glad to escape with a point from a match played before a crowd of 36,625, Norwich's highest crowd of the season so far and just 1,600 short of their record crowd for a league match.

Thompson had enjoyed a sound debut playing alongside Peter Cormack who he recalls was great to play beside. He said his first aim was to play well and get some nice headlines, and he was delighted to hear Shankly say afterwards that it still wasn't certain what his best position was. Thompson believed he could always read the game well and was capable of carrying out any instructions given to him, and that he also had an eye for goal as he often found the net for the reserves.[32] However he was realistic enough to know he may not be in the side the next week, recalling 'I knew Emlyn would be back. It was not a problem making way for the great Emlyn Hughes. I was only eighteen and I knew more opportunities would come my way'.[33] One thing that was certain was that he wouldn't be able to stand on the Kop anymore. As recently as the previous season, Thompson would attend games at Anfield if he wasn't away with the reserves, but as he was featured more and more in the local press as part of the side that reached the FA Youth Cup final he found it harder and harder to evade attention.

Despite only managing a draw, the Reds were still in a good position at the top of the league with a third of the season now having been played and having already played their two closest rivals away from home.

Liverpool: Clemence, Lawler, Lindsay, Smith, Lloyd, Thompson, Keegan, Cormack, Heighway, Boersma, Callaghan. Sub: McLaughlin.

Norwich: Keelan, Payne (Howard), Butler, Stringer, Forbes, Briggs, Livermore, Bone, Cross, Paddon, Anderson.

Referee: Mr N.Paget (Coventry).

Attendance: 36,325.

Top of the Division One Table

		Pl	W	D	L	F	A	GA	Pt
1	Liverpool	15	9	4	2	29	15	1.93	22
2	Arsenal	15	8	5	3	21	12	1.75	21
3	Leeds	15	8	4	3	28	17	1.65	20

9

The Battle of Old Trafford and Winter Warmers

Football League Division One: Liverpool 3 Chelsea 1
Saturday 4th November 1972

Bill Shankly called the result against Norwich a travesty as they prepared for the next home game against Chelsea. He believed that if Liverpool kept playing the way they were then another team would soon be sorry, on the morning of the Chelsea game the *Daily Post* reporting him as saying:

> 'Liverpool are a very dangerous team, they could be coming to their best just now. One of these days they are really going to break loose and then somebody is due for a hammering. We only need to show the form we displayed against Norwich to be capable of beating Chelsea'.

The Londoners were in fourth place, three points behind the Reds. Unbeaten in nine games, they had the best away record in the 1st Division, having been beaten only once on their travels so far. But history in the fixture was on the Reds side, with Liverpool having won eight of the nine league games at Anfield between the two sides since Chelsea were promoted in 1963.

For first time in almost two months Shankly was able to name a full strength side for a league game, John Toshack and Emlyn Hughes having come through the midweek League Cup tie with Leeds in which the big Welshman scored. They were also pleased to see Jack Whitham progressing in the A Team after nearly a year out with knee and back injuries and veteran Peter Thompson was back to full fitness and a reserves regular. Chelsea though had problems in goal, with their two first choice keepers, Peter Bonetti and John Phillips being injured, meaning only a second appearance for eighteen year old Steve Sherwood.

Chelsea's young keeper went on to produce a competent display in a game Liverpool dominated, winning 3-1 with much to spare as the Keegan-Toshack partnership created fireworks on the eve of bonfire night. They did start slowly and in the first minute Chelsea were gifted two corners when Chris Lawler needlessly put the ball out for one and then Ray Clemence conceded another when he punched clear. After this though the Reds developed a rhythm and took control of the game, Ian Callaghan firing a free kick wide, with Tommy Smith and Steve Heighway both testing Sherwood with long shots that he held well. The young keeper wasn't fazed by the atmosphere or Liverpool's possession and claimed some corners with confidence as well.

Eventually Liverpool got a reward for their dominance in the 34th minute, Keegan chesting down a Hughes pass before breaking free of his marker and passing to Toshack who calmly slotted the ball past Sherwood. Early in the second half Sherwood saved a Toshack header but just five minutes after the restart the Reds were two up, this time Toshack providing Keegan with a perfectly weighted lob over Dave Webb for him to score. After 55 minutes the Reds went 3-0 ahead, Toshack scoring from a powerful header. After an hour Chelsea finally had a shot on goal, Steve Kember trying his luck from outside the area but his effort went wide.

With a trip to Athens in the UEFA Cup looming, Liverpool eased up but did test Sherwood on occasions, the keeper doing well to turn a Lawler drive round the post for a corner. With fifteen minutes remaining the Reds defence was caught napping when a Chris Garland found space to head a Kember cross across the goalmouth for Tommy Baldwin to tap in. There was never any danger of Chelsea getting back into the game though and Toshack almost completed a hat trick with a dipping thirty yard volley that went just over the bar.

There was even better news for the Reds as news filtered through that Arsenal had surprisingly been beaten at home by Coventry, meaning the Reds were now firmly in the title driving seat with a three point lead.

Liverpool: Clemence, Lawler, Lindsay, Smith, Lloyd, Hughes, Keegan, Cormack, Heighway, Toshack, Callaghan. Sub: Hall.

Chelsea: Sherwood, Locke, McCreadie, Hollins, Webb, Harris, Baldwin, Kember, Garner, Garland, Houseman. Sub: Hinton.

Referee: Mr K. Burns (Wordsley).

Attendance: 48,932.

Football League Division One: Manchester United 2 Liverpool 0
Saturday 11th November 1972

The Chelsea game had shown the strength of the Keegan-Toshack partnership as they each laid on a goal for the other. In the ten games that Toshack had been out, Keegan had managed just two goals, one of them a penalty whereas he had now managed two in two games, having been on target against Leeds in the League Cup in midweek. His performances had confirmed a call-up for England's World Cup qualifier with Wales the following week, where he would be in opposition against Toshack if selected for the starting line-up. This time he knew he would at least be able to link up with the squad, having been forced to withdraw from the Yugoslavia friendly the previous month due to a League Cup replay with West Bromwich Albion.

As Liverpool prepared to face Manchester United at Old Trafford, the independent tribunal finally sat to consider the three-match ban that had been hanging over Larry Lloyd for nearly three months. After reviewing television evidence, they determined that, although he was not entirely blameless, in the incident a sending-off was sufficient punishment and the ban was quashed. It was a good victory for Liverpool, Lloyd being accompanied to London by Bill Shankly and director Syd Reakes. They had gone in confident mood believing that the television footage would clear Lloyd and a precedent had been set a few weeks earlier when Stoke's Geoff Hurst had a ban overturned by the FA appeals panel after a sending-off. A delighted Shankly said 'It just proves what I have always maintained, the lad did nothing to be sent off for. He was in no position to do what the referee and linesman said he had done'. Lloyd was equally happy to be able to just get on with playing knowing the threat of a ban was gone, admitting 'It has been a very worrying time but the decision has been a load off my mind'.[34] Despite the outcome Football League Secretary Alan Hardaker controversially entered the debate, claiming afterwards that the footage showed did not contain the whole of the incident and was different to what the referee actually saw[35].

The Reds were suffering a number of minor injuries in the build-up to the game at Old Trafford, the effects of playing on a hard surface in Athens in the week. Shankly expected them to clear up before the game but he did take Phil Boersma, Trevor Storton and Phil Thompson to their Cheshire hotel as a precaution.

United, European champions just four years earlier and top of the league in the corresponding weekend the previous season, were now in desperate trouble at the bottom of the table with just two wins from sixteen games. However, Shankly believed United's position was not realistic. In the *Daily Post* on the morning of the game he was quoted: 'Who would suggest they will be bottom at the end of the season. They must start rising soon. All we hope is that they don't make a start tomorrow. A glance at their team is enough to tell anybody that'.

United manager Frank O'Farrell said in his programme notes:

'The bigger you are the harder you fall and we are going through this kind of difficult experience at the moment…we are not enjoying the best of times but the barbs aimed our way have frequently been unfair and unjustified…they talk about violence on the terraces but there is such a thing about violence from the typewriters as well'.

The violence on the terraces that O'Farrell referred to unfolded before kick-off as Liverpool fans gathered in the Warwick Road/Scoreboard end, the traditional terrace for away fans, were randomly attacked by United fans after they had started chanting. Fighting spilled onto the pitch as police lost control and this led to hundreds of fans from the Stretford End jumping out of it and running over to join in the assault. Eventually police managed to restore order, making 75 arrests in the process. The trouble could have been far worse had it not been for the confiscation of several weapons beforehand, searches being standard practice at Old Trafford unlike at other grounds.

Peter Etherington was one of the Reds fans to be assaulted but eventually managed to escape and leave his attacker worse for wear. After getting into the ground two hours early due to the nasty atmosphere outside, he remembers in *One Boy and His Kop* how it all flared up minutes before kick-off:

'The Mancs must have had it all planned as they left their stations in the middle of the terrace to go round the back, come up through the entrance close to us and attack us from behind. The mayhem, with people on the running track and all over the pitch, was still going on when the players came out. Our already perilous position was worsened when hundreds ran across the pitch from the Stretford End to join in the caning of the Scousers. There was blood and snot everywhere as we were getting whacked all over the place. There was nothing else for it but to climb over the fence and into the Paddock. As we were getting over the fence the Mancs were trying to drag us back into the steaming cauldron. One of my lovely Mancunian hosts had hold of my left leg and was succeeding in dragging me back to receive my kicking. I kicked back as hard as I could with my right heel. Mine host relaxed his grip as my boot connected with his nose. I would definitely have come to serious harm if I had not lashed out so I feel no shame in saying that the noise of his nose bone splintering beneath my boot was one of the most welcome satisfying sounds I have ever heard. It was a good ten minutes into the game before the bizzies were able to restore order. They allowed the rest of the Scousers left in that mosh pit to climb over the fence and join the others already in the Paddock. There were some hard lads in that Paddock with seriously worried looks on their faces'.

Another fan, Phil Rimmer, didn't see the trouble inside Old Trafford as he got there late, but he does recall being in the Dockers' Club in Cross Lane, which was on the way to the ground from Salford Crescent station. He heard that there had been a commotion outside and next thing a Liverpool fan came in and shouted something along the lines of 'they want us out, who wants a scrap'. Next thing, half of those inside put their pints down and went out to join in. Another supporter who was fortunate to avoid the trouble, although he did see all of it happen, was Chris Wood. After taking a local train to Warwick Road from Piccadilly, he went to the Scoreboard End of the ground and was surprised to find that tickets for the stand were still on sale. He recalls:

'I bought one figuring that it might be better to sit than stand at such a high-profile and volatile fixture. What a good decision that was! I had to sit on my hands and keep my mouth tightly zipped in case I attracted any unwanted attention to myself – certainly if it was the sort of attention I saw our supporters in the enclosure below and in front of me receive. Once that enclosure started filling up, our supporters started to be attacked. The verbal attack you expect, the physical you do not. There were skirmishes all afternoon but it was particularly bad at half-time, when it was obvious that several United supporters were on the fringe of our standing block and were just randomly assaulting our people who were unlucky enough to be where they were'.

The previous season, the Scoreboard End at Old Trafford was being redeveloped and was one large terrace, but the addition of a roof and seating to the rear had inadvertently created an extra problem, as it allowed home fans sat above it to throw missiles down at the terrace where away support was gathered or go and join in the attack. Wood continues:

'I saw a few jump into the enclosure from the seated area where I was to join in. Missiles a-plenty were also flying through the air, from the seats where I was sitting as well as from home supporters in standing areas either side of the enclosure. And all this was greeted with much hilarity by the people I was sitting amongst and I had to kind of pretend that it amused me too but inside I was angry and also pretty scared because I was imagining what it might be like at full-time'.

The trouble meant neither side was able to warm up but the game, which turned out to be a bad-tempered affair that United won 2-0, was able to start just a couple of minutes late with police still escorting some troublemakers out of the ground. It was stormy all around as a high wind was ripping through the ground from the Stretford End, and United decided to use it to their advantage after they won the toss. Liverpool had the early chances, Steve Heighway mishitting a shot and John Toshack heading over from a Peter Cormack free-kick. The tackles were flying in, with Alec Lindsay being booked after eight minutes for a foul on George Best who needed treatment before he could continue, and Ted MacDougall going down in the area and appealing for a penalty which the referee ruled out on the grounds that Chris Lawler's tackle was fair.

Both teams made the most of the conditions and produced an entertaining game. Liverpool were just about on top but United looked far from a side that were bottom of the league with Best and Bobby Charlton both hitting shots just wide. Then the game turned in United's favour with two hotly-disputed decisions in the two minutes before half-time. First Heighway ran on to a good ball by Kevin Keegan and as he tried to round keeper Alex Stepney he appeared to have his legs pulled from under him, but the referee waved play on. Then MacDougall received a pass from Charlton and hit a shot that Ray Clemence saved, but Wyn Davies tapped into an empty net. Liverpool's players were furious and insisted that MacDougall had used his hand to control the ball, surrounding the referee and persuading him to consult the linesman, but even after this the goal was allowed to stand.

After 53 minutes United went further ahead when Charlton released Best on the right and his low cross wasn't dealt with by the Reds defence, rolling through to MacDougall who turned it into the net. Soon afterwards Liverpool were awarded a corner which Alex Stepney punched clear but only as far as Heighway who was on the edge of the box. His low shot through a crowded area looked like it may just sneak inside the post but the United keeper dived to push the ball away.

Liverpool piled on the pressure as they sought to preserve an unbeaten run that stretched to eighteen games in all competitions, but Martin Buchan was outstanding in defence as United restricted their chances. Liverpool's usual composed play got more desperate and they suffered a further blow with ten minutes remaining when Heighway went off injured after a challenge by Willie Morgan.

Tommy Smith put the defeat, which cut the Reds lead at the top to one point, down to just being one of those days when nothing went right. In his *Liverpool Echo* column the following Saturday, he refused to accept that MacDougall hadn't handled the ball and was convinced the Reds were denied a penalty. However, he bemoaned Liverpool's inability to take their chances, believing the reason why United were down at the bottom of the league was because they were weak at the back. As well as being livid at United's first goal being allowed to stand, Shankly was furious that nothing was given when Heighway was brought down, calling it 'one of the most blatant penalty kicks since football began'.[36] He also said that the setback would not lead to a change in the way Liverpool played as he vowed to continue the Reds attacking style:

'A mediocre team could have gone there, bogged them down in a defensive web and got a draw or win out of it. We don't do that, home or away, we aim for a result every time. We always aim to put on an attacking display'.[37]

As well as being disappointed by the defeat, Liverpool's fans then had to run the gauntlet and get away without being subject to a further beating. Chris Wood remembers:

'As soon as that final whistle went, I was gone . . . melting into the November gloom to get a bus back into the city centre and then my train back to London. The train was full of gloating United supporters, who seemed as happy about the beating they gave the Scousers as they were about the result'.

Despite attending 52 of Liverpool's competitive games that season and witnessing more unpleasant scenes at Old Trafford in 1973-74 he vowed never to attend a Liverpool v United game again and has maintained that, despite having been to many of the club's more obscure fixtures over the years. Peter Etherington and Phil Rimmer remember leaving as quickly as possible keeping their heads down and just rushing back to their transport.

Liverpool: Clemence, Lawler, Lindsay, Smith, Lloyd, Hughes, Keegan, Cormack, Heighway (Thompson), Toshack, Callaghan.

United: Stepney, O'Neil, Dunne, Morgan, Sadler, Buchan, Best, MacDougall, Charlton, Davies, Moore. Sub: McIlroy.

Referee: Mr W. S., Castle (Sedgley).

Attendance: 53,944.

Football League Division One: Liverpool 3 Newcastle United 2
Saturday 18th November 1972

Anfield and Melwood were quieter than normal during the next week with some players away on international duty. Ray Clemence, Emlyn Hughes and Kevin Keegan were with England for their World Cup qualifier with Wales in Cardiff on 15th November, where they would come up against John Toshack. It would have been more but Larry Lloyd had been omitted from the England squad and Steve Heighway was forced to pull out of the Republic of Ireland's qualifier with France in Dublin due to the injury sustained at Old Trafford.

Bill Shankly was hoping to go and watch Wales v England, but stayed at home to look after wife Nessie who was ill with tonsillitis. It was still a proud moment for him, though, that four players he had signed, three of them from lower division clubs, had gone on to represent their countries. His only surprise was that it had taken Clemence and Keegan so long to be given their England debuts. The *Liverpool Echo* reported on the morning of the game that he rang the Reds players at their Gloucestershire base and reminded them that as long as they weren't complacent they would be fine.

England won the game 1-0 thanks to a first-half goal from Colin Bell and Keegan was disappointed not to score three minutes from time, when Gary Sprake saved from a one-on-one situation. Toshack was naturally disappointed, telling the *Echo* the next day: 'We keep saying we'll give them a game but we never do. We didn't put them under any pressure and they were good value for their victory'. It meant a quiet debut for Clemence, who got the nod due to Peter Shilton being injured, although he was used to such situations playing behind Liverpool's mean defence. He told the *Echo*: 'I tried to keep up my concentration by taking up positions when the ball was in the other half of the field. I thought I would have been busier early on but the lads played well, not allowing Wales to put on any pressure'.

The four players returned to Melwood to join their team-mates in preparation for the home game with Newcastle United, who were sixth in the table. Malcolm Macdonald, never short of a quote, predicted that his team were capable of ending Liverpool's incredible winning run of home league games. Newcastle had scored more away league goals than anyone else and in the *Liverpool Echo* the evening before the game Macdonald said 'If anybody is going to beat Liverpool on their own ground it will be Leeds or Newcastle, we can score goals as abundantly as anyone'. Macdonald had managed ten goals from seventeen games so far and Liverpool knew all about him as he had hit a hat-trick against the Reds in August 1971 in his first appearance at St James' Park after his transfer from Luton Town.

Steve Heighway had recovered from an injury that had forced him off the field at Old Trafford a week earlier allowing Shankly to name an unchanged side as they sought to put that 2-0 defeat behind them. As promised by Macdonald, Newcastle got goals and he was on the scoresheet himself but the Reds won 3-2 in a game in which they were the better side, although thankful for the fortunate circumstances surrounding their two first-half strikes.

Liverpool started strongly, forcing a free-kick and corner in the first few minutes. They then got the opening goal after just five minutes, Willie McFaul and Frank Clark both leaving the other to collect a Peter Cormack cross and allowing it to end up in the net. The Reds continued the pressure and the only way the Newcastle defence could stop Heighway was by fouling him as they twice conceded free-kicks. McFaul was then involved in another calamity incident when he poleaxed his own player, Bobby Moncur, as he collected a Kevin Keegan cross. Ian Callaghan had two shots that went close, one going over and the other being tipped over the bar but the Reds were rocked after 27 minutes when Newcastle scored against the run of play. From a throw-in on the right, Jimmy Smith crossed the ball into the box and John Tudor ghosted in at the far post to head the ball home.

The scores were level for just eight minutes, with McFaul again handing Liverpool the initiative. After gathering the ball in the area he stepped outside of it while preparing to take his kick, leading the linesman to flag for a free-kick. From this Tommy Smith touched the ball to Alec Lindsay who drove a low shot into the corner of the net. As Liverpool sought to increase their lead before the break, Heighway was again the victim of a few fouls and the crowd were angered when Alec Lindsay went down in the area but the referee waved play on. It led to a chorus of boos towards the referee as the teams left the field at half-time, at which Liverpool were well worthy of their lead, despite the unusual nature of the two goals.

Within two minutes of the restart John Toshack had made it 3-1, taking advantage of the fact his marker Pat Howard had stayed behind in the dressing room for treatment, to volley in a Chris Lawler cross. Toshack had another chance but he put a header into the side netting, Cormack continued to cause problems on the right and Ian Callaghan was in total control of the midfield. But Newcastle got back into the game on 66 minutes when Stewart Barrowclough crossed from the right, Clemence failed to reach the ball and Macdonald hammered it into the net.

The Reds had a penalty awarded five minutes later for handball against Howard, an incident that only the referee appeared to see as there were no appeals from the crowd or the players. The decision may have been an attempt to make up for the failure to award a first-half penalty but Tommy Smith stepped up to take the kick and put it wide of the post. Emlyn Hughes had a good effort well saved by McFaul but Newcastle staged a late rally and the Reds were pleased to see Jimmy Smith hit a 25 yard shot straight at Clemence and Macdonald head a Frank Clark cross wide as they held on for victory.

Liverpool: Clemence, Lawler, Lindsay, Smith, Lloyd, Hughes, Keegan, Cormack, Heighway, Toshack, Callaghan. Sub: Hall.

Newcastle: McFaul, Craig, Clark, Natrass, Howard, Moncur, Barrowclough, Smith, MacDonald, Tudor, Hibbitt. Sub: Hodgson.

Referee: Mr D. Turner (Cannock).

Attendance: 46,153.

Football League Division One: Tottenham Hotspur 1 Liverpool 2
Saturday 25th November 1972

Next up Liverpool faced a tough test at Tottenham Hotspur, who were in fourth place four points behind the Reds. There were reasons to believe that something could be got from the game as Spurs hadn't won two successive matches since the opening week of the season and at home they had only once won by more than one goal. Ominously, though, Martin Chivers was returning to top form after a poor start to the season by his standards and he had played a major part in their 1-0 win at Leicester City the previous week.

A full-strength side travelled to the capital, staying at a hotel in Paddington. While on the coach to White Hart Lane, the players heard on the radio that if they could overcome Spurs in a League Cup tie in nine days' time, they'd face Blackpool or Wolverhampton Wanderers in the semi-finals of the competition.

There was again trouble on the terraces before the game, with police having to move in to segregate the crowd and one fan being carried away on a stretcher. On the pitch, though, two first-half goals put the Reds firmly on their way to victory as they maintained their unbeaten record in London. They almost took a sensational lead in the first minute when John Toshack nodded down a long throw from Steve Heighway but Kevin Keegan's shot crashed down off the bar. Spurs hit back, taking control of the midfield and in the tenth minute an Alan Gilzean header was tipped over the bar by Ray Clemence. The Reds managed to regain a foothold in the game, with Peter Cormack and Toshack both hitting efforts over the bar, although they almost went behind when Clemence was beaten by Cyril Knowles but Alec Lindsay managed to get back to clear the ball over the bar.

A minute after almost going 1-0 down, Heighway gave Liverpool the lead after a poor goal-kick by Pat Jennings fell at his feet and he created a shooting chance for himself to score with a left foot drive from the edge of the area. Five minutes before the break, Keegan dived low to head home a second from a Cormack cross to give the Reds a comfortable half-time lead. Rather than sit back in the second half Liverpool went for the jugular, dominating the midfield and creating chances for the forwards, with Toshack and Heighway both seeing efforts go inches wide and Chris Lawler getting up to go close with a shot. With seventeen minutes left Spurs were thrown a lifeline when Knowles broke up a Liverpool attack and hit a long ball to Chivers who appeared offside. The Reds appealed but there was no flag and he rounded Clemence to score.

This gave Spurs some impetus and Chivers hit a shot just wide, but no onslaught came and the Reds could have had a third only for Keegan's header to be turned over the bar by Jennings. With second-placed Arsenal losing 5-0 at Derby County, the Gunners dropped to third in the table with Leeds rising to second, two points behind the Reds.

Liverpool: Clemence, Lawler, Lindsday, Smith, Lloyd, Hughes, Keegan, Cormack, Heighway, Toshack, Callaghan. Sub: Storton.

Tottenham: Jennings, Evans, Knowles, Pratt, England, Naylor, Gilzean, Perryman, Chivers, Peters, Pearce. Sub: Holder.

Referee: Mr H. Williams (Yorkshire).

Attendance: 45,399.

Football League Division One: Liverpool 4 Birmingham City 3
Saturday 2nd December 1972

Going into December Bill Shankly set a target of six points out of eight available that month, hinting that he would be satisfied with draws in successive away games that the Reds faced against West Bromwich Albion and Ipswich Town. They would have to do this, though, without Tommy Smith, who cracked four ribs in a car accident while driving to his Crosby home after the Reds had arrived back in Liverpool from the Tottenham game. His car skidded and hit a tree and after being treated at hospital in Ormskirk he went into a nursing home in Crosby where he was expected to remain for two weeks.

Before the two away games there was a home encounter with Birmingham

City, who were sixteenth in the table and had lost eight of their eleven away fixtures so far. Kevin Keegan, who had suffered a badly bruised thigh during the midweek UEFA Cup game in Berlin, passed a late fitness test. Keegan's was the latest in a long line of injuries that had occurred in midweek games, following on from ones to Emlyn Hughes, Tommy Smith John Toshack that had forced them to miss matches. Remarkably, though, no player had so far sustained an injury in a league match that caused them to miss out on the next game.

In an amazing clash Birmingham came within a whisker of ending Liverpool's run of eighteen successive home league wins. Described by the *Liverpool Echo* that night as 'spectacular, incredible, surely one of the soccer spectaculars of the season', the visitors led 2-0 and 3-1 in the first half before the Reds stormed back to win 4-3.

Birmingham, who included Shankly's nephew Roger Hynd in their side, gave Liverpool an early scare when Gordon Taylor crossed from the left and Bob Hatton headed just over the bar. They continued to give the Reds problems and were fully deserving of their opening goal on twelve minutes, Taylor's 25 yard shot deflecting off Trevor Storton and leaving Ray Clemence wrong-footed. Liverpool responded and Keegan forced a brilliant save from Mike Kelly but in the twentieth minute Birmingham broke away again, Taylor crossing for Hatton who headed down for Bobby Hope to volley in from close range. Ian Callaghan saw a long-range effort turned away for a corner by Kelly before Alec Lindsay pulled one back for the Reds with a free-kick from just outside the box on 32 minutes.

As Liverpool pressed for an equaliser, they were dealt another sucker punch after 42 minutes, a long clearance finding Bob Latchford and he swapped passes with Hatton before shooting past Clemence. Other teams may have wilted but not Liverpool and they were right back in the game a minute before half time when Peter Cormack bundled the ball over the line after Keegan had hit in a low cross from the byline.

There was a tremendous atmosphere at the start of the second half, which kicked off in torrential rain and hard but fair tackles were flying in from both sides. In the 54th minute the Reds drew level, Lindsay again the scorer from a free-kick which he sent hard and low into the corner of the net with his left foot, which was referred to as the can-opener by Tommy Smith.[38] Most of the game was being played in the Birmingham half now as the Kop roared Liverpool on, knowing that a victory would increase their lead on at least one of their rivals as Arsenal were playing Leeds at Highbury. However, with fifteen minutes remaining the ball was in the Liverpool net, Storton again unlucky to see an effort from Gary Pendrey deflect off him. On this occasion, though, the referee awarded a foul against Hatton, who had been jostling with Storton at the time.

Three minutes after their let-off, Liverpool went ahead for the first time in the game when Keegan flicked a Clemence goal-kick into the path of Toshack, who kept his nerve to place the ball past Kelly. There was still more drama to come, with Lindsay almost getting an unlikely hat-trick only to be denied by a great save from the keeper. Both sides, whose players were caked in mud, were given a standing ovation at the end with every one of the 22 players on the pitch having given their all in search of victory.

Liverpool: Clemence, Lawler, Lindsay, Storton, Lloyd, Hughes, Keegan, Cormack, Heighway, Toshack, Callaghan. Sub: Boersma.

Birmingham: Kelly, Martin, Want, Pendrey, Hynd, Harland, Hope, Calderwood, Latchford, Hatton, Taylor. Sub: Bowker.

Referee: Mr A. L. Hart (Kent).

Attendance: 45,407.

Football League Division One: West Bromwich Albion 1 Liverpool 1 Saturday 9th December 1972

With Arsenal beating Leeds 2-1, it meant Liverpool now had a three point lead at the top over the Gunners with a game in hand, while Leeds were four points behind the Reds having played the same number of games. Tony Waddington, manager of Stoke City who had played all of the top three teams, was convinced the title was a two-horse race between Liverpool and Leeds and that the Reds would have the edge. In the *Liverpool Echo* on the evening of the Birmingham game, he was quoted:

> 'I feel the championship has got to go to Liverpool for they have developed the consistency that was such a part of the Leeds set-up. Liverpool seem to be almost invincible, even if they are not playing particularly well in a game, inevitably they will win'.

Trainer Joe Fagan, always one for detailed analysis of all things that go on in games and training, pointed out the improvements Liverpool had made on the previous season. There were now twenty games gone and Liverpool had taken two more points than they had in matches against the same teams the previous season, compared to Leeds having stayed static. He also stated that Liverpool had scored more goals than anyone else and this was down to Alec Lindsay and Peter Cormack, who had scored four and six goals respectively. Lindsay hadn't scored at all in 1971-72 but now had as many as Kevin Keegan while the player Cormack replaced, Brian Hall, had only got on the scoresheet once the season before.[39]

For the visit to The Hawthorns the Reds were again struck with the curse of injuries having occurred in a midweek game. As the Reds crashed out of the League Cup, losing 3-1 at Tottenham Hotspur, Kevin Keegan suffered a recurrence of the thigh injury that had made him doubtful for the previous game and this time he was not included in the travelling party after failing a fitness test on the Friday. There was better news, though, for John Toshack, who had suffered concussion after a clash of heads, as he was declared fit.

Amid concern at the number of goals conceded in the Spurs and Birmingham games, Trevor Storton was dropped and Phil Thompson named in the side. The Kirkby youngster had come on at half-time for Toshack at Spurs and played at the back, with Storton moving up front. He put in a competent performance against Martin Chivers but for the Albion game he was played in his usual midfield position, with Emlyn Hughes partnering Larry Lloyd in defence.

Albion were boosted by the arrival of Willie Johnston, a £135,000 capture from Rangers as they sought to pull away from the relegation zone, where they were languishing in nineteenth position just a point ahead of bottom club Crystal Palace. Every Johnston touch was cheered early on but it was Liverpool who had the better of the opening play, Phil Boersma heading just wide and Toshack hitting the post from the edge of the area. The deserved goal came after 22 minutes from a free-kick, which was floated into the box by Ian Callaghan and Peter Cormack headed the ball down for Boersma to place past Peter Latchford.

Johnston was proving a threat to Liverpool down the flanks, but Albion's forwards were not taking advantage of the crosses that he was putting in. Liverpool were happy to play a containing game, with Cormack dropping back frequently to help Chris Lawler deal with Johnston and Callaghan and Thompson maintaining midfield control. Hughes was giving extra solidity to the defence and Thompson was like a veteran in midfield, putting in a performance that belied his teenage years, creating attacks as well as breaking up opposition play. He got forward to put in a long-range effort, as did Phil Boersma, but neither were anywhere near on target.

In the second half Liverpool stepped up the pace as, helped by a strong wind, they looked to finish the game off, Steve Heighway going closest when he struck a low angled shot just wide of the post. The home crowd were getting on their team's back, but the Reds were rocked in the 69th minute when Albion scored a goal out of nothing for an undeserved equaliser. John Wile hit a long clearance upfield which was headed on by Bobby Gould to Tony Brown, who went past Lloyd and hit the ball past Clemence. Hughes got back to scramble the ball clear, but both the referee and linesman believed the ball had crossed the line and gave a goal.

Liverpool's cause in seeking a winner was not helped thirteen minutes from time when Cormack was sent off for retaliation after being fouled by Asa Hartford, the latest of many harsh challenges the Reds had been subjected to in the game. It was a stormy few minutes, as just beforehand Lloyd had injured Len Cantello with a fierce challenge, causing the Albion player to be stretchered off. The sending-off sparked angry scenes in the stands, with one fan shouting and climbing into the press box before being hauled away by police.

The game petered out with no other major goalmouth incidents and the Reds had to settle for a point which was acceptable in the circumstances of such a physical game and coming in the aftermath of having played League Cup games on the Monday and Wednesday. Afterwards Bill Shankly said that the Reds dressing room resembled a first aid tent, with six players requiring treatment for cuts. In the following Monday's *Liverpool Echo* he was quoted as saying: 'To put it bluntly they were crude. Never in all my years in football have I seen so many cuts and bruises in one match'.

The league season was now halfway through and the Reds had every reason to be satisfied with the way things had gone so far. They were top of the league, two points ahead of Arsenal with a game in hand and three ahead of Leeds, and with more goals than anyone else. There was strength in depth, as was shown by the goalscoring ability of Phil Boersma when he had come into the side for Toshack or Keegan and the emergence of Phil Thompson. Shankly now had a quandary of who to select up front and this was added to by the return to fitness of Jack Whitham. There were concerns in defence, with more goals having been conceded than in the whole of 1970-71, but it had to be taken into account that Tommy Smith had been missing for many games and Ray Clemence had been carrying an injury earlier in the season. Such defensive problems had led to the lead being surrendered in five games so far. However, looking ahead there were far less midweek fixtures to worry about and if the Reds could find a way to kill off games more often, then there was every chance the championship trophy could end up at Anfield.

Liverpool: Clemence, Lawler, Lindsay, Thompson, Lloyd, Hughes, Boersma, Cormack, Heighway, Toshack, Callaghan. Sub: Webb.

West Bromwich: Latchford, Nisbet, Cantello (Suggett), Wile, Wilson, Robertson, Brown A, Brown T, Gould, Hartford, Johnston. Sub: Suggett.

Referee: Mr T. Reynolds (Swansea).

Attendance: 27,213.

Football League Division One: Ipswich Town 1 Liverpool 1
Saturday 16th December 1972

The Reds confirmed on the Monday after the West Bromwich game that they would be appealing against Peter Cormack's impending three-match ban that came with the sending-off. Despite Bill Shankly's public show of support, Cormack recalls that privately the boss was fuming. In his autobiography *From the Cowshed to the Kop*, published by Black & White in 2012 he wrote of being summoned to Shankly's office regarding the incident and being told:

'Peter son, you let a lot of people down on Saturday. You let yourself down, your family, your Liverpool teammates, but most of all you let down the people who pay your wages – the supporters of Liverpool Football Club. Always remember that what you do on the park will determine if their next week at work will be a good week or a bad week. Next time you want to kick somebody up the backside, do it to Tommy Smith at training and after that you'll never kick anybody again. I've had a word with Bob Paisley and Doc Reid and they have made a detailed list of all the injuries and the bruises that those dirty West Bromwich players inflicted on you on Saturday. I have already sent a telegram to the FA's disciplinary committee requesting a personal hearing and that Bob and our club doctor accompany you when you appear before them. Liverpool Football Club will support you 100 per cent and do everything we can to stop them suspending you'.

There was also a strange international call-up that week with Steve Heighway being selected in the same side as Emlyn Hughes and Ray Clemence. The three Reds players were named by Sir Alf Ramsey in the squad for the Three v Six game at Wembley on 3rd January, a match between sides selected from the three countries about to join the Common Market and the six already in it.

Looking ahead to the game at Ipswich, Bill Shankly was satisfied at the Reds position and indicated that although they would be going for victory at Portman Road he would not be disappointed with a draw. He told the *Liverpool Echo* two days beforehand: 'If we don't lose on Saturday we will have done very well and will be in a very strong position. Then we will have two home games in hand because of the 22 league games we will have played, twelve have been away'.

Kevin Keegan returned to fitness in time to make the trip, but it wasn't Phil Boersma who made way for him. Shankly opted to reward him for his performances and goals in the absence of others which had amounted to eight in all so far, as he kept his place at the expense of John Toshack. This was a surprising choice considering Toshack was the leading scorer and Keegan seemed to thrive more in his presence. Steve Heighway, who was of similar style to Boersma, would have been the more likely candidate to drop out.

There was still no sign of a comeback for Tommy Smith, who had returned to light training at the start of the week but was still a few weeks away from being ready for action again. Smith had spent most of the time since the accident either in hospital or resting at home, and taken the time to respond personally to every get-well card and goodwill message that had been sent to him if an address was included. Of his return to training, he said in his *Liverpool Echo* column on the day of the Ipswich game:

'I've been training this week and feeling better every day. The first day I had a little difficulty catching my breath but each day I feel I'm getting nearer to full physical fitness. Once I get my fitness back it's just a case of waiting for the OK from the specialist that my ribs have healed sufficiently. At present I'm just running and doing exercises because obviously I must avoid physical contact'.

Ipswich were in fourth place, five points behind Liverpool, and defeat for the Reds would blow the title race wide open. Their side had been boosted by the recent signing of David Johnson, deemed surplus to requirements at Everton. He had scored four goals in his first three games since a £125,000 move and overcame a groin injury to be fit for this one. Despite his goals, he still felt his all-round game could improve and that Ipswich were underrated, promising a tough time for Liverpool. The day before the game he was quoted in the *Daily Post*:

'Everyone thinks of Ipswich as a middle-of-the-table team but they'll have to change their minds when we beat Liverpool. We're fourth now, if we beat them and keep up the good results we've been having we'll be ahead of them in the New Year. Liverpool are a great side, if we can beat them we can beat anyone'.

Johnson's manager Bobby Robson believed his side were capable of raising a few eyebrows, too, writing in the match programme: 'We consider ourselves to be live championship contenders and this afternoon's clash is a real four point affair. I consider there are eight clubs still in with a wonderful chance of capturing the title and we are one of them'

Watched by comedian Jimmy Tarbuck, Liverpool took the game to Ipswich from the start, Ian Callaghan playing a superb first-minute through ball beyond Mick Mills towards Heighway but, although he got the cross in, it wasn't powerful enough to reach Keegan and Allan Hunter cleared. Heighway gave Mills a torrid time, forcing a succession of corners but with Toshack out of the side the Reds didn't utilise them as much as they could have done. Callaghan and Phil Thompson were dominating the midfield creating attacks, one of which saw Keegan shoot just wide. For the first 24 minutes the only time Ray Clemence touched the ball was when he received a backpass and, when he finally had a save to make from a header by Bryan Hamilton, it posed no difficulty.

Immediately after Hamilton's header the Reds took the lead with a goal that started off from Clemence's kick upfield. Callaghan found a perfect pass that evaded Mills and reached Heighway, who rounded the keeper and rolled the ball into an empty net. Ipswich fought straight back, Peter Morris hitting a shot just wide from thirty yards and Mick Lambert should have done better when Hunter headed the ball down for him but his close range effort rebounded off the angle of post and bar. Callaghan and Thompson lost control of the midfield for a spell but Larry Lloyd remained dominant in defence clearing up anything that came to him. After a counter attack that saw Peter Cormack try an audacious long-range lob that stretched the keeper, Liverpool regained control of the game in the run-in to half time, Ipswich's only shot coming from South African Colin Viljoen, which was so bad it cleared the roof of the stand.

Ipswich started the better of the two teams in the second half, Trevor Whymark having a fierce low drive go just wide. After 52 minutes the equaliser came when Lloyd, impeccable until then, sliced his clearance from a cross into the path of Lambert who had the simple job of firing the ball home with Clemence stranded. Once again Liverpool had let a lead slip and with the home crowd now fired up the Reds were rattled for a while as Ipswich poured forward in search of another goal.

After weathering the initial storm the Reds were able to get back into the game and it turned into a tense end-to-end battle as both sides looked for a winner. Thompson, again displaying maturity beyond his years, hit a shot over the bar and Hunter cleared a Boersma cross that looked destined to set up Keegan to score. At the other end Viljoen hit another shot high over the bar and Chris Lawler made an excellent covering tackle after Whymark had broken free following an unfortunate collision between Lloyd and Emlyn Hughes. With Heighway not looking as dangerous as in the first half, Brian Hall came off the bench with fifteen minutes remaining but in the end both sides had to settle for a point.

Liverpool: Clemence, Lawler, Lindsay, Thompson, Lloyd, Hughes, Keegan, Cormack, Heighway (Hall), Boersma, Callaghan.

Ipswich: Best, Mills, Harper, Morris, Hunter, Beattie, Hamilon, Viljoen, Johnson, Whymark, Lambert. Sub: Miller.

Referee: Mr P. R. Walters (Bridgwater).

Attendance: 25,693.

Top of the Division One Table

		Pl	W	D	L	F	A	GA	Pt
1	Liverpool	22	13	6	3	43	26	1.65	32
2	Arsenal	23	13	5	4	31	23	1.35	31
3	Leeds	22	12	6	4	43	24	1.79	30

10

A Cup Too Far

By Christmas Liverpool had played 22 league games and six in the UEFA Cup, a punishing schedule compared to today. In 2011-12 there were seventeen Premiership rounds before Christmas, while teams competing in Europe would have generally played six or eight games. Another big difference now is in the League Cup, where teams competing in Europe now enter at the third round stage and there are no replays, meaning a maximum of three games in the competition before Christmas. In 1972-73, though, it was a different story for the Reds, as entry at the second round stage, postponements and replays stretched them to the limit before they eventually bowed out in the quarter-finals.

League Cup 2nd Round Carlisle United 1 Liverpool 1
Tuesday 5th September 1972

The campaign started on 5th September with a sentimental journey for Bill Shankly as the Reds travelled to Second Division Carlisle United, where he was manager for the 1949-50 and 1950-51 seasons when they were in the Third Division North. There was no question of this game being treated lightly, Shankly was determined to avoid a replay and the side that took the field at Brunton Park was the same as the one that had played at Derby in the league three days earlier.

The build-up to the game was overshadowed by events at the Olympic Games in Munich, where that morning members of the Black September paramilitary organisation had taken Israeli athletes hostage. The crisis would come to a bloody conclusion in the hours immediately following the game, with a failed rescue attempt leaving eleven Israelis, five Black September members and one German policeman dead.

In the game Liverpool looked to be in control only to hand the initiative to the home side and were lucky to escape with a draw. After withstanding some early Carlisle pressure the Reds dominated the first half and Kevin Keegan gave them a 41st minute lead after a John Toshack shot had been beaten into his path by the keeper. The Reds cruised through the second half and were happy just to keep possession, but they were undone after 71 minutes when Chris Lawler misplaced a pass and Les O'Neill equalised for Carlisle. With two minutes left the Reds had an almighty let-off when Frank

Lane dropped a cross into the path of Bobby Owen, who hit the post, and from the rebound O'Neill's effort was blocked by Tommy Smith.

Liverpool: Lane, Lawler, Hughes, Smith, Lloyd, Cormack, Keegan, Hall, Heighway, Toshack, Callaghan. Sub: Thompson.

Carlisle: Ross, Derrett, Gorman, Laidlaw, Winstanley, Ternent, Train, Martin, Owen, Bowles (O'Neill), Balderstone.

Referee: Mr K. Styles (Barnsley).

Attendance: 16,257.

League Cup 2nd Round Replay: Liverpool 5 Carlisle United 1 Tuesday 19th September 1972

By the time the replay came around two weeks later Carlisle's most dangerous player, Stan Bowles, who had been substituted in the first game due to a stomach complaint, had joined Queens Park Rangers for £110,000. The game or competition didn't catch the fans' imagination at this stage – no tickets at all were issued for the replay and the attendance of 22,128 was the lowest at Anfield since the Reds returned to the First Division in 1962. But Shankly made it clear it was a competition he wanted to win, even suggesting that he preferred it to Europe. The evening before the game the *Liverpool Echo* quoted him as saying:

'We have a young team and we have not yet had a midweek without a match this season. In fact the season will be at least eight weeks old before we get a break. We could have done with being out of one of the competitions this season and if it was my choice it would be Europe which we didn't play in. By missing Europe we would eliminate a lot of tiring travelling. Our bread and butter is here and because there is not the travelling expenses involved you can make a lot of money in the later rounds of the League Cup. You can get about £40-50,000 in the final'.

A full-strength Liverpool beat Carlisle 5-1, a result that didn't do the Second Division side justice. 2-0 down at half time to goals from Kevin Keegan and Phil Boersma, they pulled one back five minutes after the restart through Bobby Owen. The visitors then wouldn't give the Reds any room on the ball, forcing a fine fingertip save from Ray Clemence and also hitting two shots just wide. After weathering the storm, Liverpool's superior fitness showed and they regained command in the last quarter of the game. Although Tommy Smith had a penalty saved, goals in the last fifteen minutes from Chris Lawler, Boersma and Steve Heighway gave them a flattering margin of victory.

Liverpool: Clemence, Lawler, Lindsay, Smith, Lloyd, Hughes, Keegan, Cormack, Heighway, Toshack (Boersma), Callaghan.

Carlisle: Ross, Derrett, Gorman, Laidlaw, Winstanley, Ternent, Train, Martin, Owen,

O'Neill, Balderstone. Sub: Delgardo.

Referee: Mr R. Tinkler (Lincolnshire).

Attendance: 22,128.

League Cup 3rd Round: West Bromwich Albion 1 Liverpool 1
Tuesday 3rd October 1972

The third round draw handed Liverpool a tricky away tie at West Bromwich Albion. The Reds allocation of stand tickets arrived in unusual fashion courtesy of Chester, whose second round second replay against Southampton took place at Albion's Hawthorns ground the day after the Reds had beaten Carlisle. The Fourth Division side brought back the tickets, which ranged in price from 75p to £1.25, on Liverpool's behalf, delivering them to Anfield the next day.

Despite the game coming four days before the derby with Everton, Shankly resisted the temptation to rest Steve Heighway and Ian Callaghan, who were carrying niggling injuries, as he sought to get the tie over and done with at the first attempt to avoid a replay. However, the Reds missed a host of chances before Asa Hartford gave Albion the lead in the 66th minute. Eventually Heighway rescued the tie in the 87th minute when he beat two defenders and hit a low shot into the corner of the net to earn the Reds a replay.

Liverpool: Clemence, Lawler, Lindsay, Storton, Lloyd, Hughes, Keegan, Cormack, Heighway, Boersma, Callaghan. Sub: Hall.

West Brom: Latchford, Nisbett, Wilson, Cantello, Wile, Robertson, Suggett, Brown T, Gould, Brown A, Hartford. Sub: Merrick.

Referee: Mr R. E. Lee (Cheadle).

Attendance: 17,756.

League Cup 3rd Round Replay: Liverpool 2 West Bromwich Albion 1
Tuesday 10th October 1972

The replay took place the following Tuesday meaning Ray Clemence, Emlyn Hughes, Kevin Keegan and Larry Lloyd were unable to play for England in a friendly with Yugoslavia. Sir Alf Ramsey's initial squad of 22 was slashed to just eleven, including two goalkeepers, due to the impact of League Cup replays.

The game was again a cash-only affair with no tickets being issued and those who turned out saw Liverpool need a winner late in extra time to avoid the tie going to a second replay. The Reds looked jaded after a tough game against Everton the previous Saturday and went behind to an Alastair Robertson strike on fifty minutes. This sparked the Reds into life and Emlyn Hughes equalised in the 62nd minute with a fierce drive that gave Peter

Latchford no chance. The Albion keeper then put in a heroic goalkeeping performance to keep the scores level. Liverpool also hit the bar twice before Keegan finally broke the deadlock with thirty seconds of extra time remaining when he headed in an Alec Lindsay cross.

Liverpool: Clemence, Lawler, Lindsay, Storton, Lloyd, Hughes, Keegan, Cormack, Heighway, Boersma (Hall), Callaghan.

West Bromwich: Latchford, Nisbet, Wilson, Cantello (Woolgar), Wile, Robertson, Suggett, A Brown, Gould, T Brown, Hartford.

Referee: Mr A. E. Morrisey (Bramhall).

Attendance: 26,461.

League Cup 4th Round: Liverpool 2 Leeds United 2
Tuesday 31st October 1972

The reward for beating West Bromwich was a home game with Leeds, who overcame Aston Villa in their replay the following night. There was no apathy for this one, although the attendance of 44,609 was still not as high as the record League Cup crowd at Anfield of 45,957 that had attended against Bolton in 1967-68.

Again, Liverpool paid a price for failing to finish Leeds off after taking the lead and had to settle for a draw. The Reds dominated the first half, John Toshack heading just wide and Kevin Keegan forcing a point-blank save from David Harvey before meeting Steve Heighway's cross with a powerful header on the half-hour to make it 1-0. Harvey saved from Emlyn Hughes and Heighway before the break, only for Leeds to score a freak equaliser with the final kick of the half. Chris Lawler conceded a corner which Eddie Gray took and his inswinging kick deceived the Reds defence before being helped over the line by Mick Jones.

Leeds were rejuvenated by their good fortune and started well in the second half, taking the lead on the hour when Peter Lorimer turned in a Gray cross. For a period Liverpool looked likely to concede another as they failed to string more than a couple of passes together, but Leeds's cockiness was their downfall and the Reds managed to regain a stranglehold. Toshack had a great chance when he forced a save from Harvey from a tight angle, then stabbed home an equaliser with ten minutes remaining. Afterwards Shankly said that the Leeds keeper was the difference between the two sides, saying: 'The misfortunes against Leeds were unbelievable, the goalkeeper got them a draw. It was Harvey against Liverpool'.[40]

Liverpool: Clemence, Lawler, Lindsay, Smith, Lloyd, Hughes, Keegan, Cormack, Heighway, Toshack, Callaghan. Sub: Boersma.

Leeds: Harvey, Madeley, Cherry, Bremner, Ellam, Hunter, Lorimer, Clarke, Jones, Bates, Gray, Clarke. Sub: Yorath.

Referee: Mr J. Holmewood (Middlesex).
Attendance: 44,609.

League Cup 4th Round Replay: Leeds United 0 Liverpool 1
Wednesday 22nd November 1972

A draw was the result neither side wanted, with the following two midweeks being taken up by European and international fixtures respectively meaning it was not known when the replay would take place. The following Sunday the League Management Committee made the decision both sides feared when they announced the replay must take place on Monday 20th November, with the winners playing their fifth round tie at home to Tottenham two days later. Although both clubs were naturally unhappy with this decision, it was not unexpected as Spurs had been victims of the same situation themselves, having had to play a third round second replay on the Monday before their fourth round game. Liverpool Secretary Peter Robinson's appeal that two games in three days would lead to mountainous organisational difficulties, a strain on financial resources of supporters and devalue the competition, had fallen on deaf ears.

The League then had even worse news for Liverpool in the event of the Leeds game needing a second replay. They announced that it would take place at Old Trafford on the night of the fifth round ties on Wednesday 22nd November, with the winner taking on Spurs the following Monday, 27th November, just two days before a potential UEFA Cup tie for the Reds. Such a decision posed Spurs with an even bigger problem, as they faced the possibility of travelling 200 miles north on the Monday, then on to an as-yet unknown European destination for a game on the Wednesday. Further complications were faced when five hours of torrential rain on 20th November meant Elland Road was waterlogged, forcing the postponement of the replay at two hours before kick-off. Despite the additional problems this caused, Shankly admitted there was no way the game could have gone ahead and refused to worry about possible fixture congestion, telling *Daily Post* reporter Horace Yates that there was no point in conjecture.

The game was re-scheduled for two nights later, with League Secretary Alan Hardaker promising that the winners wouldn't now need to play Spurs in the same week as European ties. Writing in the *Liverpool Echo* on 21st November, Chris James wondered why the Football League were causing so much of a fuss over getting the games played, as there were plenty of dates from mid-December when ties could take place. While it would mean the semi-finals, scheduled for 6th and 13th December, being put back, the final wasn't until 17th February and so there would be plenty of time to resolve everything.

At Elland Road on 22nd November, a last-gasp goal from Kevin Keegan gave the Reds victory to take them into the quarter-finals for the first time. It was a hard-fought game that threatened to spiral out of control at times as tackles flew in from both sides. A lunge by Allan Clarke on Ian Callaghan went unpunished after nine minutes and that set the tone for the tackles that followed, one of which from Emlyn Hughes on Billy Bremner led to a booking. Tommy Smith was also booked for dissent in a game when heads were shaken at many of the referee's decisions, including the one to award a penalty to Leeds in the 63rd minute after Smith had made a superb tackle on Bremner. After making the challenge Smith was stunned to see the referee pointing to the spot as none of the home players had appealed for a penalty. Justice was done, though, when Johnny Giles struck the kick against the bar.

Liverpool had opted for containment in the first half, where most of the game was played in midfield, although Peter Cormack did try a long-range effort that hit the bar. They were more adventurous in the second half but with both defences firm and Larry Lloyd especially outstanding for the Reds, it was going to need either a piece of magical play or a mistake to see the deadlock broken. That came in the 90th minute from Jack Charlton, who overhit a backpass that went just past the post and out for a corner. Steve Heighway took it and from eight yards out Keegan headed it past David Harvey, a well-deserved goal for a player who had run his heart out in pursuit of the Reds cause.

Bill Shankly, though, had missed the goal, having been on his way down to pitchside from the directors' box so he could give instructions for extra time. Naturally delighted, he told the *Liverpool Echo:* 'What a great finish to a fantastic game. What a tremendous show of strength these teams put up. I could write a book about our games with Leeds'. Leeds boss Don Revie agreed but felt it would have been different if the penalty had gone in. He said: 'It was just one of those things, if the penalty had have gone in I reckon we would have had them rocking. But anyway it was a great game'. Despite the penalty miss Smith was still fuming about the decision afterwards, saying: 'I thought it was a goal kick. I was staggered when the referee pointed to the spot because Billy Bremner had gone one way and I went the other and I got the ball'.

Liverpool's army of supporters who crossed the Pennines had difficulty getting home that night thanks to a national rail strike, which was to take effect from midnight. During the second half an announcement came over the tannoy that the special train would be leaving at 9pm to make sure it got back to Liverpool in time and as such the exit gates had been opened. This led to many Leeds fans coming round to infiltrate the end but they were quickly repelled. With the game so precariously poised hardly any took the option of leaving the ground, preferring instead to pile onto the coaches later. There was no issue with this amongst drivers and fans already booked on them, it was a case of getting everybody home safely after an important match, with those who had train tickets making do with standing up, sitting on the floor or even curling up in the boot as those who'd travelled over by coach took the seats for themselves. That was, once the coaches were on their way out of Leeds. In *One Boy and His Kop* Peter Etherington recalls that getting to the coach park safely was a problem:

> 'I'd seen some big Leeds mobs before but never this big. The best thing we could do was stick together and fight our way through them and onto the coaches, which we did. I wouldn't have liked to have seen the repair bills for them coaches the next day as every one of them got bricked. Ours had three windows put in, there was glass everywhere. Some lads on the coach had been cut by flying glass, one quite badly having a massive gash on his head. Still we'd won and all arrived home in virtually one piece even if there were sixty odd people on each coach designed to hold 42. Tales of that night have been told and exaggerated over the years but that's a truthful account of how it was. It was f*cking freezing coming home over those Pennines!'

Liverpool: Clemence, Lawler, Lindsay, Smith, Lloyd, Hughes, Keegan, Cormack, Heighway, Toshack, Callaghan. Sub: Hall.

Leeds: Harvey, Reaney, Cherry, Bremner, Charlton, Hunter, Lorimer, Clarke, Jones, Giles (Jordan), Madeley.

Referee: Mr B. Homewood (Sunbury).

Attendance: 34,856.

League Cup 5th Round: Liverpool 1 Tottenham Hotspur 1
Monday 4th December 1972

The day after the victory at Leeds the Football League came up with what Peter Robinson called a realistic and fair solution for the dates for the next round. It was decided that Liverpool would meet Tottenham Hotspur at Anfield on Monday 4th December, with any replay taking place two nights later. However, if the tie was settled at Anfield the winners would not be expected to play the first leg of their semi-final on 6th December. Instead, the semi-final dates were put back to 20th December and 1st January. Despite Robinson's satisfaction Bill Shankly made his feelings known about being forced to play Mondays and Wednesdays, telling the *Liverpool Echo* on 23rd November 'If players were animals there would be complaints to the RSPCA. The players are expected to go out and entertain but if they are asked to play four matches in eight days they can't do that'.

The Reds were in the quarter-finals of the League Cup for the first time and if they were able to overcome Spurs they faced a last-four encounter with Wolverhampton Wanderers. There was now great interest in the competition, an Anfield League Cup record of 48,677 turning out for the game, which came just two days after the energy-sapping 4-3 win over Birmingham City in the league. Spurs hadn't won at Anfield for sixty years and the Reds had won 2-1 in the league at White Hart Lane nine days earlier, but Shankly knew the task was still huge, telling the *Liverpool Echo* on the day of the game: 'We have a tough job on our hands, Spurs are a good side and we have a great respect for them'.

For the fourth round in succession, Liverpool had to settle for a draw, needing an Emlyn Hughes equaliser to rescue the game. The Reds looked jaded and Spurs were the better team in the first half, Martin Peters heading over and Martin Chivers somehow missing from six yards. Only John Toshack tested the visiting keeper, Pat Jennings diving to save a flicked header. In the 54th minute Peters gave Spurs the lead from a corner, which stuck in the mud before he scrambled it over the line. This led to them pulling all men back behind the ball and Liverpool rarely looked like breaking the resistance, although a fierce Ian Callaghan drive was spilled by Jennings. As Toshack closed in, the keeper managed to recover and gather the ball.

When the equaliser came it was a spectacular effort from Emlyn Hughes, who collected a short corner from Heighway before moving to the edge of the area and unleashing an unstoppable shot that Jennings didn't even have time to dive for. After the game, Shankly admitted that as Liverpool's schedule grew even more punishing, with the replay taking place two days later, he wouldn't have been too upset at a defeat. The following evening's *Liverpool Echo* reported him as saying:

> 'I wouldn't have minded if we had lost tonight for the safety of the players. We are involved in too many competitions but the league, of course, is our prime target. The more games they play, the more tired players become and the more liable they are to injuries'.

Such words would normally be unthinkable from Shankly, but the Reds were now about to play their 33rd game in just 117 days, with the weather now having a big impact on the pitches and sapping the players' energy even more.

Liverpool: Clemence, Lawler, Lindsay, Storton, Lloyd, Hughes, Keegan, Cormack, Heighway, Toshack, Callaghan. Sub: Boersma.

Spurs: Jennings, Evans, Knowles Pratt, England, Naylor, Gilzean, Perryman, Chivers, Peters, Pearce. Sub: Kinnear.

Referee: Mr J. Taylor (Wolverhampton).

Attendance: 48,677.

League Cup 5th Round Replay: Tottenham Hotspur 3 Liverpool 1
Wednesday 6th December 1972

On the afternoon of the replay torrential rain put it in serious doubt.

Chelsea's semi-final first leg with Norwich City had already been called off in the morning but the White Hart Lane pitch passed an inspection to the relief of Liverpool's fans and players, who hadn't faced a wasted journey. Fan Chris Wood remembers that not many Reds fans made it to the game due to the short notice and also the fact that Spurs, who had won the competition in 1971 and reached the final the year before, were likely to be taking the game far more seriously. Of 1,000 tickets allocated to Liverpool, only 400 were sold although more would have paid cash at the turnstiles.

Despite his comments after the first game and speculation in the *Liverpool Echo* that some changes may be made to give players a rest, Bill Shankly opted to field his strongest available side. He believed he owed it to fans making the journey at such short notice to do all he could to win the game and told the *Daily Post:* 'The fixture pile-up sees us up to our neck in matches, so we may as well be in it over our heads. The players must be very tired but they know they can't let down the fans who have been so wonderful'.

Fifteen minutes into the game, though, the Reds may have wished the game had been called off as amid a thunderstorm Spurs raced into a 3-0 lead. A Martin Chivers' deflected free kick, an unstoppable drive from John Pratt and another from Chivers after he dispossessed Trevor Storton, put the game out of Liverpool's reach.

Nine years earlier the Reds had suffered a 7-2 hammering at White Hart Lane on Easter Monday and a repeat was feared and only Spurs' carelessness prevented this happening. The Reds were dealt a blow at half time when John Toshack was forced off following a clash of heads with Mike England, causing a wound that required three stitches.

In the second half Kevin Keegan suffered a thigh injury but, with Toshack already off, he was forced to limp on – and Ian Callaghan developed cramp. By the time Liverpool's consolation came, when Emlyn Hughes set up Callaghan to score five minutes from time, it was not necessarily even deserved for the performance was sluggish and lethargic in all areas of the field. However, it didn't stop one Reds fan running out of the Paxton Road end and giving an embarrassed scorer a big hug. There was no late comeback, though, and it seemed that collectively the players had just run out of gas as they played a third game in five days on a very heavy pitch.

As the team travelled home Shankly conceded that perhaps defeat may have been for the best as it meant a clear run of no midweek fixtures, barring FA Cup replays. He told the *Liverpool Echo:*

'We always go out to win and we are disappointed when we lose. But perhaps some good will come out of it. The players badly need a rest and perhaps they will now be able to get it. Once we have played Dynamo Berlin next week and got over Christmas, we may not have another midweek match until March. The one thing that every team would like to win is the league and we are no exception. If we go on to win it, then perhaps tonight's defeat will not be so disappointing after all. The players have done a remarkable job in playing so many matches as they have done and in getting so far. What they need now is a rest and they will be able to have it'.

Liverpool: Clemence, Lawler, Lindsay, Storton, Lloyd, Hughes, Keegan, Cormack, Heighway, Toshack, Thompson, Callaghan.

Spurs: Jennings, Evans, Knowles, Pratt, England, Naylor, Gilzean (Neighbour), Perryman, Chivers, Peters, Pearce.

Referee: Mr J. Taylor (Wolverhampton).

Attendance: 34,565.

Liverpool's plight in the League Cup had attracted sympathy from Everton's Brian Labone. He wrote in his weekly *Liverpool Echo* column two days after the defeat: 'This regular midweek stint makes it impossible for players to recover from injuries. The finest physio set-up in the world can't get players fit in two days if they suffer an injury'. Tommy Smith, forced to sit the game out due to his injury sustained in a car accident, wrote in his column the following Saturday that he believed Spurs were lucky with their first two goals, referring to a deflection and bad bounce that deceived Storton. However, he believed the defeat could prove to be a blessing in disguise and that it meant the players were now left to focus on the league and Europe.

Despite the fixture chaos the League Cup caused, not once did Shankly make a change for the sake of it. He only did so if it was needed due to injury or loss of form. Tommy Smith wrote in his column on 17th January 1973 that the answer to the tiredness some players were feeling was for two substitutes to be allowed in games, allowing for managers to make changes earlier on for tactical reasons or to give a player a break. However, it would be fifteen more years before this proposal was introduced.

When Liverpool suffered a downturn in results during January and February, Shankly identified the number of replays required in the League Cup as a factor that had eventually drained them and felt Tottenham were also suffering as a result. After the Reds were beaten 2-0 by Arsenal on 10th February, the *Liverpool Echo* quoted him two days later:

'The draws and replays in the League Cup were the real killer. At Carlisle and West Bromwich we should have killed them off early on. The mental strain of playing a match takes a lot out of you. These lads have been playing twice a week so they have been getting a double dose. Perhaps it is no coincidence that Tottenham are not doing too well at the moment. They conceded eight goals in two home matches last week, including five in one match. When they are fit no team in the world can go to White Hart Lane and score five goals, you have to work hard to get even five shots. They seem to be suffering as we are from the number of matches they have had to play'.

11

Christmas Crackers

Football League Division One: Liverpool 2 Coventry City 0
Saturday 23rd December 1972

The Christmas period began with a home game against Coventry City, which was just too early for Tommy Smith's return after he received the all clear from a specialist. Bill Shankly told the *Liverpool Echo* on 21st December that although Smith was the type of player who could step straight back into the side after injury, he felt a few more days' intensive training was needed and the Boxing Day fixture at Sheffield United was a more realistic target.

Shankly predicted a tough game against a Coventry side jointly managed by ex-Reds midfielder Gordon Milne and ex Manchester city boss Joe Mercer. They were tenth in the table and in good form, having taken sixteen points from the last 22 available to move them away from a position of second to bottom at the beginning of October.

John Toshack was recalled to the side with Phil Boersma dropping to the bench and the big Welshman justified his inclusion with two first-half goals to give Liverpool a 2-0 win. The game started slowly, Steve Heighway's dipping volley on five minutes being the first real action but just a minute later the Reds were ahead when Ian Callaghan crossed from the right and with the visitors' defence concentrating on Kevin Keegan, Toshack stole in unnoticed to score with a diving header. Liverpool maintained the pressure, with Keegan and Peter Cormack being particularly impressive, and although Coventry tried to play decent football, most of their time was spent behind the ball keeping the Reds at bay.

In the 21st minute Toshack got his second, starting and finishing a brilliant move. He played a ball out to Cormack, who crossed into the box for Keegan who headed it across the face of goal for Toshack who came in from the blind side to head home. A minute later, only the quick thinking of Neil Ramsbottom, diving at Keegan's feet after Toshack had headed down a corner, prevented a third goal. With half-an-hour gone Ramsbottom punched a Cormack free-kick clear only as far as Emlyn Hughes but his fierce volley went inches over the bar. Up to then Ray Clemence still hadn't made a save as Coventry had managed just two shots, one of which was blocked by Chris Lawler and the other going well wide.

In the second half, crosses were flying in but Ramsbottom wasn't afraid to come off his line and deal with them despite the menacing presence of Toshack. The Reds were clearly feeling the benefit of having had no midweek game as they continued their onslaught, showing no signs of sluggishness. Phil Thompson found himself clean through on goal in the 65th minute but his effort was weak and easily saved. With the Coventry defence in disarray Ramsbottom was the only person between Liverpool and a cricket score, bravely diving at the feet of Toshack to deny him a hat-trick and making a double save from Callaghan and Toshack. There was a comedy moment when Cormack mishit a shot but, as a relieved Roy Barry went to head it back to Ramsbottom, he miscued as well into the path of a surprised Toshack only for the keeper to dive and get the ball from the striker's feet.

Toshack almost got his hat-trick in the 80th minute but his shot was cleared off the line by Barry and Heighway hit a hard low shot that beat Ramsbottom but went just wide of the post. Coventry scarcely troubled the Reds, Clemence's activity being limited to touching a Tommy Hutchison effort round the post and then blocking a Colin Stein shot with his legs after a defensive lapse had let the striker clean through. To their credit Coventry never stopped trying, they just weren't good enough to trouble a hungry Reds side. They saved their best chance to the last minute but Willie Carr headed Hutchison's cross over the bar.

Liverpool: Clemence, Lawler, Lindsay, Thompson, Lloyd, Hughes, Keegan, Cormack, Heighway, Toshack, Callaghan. Sub: Boersma.

Coventry: Ramsbottom, Coop, Caitlin, Smith (McGuire), Barry, Parker, Mortimer, Alderson, Stein, Carr, Hutchison.

Referee: Mr A.E. Morrisey (Bramhall).

Attendance: 41,500.

Football League Division One Sheffield United 0 Liverpool 3
Tuesday 26th December 1972

With both nearest rivals drawing, the win over Coventry meant the Reds were two points clear of Arsenal at Christmas with a game in hand, and three ahead of Leeds. In his *Liverpool Echo* column that was published on the evening of the Coventry game, Tommy Smith pointed to three reasons why he believed the championship trophy would end up at Anfield. Firstly, he believed the number of games to come at Anfield would be a factor as the Reds had ten home matches remaining, compared to Arsenal's eight and Leeds's nine. Secondly, Liverpool had played all their difficult away fixtures, having visited all of the other top six teams, losing only at Derby. Thirdly, following on from his second reason, it meant that four of the five teams immediately below them still had to come to Anfield, the exception being Chelsea who Liverpool had already played twice.

In the same edition of the *Echo*, Chris James looked ahead to the games that would decide the outcome of the title, which now looked certain to be a three-horse race. The visit of Arsenal to Anfield on 10th February was clearly going to be a crunch game, but it already looked like the key clash would be Liverpool v Leeds on Easter Monday, 23rd April. James wrote:

'It could well be that as in 1969 Liverpool and Leeds will contest the title between themselves at Anfield. If it is and it goes Liverpool's way then they have one more home match on the following Saturday against Leicester which may well see the presentation of the trophy and great celebrations'.

James also identified the possibility of Leeds and Arsenal meeting in the last match of the season. They were scheduled to meet at Elland Road on 7th April, which was FA Cup semi-final day and therefore there was every possibility one of the two sides may be involved.

On Boxing Day Liverpool faced Sheffield United at Bramall Lane, which was then still a three-sided ground as it was also a cricket venue for Yorkshire. Tommy Smith failed a fitness test and Phil Thompson continued to deputise, while a stomach upset forced John Toshack to drop out, with Phil Boersma stepping in. On Christmas Eve Little Jimmy Osmond's *Long Haired Lover From Liverpool* had been revealed as the Christmas Number One hit and fan Peter Etherington admits to starting the song on the terrace where it was soon being belted out, although he does concede in *One Boy and His Kop* that Little Jimmy was 'an irritating little tw*t'

United were by far the better side for the first quarter of the game but Liverpool withstood the pressure and took advantage of a defensive mistake in the 27th minute to take the lead. Boersma was quick to seize on a poor backpass by Alan Ogden and kept his cool to slide the ball past the advancing Tom McAlister. The home side almost got straight back into the game when Alan Woodward hit a rocket of a thirty-yard shot that Ray Clemence couldn't hold. The ball fell to Bill Dearden but he prodded it wide. Just before the break Boersma almost had a second, this time Trevor Hockey underhitting a backpass but on this occasion McAlister managed to close him down and block his shot.

Liverpool began the second half confidently, passing the ball around with some style. In the fiftieth minute the lead was increased thanks to a wonderfully worked free-kick. With Peter Cormack, Emlyn Hughes and Alec Lindsay standing over the ball twenty yards out, a shot looked inevitable, but then Kevin Keegan moved towards the near post taking a defender with him. This left the centre of the area exposed and Cormack chipped the ball into that space where Chris Lawler ran in to head it into the net off the post.

There was no danger of a United fightback now as the Reds took charge of the game, happy to sit back and control the midfield and stop anything getting through. Cormack was outstanding, showing that his defensive abilities were as good as those going forward, and Lawler had another solid display against Geoff Salmons. In the 81ˢᵗ minute, a superb counter-attacking goal confirmed an emphatic victory for the Reds. Larry Lloyd cleared from defence to Keegan who headed it to Steve Heighway. He passed to Boersma before running into the box and collecting the ball back and scoring from an acute angle. United did have the ball in the net before the end of the game, Dearden volleying in the rebound after Woodward had hit the post, but it was ruled out due to offside.

Liverpool: Clemence, Lawler, Lindsay, Thompson, Lloyd, Hughes, Keegan, Cormack, Heighway, Boersma, Callaghan. Sub: Hall.

Sheffield Utd: McAlister, Badger, Ogden, Flynn (Holmes), Colquhoun, Hockey, Woodward, Salmons, Dearden, Curry, Warboys.

Referee: Mr P.Partridge (Middlesbrough).

Attendance: 34,040.

Football League Division One: Liverpool 1 Crystal Palace 0
Saturday 30ᵗʰ December 1972

The 3-0 win at Sheffield United was Liverpool's biggest away win of the season and although it hadn't been their best performance on the road, they had been ruthless in taking their chances when presented with them and gave nothing away at the back. It meant they were the only side in the First Division to win both Christmas fixtures as they looked forward to their final fixture of 1972. This was at home to relegation-threatened Crystal Palace, a side who were struggling to make players gel despite having spent almost half a million pounds since summer.

Although things were rosy for the Reds at the top of the league and the club's finances were sound, the game in general was facing problems. Many clubs were suffering falling attendances, hooliganism was on the rise and several clubs were at risk of going to the wall. On 29ᵗʰ December the Football League launched a blueprint for the future, which was to be considered by all chairmen on 10ᵗʰ January. The report suggested having the season run from September-May and not August – April to avoid clashes with cricket and holidays; reducing the First Division to twenty clubs; regional Third divisions; no offsides; and playing the League Cup on Saturdays. There was naturally a mixed reaction to the report. Wolves forward Derek Dougan questioned why chairmen should be discussing and making decisions regarding the game, rather than the Professional Footballers' Association and Managers' Association. As a striker, though, he was more than happy with proposed changes to the offside rule.[41]

No further injuries were reported from the Boxing Day game and, with Toshack getting over his stomach upset, Bill Shankly faced a selection problem for the Palace match. He opted to recall Toshack, despite Phil Boersma's excellent record of nine goals in fourteen games, including one at Sheffield United. Tommy Smith, after seeing a specialist two days before the game, was told that his ribs had fully healed and he was included in the reserve side to face Derby County at the Baseball Ground.

Although they were struggling, Palace had two players in their side who had caused Liverpool problems in the past. Former Everton striker Alan Whittle had twice scored for the Blues against Liverpool at Anfield, including the 2-0 victory for them in 1969-70, and Don Rogers, a recent £150,000 buy from Swindon, had hit two against the Reds in 1970-71 to knock them out of the League Cup.

However, the two former demons didn't come back to haunt the Reds as, from the kick-off, Palace set out their stall to defend. The first real Reds opportunity came in the eighth minute when Emlyn Hughes, still standing in for Smith at centre back, got forward to swap passes with Toshack but his shot was blocked by the keeper. Such was Palace's lack of adventure that Larry Lloyd joined in attacks as well but two of his shots failed to reach the goal due to the penalty area being packed with defenders. Keeper John Jackson confidently dealt with any shots and crosses that did make their way to him, his best coming when he tipped a low shot from Steve Heighway around the post. From the resultant corner Chris Lawler tested Jackson, but he was again equal to the shot and pushed it away. Liverpool got more frustrated as the first half went on, Kevin Keegan struggling to escape his man-marker Tony Taylor and Ian Callaghan resorting to a long-range effort from more than thirty yards that dipped just over the bar.

The second half was the same story, Palace getting every man behind the ball and in the way of everything Liverpool tried. Early on a great chance fell to Lawler from a throw-in but although his shot beat Jackson, it went across the face of goal with nobody being there to turn it into the net. Eventually the breakthrough came after 67 minutes, Peter Cormack sneaking in unnoticed to score with a glancing header from Alec Lindsay's cross. Forced to break off their shackles, Palace looked certain to equalise when Hughes blocked a shot and it fell to Alan Pinkney, but Ray Clemence somehow turned his point-blank range shot over the bar. Otherwise, Liverpool held on to win comfortably, almost adding to their advantage in the last five minutes when Toshack headed just wide and Keegan, now free of his marker, curled a great effort just past the post.

It was revealed afterwards by Bill Shankly that Cormack, whose goal against Palace was his eighth of the season in all competitions, had overcame a stomach upset to play in the game. The Scottish midfielder set himself a target of finishing the campaign on fifteen goals and said of his Palace winner 'That one was certainly a relief as we were beginning to get a bit frustrated'.[42]

Liverpool: Clemence, Lawler, Lindsay, Thompson, Lloyd, Hughes, Keegan, Cormack, Heighway, Toshack, Callaghan Sub: Boersma.

Palace: Jackson, Payne, Taylor, Phllip, Bell, Blyth, Pinkney, Roffey, Whittle, Cooke, Rogers. Sub: Hughes.

Referee: Mr G.W. Hill (Lancashire).

Attendance: 50,862.

Football League Division One: West Ham United 0 Liverpool 1
Saturday 6th January 1973

The victory over Palace was Liverpool's 21st in succession in the league at Anfield, the last team to escape with any points being Leeds the previous New Year's Day. It also meant the Reds had accumulated 67 points in their last 42 league games across the two seasons. This was equal to Leeds record-breaking haul when they won the title in 1968-69 and a clear sign that the Reds were the team everyone else had to beat if they were to be champions. Their points total of 38 after 25 games was two more than they had in 1965-66 and four more than 1963-64, Bill Shankly's other title-winning seasons. The fact that they had achieved this despite being pushed to the limit during the first half of 1972-73, in which they played fourteen midweek cup ties, was even more remarkable.

If there was one thing that may hinder Liverpool, it was the impact of the cups. Brian Labone had expressed caution in his *Liverpool Echo* column on 29th December, writing: 'If they didn't have their sights switched from time to time in the New Year I would rate them as odds-on favourites'. However, he felt the Reds still had the strength to pass the finishing line first, continuing: 'Liverpool have kept such an unrelenting pace that they'll outstrip their challengers if they can keep it up. They have all the assets available to do just that'. As an ex-Everton player, Labone's comments did not convince many Reds, who believed he was only showing such opinions with a view to boosting his testimonial fund as Liverpool were providing the opposition for the game the forthcoming March. One fan, a Mr Wedgwood from Wavertree, wrote to Labone reminding him that he used to state he only went to Anfield once a year and only because he had to play there, and that Reds fans were not so gullible as to fall for his public relations exercise. Labone responded using his column on 5th January, replying:

'I am a dyed in the wool Evertonian and will continue to be. But this doesn't prevent me from discussing the Liverpool team, they are a very good team and will probably win the league. I only wish the positions of Liverpool and Everton were reversed at the moment'.

After being given New Year's Eve and New Year's Day off, the Reds players returned to training on Tuesday 2nd January. Emlyn Hughes and Ray Clemence weren't present, being away for the 'Three v Six' game, arranged to celebrate the expansion of the Common Market and consisting of teams representing the new and old members. Ireland's Steve Heighway was refused permission to play due to him having been suffering the same stomach complaint that had troubled Peter Cormack. Just 36,500 turned out at Wembley to see The Three win 2-0 thanks to goals from Scotland's Colin Stein and Denmark's Henning Jensen. Hughes played but Clemence was left out of the side in favour of Northern Ireland's Pat Jennings as Sir Alf Ramsey sought to give players of all nations a chance.

With Tommy Smith having successfully come through the reserve game at Derby, it gave Shankly a selection poser for the away game at West Ham United on 6th January as the Reds had been unbeaten in his absence. Teenager Phil Thompson had done well as Smith's replacement; well enough for it not to be a straightforward decision that it would be him who made way. In each of the past three seasons a previously unknown gem seemed to have been unearthed by Shankly – Ray Clemence and Larry Lloyd in 1969-70, Steve Heighway in 1970-71 and Kevin Keegan in 1971-72. Now in 1972-73 Phil Thompson appeared to be that player.

On 1st January *Liverpool Echo* sports columnist Michael Charters wrote of his performance against Palace: 'Bill Shankly looks to have unearthed another gem in nineteen-year-old Phil Thompson. This slim young man does the right things quickly and instinctively'. Praise was coming from outside Liverpool too with Coventry joint boss Gordon Milne, who had managed Thompson during an England youth tournament in the summer, saying of him:

'All around he is an exciting proposition, the most exciting feature about him for me is his enthusiasm for the game and the fact that he doesn't like losing. Put those qualities with experience and a little more physical strength and he will be a very good player indeed. He can tackle and win the ball and use it well too'.[43]

Thompson himself recalls of that first run in the team how important it was to get those tackles in:

'I'd had a few away starts and then I made my first appearance at Anfield in the league against Coventry. I felt the fans were looking at me as just some skinny kid, which made me determined to prove a point that I deserved to be in the side. I knew putting a tackle in was always a good crowd pleaser'.[44]

In the end Shankly's selection decision was made easier for him when Alec Lindsay, who was confined to bed on the Wednesday and Thursday with the same stomach bug that had hit Cormack and Heighway, was left behind as the team travelled to London on the Friday. It meant Hughes could switch to left back, the position he played for England, with Smith slotting back into central defence and Thompson remaining in midfield.

As the train carrying the Reds rolled into Euston Station, there was a camera crew on the platform leading Shankly to comment that there must be some film stars aboard. But he soon realised that the film crew was there for him, as Eamonn Andrews stepped onto the carriage with his red book and spoke the immortal words 'Bill Shankly This Is Your Life'. Shankly and the team were bussed to the studios of Thames Television and as old friends came through the doors to meet him, he was still able to get in some quips. One classic was when he told Andrews that he had been transferred from Carlisle to Preston for £500, but it would now cost that much in rail fares to get from one to the other. Amongst those in the studio were football legends Tommy Lawton, Sir Matt Busby, Billy Liddell, Tom Finney, Stan Mortensen and, from the world of showbiz, Cilla Black.

Shankly said afterwards that as soon as he saw Andrews it gave him an explanation for several strange goings on of late and described seeing so many old friends as one of the most memorable moments of his life.[45] Two of the strange things Shankly referred to were the players turning up for their train in suits rather than the usual casual gear for travelling, and wife Nessie having left him a note saying she'd gone shopping when he briefly returned home from Melwood to say goodbye before heading to Lime Street.

In *The Real Bill Shankly*, published by Trinity Mirror Sport Media in 2006, Shankly's granddaughter Karen Gill recalls how she had been told to keep things quiet:

'The only piece of information we were given was that we were going on a surprise journey and we weren't to say a thing about it to anyone. It was all very mysterious and exciting for an eight year old. The whole family travelled to London by train and we were put up in a very luxurious hotel. I remember rehearsals when we had to pretend that one man was my granddad. Over and over we had to walk over and give him a kiss – very unpleasant! There was a big party later and I remember that me and my sister Pauline must have sat on every Liverpool player's knee! We also tried to talk to some of the other famous people there and realised for the first time that not all celebrities were as warm and genuine as my granddad. It was a wonderful night and we felt really proud of him. It was something he deserved and I know that he thoroughly enjoyed having everybody he loved and respected gathered in his honour'.

Others who'd been told to keep quiet were fans from the London branch of the Liverpool Supporters Club, some of whose members were in the studio audience. Chris Wood recalls:

'I was in the audience, along with many other members of the London Branch. Thames Television had rung our headquarters, a pub in the Aldgate part of the City of London that was managed by our chairman, who was told what it was about and asked if we could provide some members of the audience. Could we ever! After the show had been broadcast, we got a terrible ear-bashing from the main supporters club in Lower Breck Road, absolutely furious than none of their committee had been invited too. But Thames had sworn us to secrecy so we could not pass the information on, not to them anyway'.

Such was the secrecy involved that only Peter Robinson, Eric Roberts and Bob Paisley at the club had been aware of the making of the programme, with Tommy Smith and the players being told two days before. Initially Robinson suggested to the programme makers that Shankly be summoned to Anfield for a bogus board meeting before being whisked off to Manchester, but when it became apparent the programme had to be recorded in London, doing it when the Reds were playing down there became the best option.

When attentions turned to the game the next day, it should have promised plenty of goals, with West Ham having scored more than anyone else in the First Division except for Liverpool and Leeds and their side containing the league's leading scorer Pop Robson who had got seventeen goals so far. However, as so often in these cases, it was a solitary goal that won the game, Kevin Keegan's second-half strike being enough for the Reds to return home with both points.

As well as Smith coming in for Lindsay, Shankly made another change when he dropped John Toshack for the second time of the season, preferring Phil Boersma instead. Despite Billy Bonds and Trevor Brooking both being missing from the West Ham midfield, the Reds struggled to get a grip of the game in this area during the first half. Clyde Best and Dudley Tyler both managed shots on goal in the first five minutes but they posed Ray Clemence no difficulty. Liverpool's first chance came after an uncharacteristic slip by Bobby Moore allowed Peter Cormack a shot, but it went just over the bar.

Smith's first major contribution came after a quarter of an hour when he played a chipped pass to Kevin Keegan on the right. He dummied the ball allowing it to run on to Steve Heighway who beat Frank Lampard but curled his shot well wide. In a first half that was played in drizzly conditions West Ham were the better side, Moore getting forward to spray passes around and set up attacks, with Liverpool's chances being limited to breakaways. Despite this, Liverpool's defence was solid and the home side weren't allowed any clear-cut chances to score until the half-hour, when a ball over the top by Moore found Best who, after first being deceived by an awkward bounce, then slipped as he was about to shoot. Liverpool's best chance of the first half came when Heighway and Cormack combined to set up Boersma but his shot was blocked and then Chris Lawler fired the rebound wide.

Early in the second half Lampard went on a good run to the byline and his cross beat both Lawler and Larry Lloyd but, although Tyler got his head to it, Clemence saved well. From then on Liverpool took much more command of the game, Ian Callaghan and Phil Thompson beginning to assert more authority in midfield. Just before the hour Keegan picked out Heighway who was making a clever run from the left, but although he beat a defender and got a shot in, it was straight at keeper Bobby Ferguson. Liverpool were showing more spark in the second half, but the Keegan-Boersma combination in attack wasn't working on this occasion and they were grateful for a let-off when Clive Charles completely miscued when he went for a spectacular volley rather than control the ball first.

As the half wore on West Ham did begin to run out of ideas as the Reds defence was having little problem in containing them and in the 75th minute Keegan made it 1-0, rising to meet Heighway's cross from the left with a powerful header that gave Ferguson no chance. Tyler responded with a thirty-yard drive that Clemence held well but Liverpool looked more likely to add to their lead before the end rather than West Ham find an equaliser. Keegan had another header from a Boersma cross go just wide and Heighway was brought down by Taylor in full flight with Keegan lurking ready to receive the pass. All in all it was a very satisfactory victory for Liverpool, their fourth in succession without conceding a goal and one achieved while not playing particularly well.

Liverpool: Clemence, Lawler, Thompson, Smith, Lloyd, Hughes, Keegan, Cormack, Heighway, Boersma, Callaghan. Sub: Hall.

West Ham: Ferguson, McDowell, Lampard, Lock (Charles), Taylor, Moore, Ayris, Best, Holland, Tyler, Robson.

Referee: Mr R. Tinkler (Boston).

Attendance: 34,480.

Top of the Division One Table

		Pl	W	D	L	F	A	GA	Pt
1	Liverpool	26	17	6	3	50	26	1.92	40
2	Arsenal	27	15	7	5	37	25	1.48	37
3	Leeds	25	14	7	4	47	26	1.81	35

12

January and February Blues

After just three league defeats in their opening 26 games, putting them three points clear of nearest challengers Arsenal at the top of the league table, Liverpool came seriously unstuck during January and February. After beating West Ham on 6th January, they won only one of their next five league games and crashed out of the FA Cup amid a war of words with Manchester City manager Malcolm Allison. There was also a period of discontent amongst some players left out of the side as Arsenal and Leeds closed the gap to turn the championship into an extremely tight three-horse race, plus the frustration of losing out to Manchester United in the transfer market.

FA Cup 3rd Round: Burnley 0 Liverpool 0 Saturday 13th January 1973

In the FA Cup third round Liverpool were paired away to Second Division Burnley, the sixth time they had faced the Clarets in the competition. It would be a tough game as Burnley were four points clear at the top of the table and had only been beaten once at Turf Moor all season. It was an example of keeping faith with the manager, as Jimmy Adamson had taken Burnley down in 1971 and they failed to make a promotion challenge in 1972, but he was moulding a side together and that patience paid off. However, William Hills didn't see the tie as too hazardous, installing the Reds as 8/1 joint favourites to win the competition along with Leeds.

Although he would have preferred to be at home, Bill Shankly believed it was as good an away draw as you could hope for given the short distance involved and the fact plenty of Reds fans would be present. However, at the beginning of the week of the game, Shankly became pre-occupied with plenty of other matters, namely Peter Cormack's appeal against his sending off at West Bromwich Albion, John Toshack's discontent at being dropped and a possible transfer bid for Celtic's Lou Macari.

Shankly travelled to Birmingham on Monday 8th January for Cormack's appeal, which saw a club doctor give evidence at an FA disciplinary hearing for the first time. The doctor explained the nature of the cuts and bruises to Cormack's legs as proof of the provocation he had received prior to kicking out at Asa Hartford in retaliation. This was enough for the commission to quash the impending ban.

After being dropped for the second time, Toshack sought talks to clarify his position with Shankly when training resumed. Despite averaging a goal every other game, this was the second time he had been dropped as he became a victim of differing tactics for home and away games. At home, with the emphasis on constant pressure and bombardment of the opposition penalty area, his physical nature and aerial presence was essential, but in away games where counter-attacking was more common, the speed of Phil Boersma was preferred. On 8th January the *Daily Post* reported that Toshack was desperately disappointed at being left out of the side and the following day Shankly confirmed to the *Liverpool Echo* that he had spoken with the striker, but would not elaborate on what was said between the two of them.

With neither Toshack nor Boersma having a permanent claim on the number 10 shirt, there was speculation that Shankly would look to sign somebody else. One name linked with Liverpool was Manchester United's Ted MacDougall, who had been at Anfield as a youngster in the 1960s. He was now struggling to live up to the reputation of George Best and Denis Law after a £200,000 move there from AFC Bournemouth earlier in the season and new manager Tommy Docherty, who had replaced Frank O'Farrell, didn't appear to want him in his plans. But on 8th January the *Daily Post* was quick to quash any rumours that the Reds may be interested in bringing him back to Anfield.

One player that Shankly would be interested in, though, was Lou Macari, who the *Liverpool Echo* reported that Celtic were willing to sell for £200,000 on the same day as the Post dismissed any move for MacDougall. However, Reds correspondent Chris James hinted that Macari may prefer a move to Manchester United due to the number of Scottish players at Old Trafford, something he had stated would help determine who he signed for.

With Celtic manager Jock Stein in hospital and fourteen days' prior registration being required for FA Cup games, there was no immediate move for Macari and thoughts turned to the Burnley tie instead. It's an indication of how big the FA Cup was for players and fans alike that the press build-up to the game began at the start of the week, whereas for run-of-the-mill league games it was usually Friday, Thursday at the earliest. With Alec Lindsay recovering from the stomach bug that had ruled him out of the West Ham game, it meant Shankly had to choose eleven from thirteen, not including the now perennial unused substitute Brian Hall.

As Shankly pondered his team selection, Burnley's manager Jimmy Adamson made his known three days before the game. He stuck with the side that had impressively beaten Aston Villa 3-0 away from home the previous Saturday, with Billy Ingham continuing to replace the suspended Doug Collins in midfield. The player to watch was nineteen-year-old Welsh international Leighton James, who had made his debut in November 1970 but only established himself as a regular in the side this season. Despite his young age James was confident enough to face the press and answer questions in the lead-up to the game. Admitting Liverpool were a great side, he stated Burnley were, too, and could cause an upset. James told a press conference: 'Football is all about goalscoring and that's all I'm interested in. We've played 25 games and lost only once, that's better than Liverpool. Luck, run of the ball decides an awful lot of matches.' Although Kopites had seen nothing of James, one familiar face would be ex-Everton player Keith Newton, who had joined Burnley the previous summer and at 31 was the veteran of their side.

Burnley's players turned down the offer of three days in Blackpool to prepare for the game, preferring their normal routine instead. It was not uncommon for teams to prepare for cup-ties by going away to a hotel or special training camp for a few days but that was not the case at Liverpool, where preparations were the same as for any normal league match.

Liverpool looked set to be backed by almost half the crowd at Turf Moor, which held 38,000. The Echo reported two days before the game that they had sold 11,000 tickets themselves, having requested an additional batch after selling the initial 9,500 allocation. With no segregation and tickets being on open sale in Burnley and no restrictions on numbers bought, up to 5,000 more were believed to have been sold to Liverpool fans who had travelled there to buy them and distribute on Merseyside. While travelling Reds would be going to Burnley by a combination of special train, coaches and car, the team would be ferried in their luxury new Leyland Leopard coach that was being supplied by local company Blundells. Acquired at a cost of £15,000, the coach was fitted with a television and cassette recorder as well as the normal card tables.

The day before the game Shankly put a stop to any further speculation regarding his team selection when he announced that he was opting for experience, recalling Alec Lindsay and John Toshack to the side at the expense of Phil Boersma and Phil Thompson. Extra care was taken to prevent Ray Clemence from coming into contact with anybody carrying germs, as both reserve and A Team keepers, Frank Lane and Grahame Lloyd, were ill with the mystery stomach bug. Shankly said he hoped Lane would recover in time if he was needed but the B Team keeper, 16 year old Dave Redhead, was on standby. Although Thompson would have been naturally disappointed to drop out of the side as Hughes returned to midfield from defence, Shankly had some words to boost his confidence, telling the Echo the day before the match that he was 'brilliant and someone who is going to have a big future in this game'.

Burney boss Adamson had promised to 'lick Liverpool' before the game and his side got off to a bright start, Frank Casper posing problems down the flanks and testing Clemence with a curling shot. Liverpool responded when Ian Callaghan crossed for Kevin Keegan, who headed down for Peter

Cormack but his volley was over the bar. It was an entertaining first half, with Burnley taking the game to the Reds as Adamson had promised, but Liverpool responding with plenty of attacks of their own. With Toshack restored and his marker Mick Docherty not being of great height, plenty of crosses were sent into the box which posed a threat for the defence. On one occasion a poor clearance by Colin Waldron fell at Cormack's feet but his effort went just over the bar. Leighton James showed what he could do when he beat Lindsay and Larry Lloyd but his low shot was easily saved by Clemence.

Neither side appeared to want a replay, with shots from Emlyn Hughes and Cormack being blocked by Geoff Nulty, and Casper heading just over from a James cross that had evaded Clemence. Alan Stevenson was performing well in the Burnley goal, making a great save from a fierce Hughes shot and palming away a Toshack header. The last action of the half was a Burnley free-kick, which Casper chipped to Waldron whose volley was just over the bar.

There was no let-up in the end-to-end attacking play when the second half began. Nulty tried an overhead kick that was saved by Clemence and Steve Heighway fired just over from 25 yards. Burnley then forced three quick corners and Tommy Smith slipped in the area allowing Nulty a shooting chance but his shot went wide. Just past the hour mark Hughes's shot was turned past the post by Stevenson, Liverpool being forced into longer-range efforts on occasions due to an excellent shackling job being done on Keegan by the home defence.

The game was played in a clean fashion, the first booking coming after 68 minutes when Heighway was brought down by Docherty, who had been identified as a weak link by the Reds attack and was the focus of many of their runs forward. After being treated, Heighway helped set up the best chance of the game in the 71st minute, his cross being headed down by Toshack but Cormack failed to connect with the goal gaping. The sheer pace of the game meant that it couldn't be expected to continue for the full ninety minutes and towards the end it did tail off, becoming much more of a midfield battle. There were still chances for either side, though, Casper wrong-footing Smith before shooting just past the post and Hughes finally beating Stevenson, only for Nulty to clear off the line. Liverpool didn't sit back and accept the draw, having the better of the play for the last ten minutes but they were unable to create any meaningful chances and both sides would have to try again at Anfield the following Tuesday.

Sadly, the pulsating game hadn't been captured by television cameras. Although the BBC had wanted to record the game for *Match of the Day*, they were barred from doing so by Burnley chairman Bob Lord. A strong opponent of televised football, Lord was also vice-president of the Football League and he made his reasons quite clear for turning the BBC down:

'Nobody will convince me that people will turn out on a mucky, murky day to watch a live match when they can, absolutely free, watch an hour's football in the evening. We must keep televised soccer to reasonable proportions, at the moment it has got out of hand. This, to my mind, is the start of a total ban at Burnley. Too many people seem to stand by and talk about the game dying without doing anything about it. Well, we are going to make a stand and it's up to others to follow our lead'.[46]

Liverpool's huge following at Burnley was praised by the police chief in charge of the game, superintendent Maurice McKenzie-Folan, who said they lived up to their claim to be the best behaved supporters in the country.[47] Thousands packed the pubs near the ground engaging in good-humoured singing and there were only two arrests all afternoon for disorderly behaviour. Unfortunately some fans found themselves on the receiving end of trouble when a special train was stoned at Rishton, just east of Blackburn, but nobody was hurt.

Liverpool: Clemence, Lawler, Lindsay, Smith, Lloyd, Hughes, Keegan, Cormack, Heighway, Toshack, Callaghan. Sub: Thompson.

Burnley: Stevenson, Newton, Docherty, Dobson, Waldron, Thomson, Nulty, Casper, Fletcher, Ingham, James. Sub: West.

Referee: Mr H. Williams (Sheffield).

Attendance: 35,730.

FA Cup 3rd Round Replay: Liverpool 3 Burnley 0 Tuesday 16th January 1973

The prospect of the sides meeting at Anfield evoked memories of a fourth round replay ten years earlier, when a Ronnie Moran penalty at the Kop end in the last minute of extra time had given Liverpool a 2-1 victory. The attendance for that game was 57,906, a crowd that has never since been matched at Anfield. None of the Burnley side were still there in 1973, but Ian Callaghan lined up for Liverpool in both games. The most senior fans of both sides would be also able to remember the 1914 FA Cup final in which Burnley had beaten the Reds 1-0 at Crystal Palace in front of King George V. Despite the fact the Reds still had to get through the third round, the *Daily Post* reported on 15th January that the bookmakers still made them 7/1 joint favourites with Leeds.

On the day before the replay the draw paired the winners at home to Manchester City in the fourth round, while the *Liverpool Echo* reported that Bill Shankly needed to choose whether to bring back Phil Boersma after John Toshack had had a quiet second half at Burnley. For the visitors, Jimmy Adamson had to decide whether or not to recall Doug Collins to the midfield or allow Billy Ingham to keep his place and he opted to go with experience, with twenty-year-old Ingham dropping back to the bench. The Reds may have had a tremendous home record over the last year but nothing could be taken for granted as Burnley were so far unbeaten on the road in the league, although they had gone down 4-0 at Leeds in a League Cup tie.

As well as preparing for the replay, Shankly made his move for Lou Macari, taking advantage of a gentlemen's agreement with Jock Stein that gave Liverpool first refusal to make a £200,000 bid. Manchester United, having spent £900,000 since the summer, were struggling to raise funds and couldn't get involved in a bidding war, meaning it now seemed just a formality of agreeing personal terms. After a transfer fee was agreed, Macari was in the stands at Anfield where he saw Toshack retain his place in the side and send out a clear message as he scored two goals and made another in a 3-0 win.

The appeal of the cup was demonstrated by the fact more than 56,000 were present for the replay, several hundred stand tickets that were returned by Burnley being snapped up by home fans on the day of the game. Liverpool forced them onto the back foot from the start, Ian Callaghan, Peter Cormack and Emlyn Hughes taking total control of the midfield and Kevin Keegan running the defence ragged. The Reds forced seven corners in the first half-hour and Alan Stevenson made good saves from Cormack, twice, Keegan, Chris Lawler and Alec Lindsay as both full backs joined in the attacks. In the 36th minute the breakthrough finally came when Toshack stooped at the back post to head in a Cormack corner, leaving Stevenson mesmerised at how he had sneaked in unnoticed. However Burnley didn't lie down and twice came close to equalising before half time, Martin Dobson having a shot cleared off the line by Cormack and Paul Fletcher incredibly hitting over the bar from a great position after a cross by Frank Casper.

Three minutes into the second half Toshack gave Liverpool some breathing space from a free-kick that was taken very quickly after Tommy Smith had been brought down by Leighton James. Cormack chipped the kick to Keegan at the far post and the ball was headed goalwards, Toshack helping it on its way into the back of the net. Burnley protested fiercely about the goal due to the free-kick being taken so quickly but after consulting with his linesman, referee Mr Williams still allowed it to stand. The second goal took the sting out of the game and the second half was played at a much slower pace than the first. With fifteen minutes remaining Toshack turned provider for Cormack, heading Steve Heighway's centre across the goal for the Scot to nod the ball home. With the result now beyond doubt, the Reds players tried to tee up Toshack for his first Liverpool hat-trick and on one occasion he was lining up his shot only for Jim Thomson to rob him of the ball at the last second.

Liverpool: Clemence, Lawler, Lindsay, Smith, Lloyd, Hughes, Keegan, Cormack, Heighway, Toshack, Callaghan. Sub: Boersma.

Burnley: Stevenson, Docherty, Newton, Dobson, Waldron, Thomson, Nulty, Casper, Fletcher, Collins (Ingham), James.

Referee: Mr H Williams (Sheffield).

Attendance: 56,124.

Football League Division One: Liverpool 1 Derby County 1
Saturday 20th January 1973

Whether or not watching John Toshack's display against Burnley had led Lou Macari to believe he wouldn't be a regular starter nobody could be sure, but the following afternoon he was on his way back to Glasgow with the deal firmly on ice. After talks with Bill Shankly and a tour of Melwood, Macari asked for time to think over the deal and was smuggled out of Anfield through a side door at lunchtime. This led to Shankly issuing a very brief statement that the *Liverpool Echo* reported as saying: 'The player has gone back to Scotland to see his club and think over what was discussed'.

When Liverpool informed Celtic at 6pm that they were no longer interested in signing Macari, it left the door open for Manchester United to make their move. Macari may well have had opportunity to speak with their manager Tommy Docherty, who had also been at Anfield the previous night with assistant Paddy Crerand, and actually sat next to him. When Macari returned to Glasgow, Docherty followed him up there and agreed terms at midnight, before they both travelled to Manchester the following day where he signed on the dotted line before the deadline for playing in Saturday's game. The £200,000 was a record fee for a transfer from a Scottish to an English club and a major snub for Liverpool, who were not used to players showing little enthusiasm in joining them. Even though Macari had played under Docherty for Scotland and was joining a club where there were a number of other Scottish internationals present, he was still swapping a treble chase for a relegation dogfight.

Fan Chris Wood, who had attended the Burnley game, remembers how there was much talk of Macari amongst fans, but believed that if the deal had been cut and dried the player would have been paraded on the pitch in front of fans. He also remembers the prophetic words of one fan who told him: 'Macari is alright but I would rather have his mate, who is slightly younger and called Kenny Dalglish'. History has showed that the failure to complete the deal was Macari's loss not Liverpool's. At Manchester United he won just one medal in eleven years, ironically against Liverpool in the 1977 FA Cup Final. In the same period, Liverpool won eighteen major trophies and when United won the FA Cup in 1983, Macari was not in the side.

But back to January 1973 and Liverpool had to put the disappointment of failing to secure Macari behind them and prepare for the next league game, at home to reigning Champions Derby County. It was clear that unless there was a dramatic collective slump in form amongst the top three then Derby would be abdicating in April, as they were eleven points behind Liverpool with just fifteen games remaining.

Tommy Smith identified the next six league games as Liverpool's most difficult of the season, barring the Leeds game that was to take place on Easter Monday. As well as the impending game with Derby, they would be at home to close challengers Arsenal and dark horses Ipswich Town. He believed it was essential that the Reds took six points from them to maintain their position as at the head of the pack. He had written in his *Liverpool Echo* column on 6th January:

'If we are to win the league comfortably then we need to take at least nine or ten points out of the twelve at stake. If we did achieve that target then it would need something really drastic to happen for us not to win the league. It is important that we win the home games against Derby and Ipswich. Victory in those matches would be likely to reduce the title chase to a two-horse race between Leeds and ourselves'.

Bill Shankly believed 58 points, the same number as Derby won the title with the previous season, would be enough to be champions. This meant that if the Reds kept winning their home games, which included ones against Arsenal and Leeds, then they could afford to lose all their away ones and still be champions. However, Shankly was not looking to keep it that close:

'If we beat these teams and get a good return from the rest of our home programme we would almost clinch the league. I think 58 points could clinch the title again but we have the best away record too, don't forget, and we won't be taking any chances'.[48]

Against Derby at Anfield Tommy Smith's plan fell flat at the first hurdle. Despite being without leading scorer Alan Hinton due to a groin strain, the visitors became the first side to come away with a point for more than a year after holding the Reds to a 1-1 draw on a snow covered pitch.

Both sides struggled to deal with the conditions early on and Derby defender Roy McFarland almost paid a high price for attempting a back pass along the ground when the ball stuck in the snow, only for Colin Boulton to quickly gather the ball as John Toshack pounced. Toshack then had the ball in the net after five minutes, scoring from an Emlyn Hughes pass but the goal was ruled out for offside and he was then denied a penalty despite loud appeals after going down under a challenge from Colin Todd. In the fourteenth minute Derby took the lead in controversial circumstances, McFarland playing a long ball to Roger Davies who looked yards offside but the referee further antagonised the crowd when he waved play on and the young forward gave Ray Clemence no chance.

Liverpool were struggling to deal with the slippery conditions which weren't suited to a quick-passing game but they found an equaliser just eight minutes after Derby's goal. Kevin Keegan beat David Nish on the right and crossed for Toshack who scored with a glancing header to serve Shankly with another reminder that he didn't need to dip into transfer funds. Toshack was saving the Reds money in other ways, too, as he was the only player to turn out in short sleeves, Shankly explaining to the *Liverpool Echo* the following Monday that his shoulders were so broad even the largest long-sleeved one still ended up near his elbows. The rest of the half was a midfield battle, with few chances being created due to the snow and any opportunities being limited to long-range shots. Derby did have one great chance five minutes before half-time when Kevin Hector played a ball into the box past Smith towards John O'Hare. With Clemence isolated Lindsay managed to get across to cover and concede a corner.

Things got worse in the second half as snow began to fall again and both sides were struggling to put passes together ruining what had promised beforehand to be an entertaining game as Derby were renowned for attacking football. Cormack did manage to create two opportunities for Toshack, one which led to a shot going wide and the other a dangerous header that was well saved – but there was little else at either end. With Liverpool resorting to high balls to keep the ball off the ground, Todd and McFarland were doing a good job of containing Toshack. Heighway and Keegan were ineffective due to the state of the pitch and with Derby happy to sit back for a point the game fizzled out into a draw as the Reds lead at the top was cut to two points.

Despite the winning home run coming to an end, Shankly joked to the *Daily Post* that even he had had bad games in the snow. He had nothing but praise for his players given the slippery conditions they had to contend with, the *Liverpool Echo* quoting him on the Monday:

> 'It's alright if snow falls on a hard pitch because players can keep their feet. But on Saturday the ground was soft underneath and the pitch was really unplayable. We were reasonably happy to take a point, there were some really tired players leaving the field'.

In his *Echo* column the following week Tommy Smith claimed that he had never played in conditions as bad and had nothing but praise for the fans who braved the conditions to attend Anfield. He believed that nothing deterred them and their support was a big reason for Liverpool's consistency over the years as it is a tremendous boost to receive such consistent support. He said he would not be surprised if Liverpool played a friendly in Timbuktoo to see fans there, and recalled how in 1966 five Kopites had made it to Ploesti in the European Cup travelling across Europe by car.

Liverpool: Clemence, Lawler, Lindsay, Smith, Lloyd, Hughes, Keegan, Cormack, Heighway, Toshack, Callaghan. Sub: Thompson.

Derby: Boulton, Webster, Nish, Hennessey, McFarland, Todd, McGovern, O'Hare, Davies, Hector, Powell Sub: Durban.

Referee: Mr K. Styles (Barnsley).

Attendance: 45,996.

Football League Division One: Wolverhampton Wanderers 2 Liverpool 1 Saturday 27th January 1973

Liverpool's position at the top of the First Division was recognised by the Sportsmen's Club of London, who awarded them Team of the Month for December. It was the first time a club outside London had won the award and with it being international week Shankly travelled to collect it from them in person. There was no joy for the Reds, though, when the winner of the *Liverpool Echo* Sports Personality of the Year was announced the same week, Emlyn Hughes having to settle for second place behind Everton's Howard Kendall.

Melwood was quieter than normal with five players away for the England v Wales World Cup qualifier. Ray Clemence, Emlyn Hughes, Kevin Keegan and Larry Lloyd were in the England squad and John Toshack had been called up by Wales. Knowing Wembley was an extremely tiring pitch, Shankly was hopeful the weather wasn't bad and his players came back without any injuries. However, he must have been livid when he heard the day before the England game that Clemence had twisted his ankle in a training match in which Sir Alf Ramsey asked him and the other keeper, Peter Shilton, to play outfield. Thankfully, Clemence's injury wasn't as bad as first thought and he was named as England keeper for the game, which was drawn 1-1. Hughes and Keegan also played for England, the latter in an unfamiliar right wing position where he made little impact, while Toshack struck the Welsh goal.

With all the players involved in the World Cup qualifier coming through unscathed, Shankly was able to announce that the side would be unchanged as they set off for Wolverhampton on the Friday with Toshack being preferred to Phil Boersma in attack. Phil Thompson travelled as substitute and youngster John Webb was taken along to be given another taste of the first-team atmosphere. Wolves were eleventh in the table with a mixed home record, winning seven and drawing five so far but, writing in the *Liverpool Echo* the evening before, Ken Rogers, usually the Tranmere correspondent but deputising for Chris James, said they were difficult to beat and the Reds may have to settle for a point. Their dangerman was twenty-two-year old forward John Richards, whose performances had earned him a call up to the England squad for the Wales game.

Liverpool made a slow start at Molineux and Clemence had to be on hand to make saves from Richards and Derek Dougan. They were also fortunate when, after wasting a free-kick, Chris Lawler was on hand to clear after the ball was pumped upfield towards Richards. After ten minutes Wolves took the lead when Dave Wagstaffe crossed from the left. Jim McCalliog missed his kick but Hughes, not realising Clemence had left his goal line, turned the ball back to where he thought the keeper would be but instead into an empty net. Just seven minutes later Liverpool were level from a free-kick by the halfway line which Lawler hit long into the box, where Toshack rose to head it across goal and Keegan fired an unstoppable shot past Phil Parkes.

Both sides went on to make a good contest of it for the rest of the first half, Alan Sunderland having a good dipping shot saved by Clemence and Ian Callaghan being denied by Parkes after a similar effort. Peter Cormack had a shot that was easily held by Parkes after some good work by Heighway, but the Reds were lucky not to go behind again on the half-hour when Richards crossed for Dougan who was just unable to reach the ball when a goal looked certain. Three minutes before half-time, Alec Lindsay's cross was spilled by Parkes to the surprise of Toshack who failed to react quickly enough and the ball was scrambled to safety.

Five minutes into the second half Wolves had the ball in the net when Richards headed in Wagstaffe's cross but to the relief of the Reds players the goal was ruled out for offside. This angered the Wolves fans, who were booing every Liverpool touch and they were further enraged after an hour when Larry Lloyd hauled down Dougan as he was clean through on goal. Lloyd was booked for his challenge and from the free-kick Bernard Shaw tried a chip which failed to fool Clemence. Wolves were causing Liverpool all sorts of problems, with veteran Dougan showing no signs of age to run Lloyd ragged.

Midway through the second half the Reds finally managed to get back into the game and apply some pressure, with Heighway having some good runs down the left flank. However, Toshack was often getting caught offside. Wagstaffe tested Clemence with a long-range effort which he tipped wide and when Wolves did take the lead again in the eightieth minute, Liverpool could have no complaints. Shaw found Richards just inside the area and he turned and struck a first-time effort that gave Clemence no chance. Richards almost made it 3-1 just afterwards but Clemence managed to dive at his feet and although the Reds piled on the pressure in the last five minutes, no equaliser was forthcoming as the Midlands hoodoo continued, this defeat following on from earlier ones at Derby and Leicester.

Shankly had praise for Wolves afterwards but felt Liverpool's preparations hadn't been helped by the international. He told the *Daily Post*:

> 'When you're on the top, mid-table sides raise their game and come at you hard. It's bound to disrupt training having Clemence, Hughes, Keegan, Lloyd and Toshack away for half a week. We were lucky not to have them injured at all, but international call-ups are no good for a team going for

honours. When you are playing for another side you get told different things and this must affect you when you come back to your own club".

Although dropping three points in the last two games had seen the Reds lead at the top cut to one point, Tommy Smith still believed they would win the title. He said of the situation in his *Liverpool Echo* column the following Saturday:

'The only teams who are a major threat to us have got to come to Anfield. Earlier in the season Arsenal had a bad spell when they picked up only two points in four games while Leeds had a spell of picking up three from four. Never in modern football has a team gone through a season unbeaten. We were due to drop a point at home, after all it was more than a year since we had done so in a league match'.

Liverpool: Clemence, Lawler, Lindsay, Smith, Llolyd, Hughes, Keegan, Cormack, Heighway, Toshack, Callaghan. Sub: Thompson.

Wolves: Parkes, Taylor, McAlle, Shaw, Munro, McCalliog, Jefferson, Sunderland, Richards, Dougan, Wagstaffe. Sub: Kindon.

Referee: Mr H. T. Hackney (Barnsley).

Attendance: 32,957.

FA Cup 4th Round: Liverpool 0 Manchester City 0
Saturday 3rd February 1973

After the disappointment of the Wolves and Derby games, Bill Shankly decided the best way to prepare for the upcoming FA Cup fourth round tie with Manchester City was relaxation. With no midweek game to worry about, the players were given the Monday off and then headed to Blackpool for a day on the Tuesday for some sea-air and meal in a hotel. Of the plans for the trip, Shankly told the *Liverpool Echo*: 'We will not be doing any training on the beach or anything like that. This will be a bit of a change because we have been at it all the time'.

As Liverpool prepared for the tie in low-ley fashion, City were firing a verbal broadside. As soon as the Reds had overcome Burnley in their replay City manager Malcolm Allison claimed a strong referee was needed as the crowd could influence decisions at Anfield.[49] Vice-chairman Peter Swales then joined in, stating that Liverpool's decision not to make the tie all-ticket was a joke. City were allocated 5,000 stand tickets, but Swales said that their fans would be discouraged from travelling and paying at the turnstiles for the terraces in case they failed to gain entry. Peter Robinson defended the decision, pointing out that in the previous two seasons' big FA Cup games against Leeds and Tottenham it had been pay at the gate and that it was a system that suited the club and fans best. The *Daily Post* reported his comments on 23rd January as:

> 'Our fans prefer to come along and pay at the turnstiles on the day of
> the match rather than queue twice to get in. It is also a safeguard against
> the setting up of any black market in ticket sales. We don't like our fans
> having to pay over the odds to see the team they follow regularly through
> the season'.

Given City had attracted just 38,648 for their fourth round game at home to
Stoke and were not known for such a large away following, Swales may well
have been over-optimistic about the size of the following his team would
have at Anfield. Allison was so confident of success that he announced his
team for the game on the Wednesday and told the national press what
they intended to do at Anfield. The day before the game Shankly finally
responded to all of the taunts, saying that Liverpool intended to do their
talking on the pitch and telling the *Liverpool Echo:* 'No matter what they say
they have still got to come here and play. This week it's been all Manchester
City and what they intend to do. You'd hardly think there was another game
on in the North West'

Shankly named a squad of fourteen for the game, with Phil Boersma and
Brian Hall being added to the twelve who had been involved against Wolves.
Failure to confirm that the same eleven as last week would be starting often
indicated that Shankly was planning a change. Although it was known
Chris Lawler had been struggling with a foot injury, the *Echo's* Chris James
speculated the evening before the game that Tommy Smith may be dropped
as Shankly sought to shore up the defence that had been impregnable while
he was out with injury.

Shankly did indeed decide to leave Smith out of the side, recalling Phil
Thompson in his place and informing his captain of the decision the night
before. Shankly stressed that Smith hadn't been dropped, but was instead in
need of a rest as the injuries and car crash had taken more out of him than
previously thought.[50] When the teams were announced over the tannoy by
George Sephton there was a stunned silence around the capacity crowd,
the gates having been locked half-an-hour before kick-off. Smith himself
wasn't even in the ground then, having returned home in disappointment
as he couldn't bear the thought of watching a match he wasn't playing in.[51]
Sephton, who is still the announcer at Anfield today after more than forty
years in the role, explains that although nowadays most of the crowd does
not get into the stadium until a few minutes before kick-off, his routine
remains very similar to what it was then. He says:

> 'The difference now is that the gates open ninety minutes before kick-
> off whereas then the gates opened when there were people waiting to
> come in. Sometimes I would be in my seat at noon for a three o'clock
> kick-off and slump into my seat shattered at kick-off time. I still play music

from the time the gates open but in these days of all-seater stadiums the audience is usually quite sparse early on but I use the maxim that I had when I was on Dune FM in Southport. You carry on as if you're talking to one particular listener regardless of the actual figure'.

The Kop sang 'Allison Shut Your Mouth', which was lapped up by the City boss, but after all the build-up the first half proved to be a drab affair that hardly flowed, with Chris James describing it in that night's *Echo* as a 'disgraceful shambles'. Liverpool lost the toss and were forced to kick into the Kop and it was a scrappy affair, in which City committed 23 fouls and were fortunate that only Tony Book was cautioned for a late tackle on Steve Heighway. When Keegan reciprocated a foul on Derek Jeffries in the tenth minute a fracas broke out between many of the players. It seemed inevitable that the first real chance would come from a free-kick and just after a quarter-of-an-hour had gone Ian Callaghan floated a ball into the box and Peter Cormack's header was well saved by Joe Corrigan. Shortly after this Callaghan tried his luck with a thunderous volley from thirty yards that went just wide.

At the other end, the main danger was coming from Mike Summerbee who was giving Alec Lindsay a hard time, while in the nineteenth minute Rodney Marsh bundled the ball into the net but in doing so committed a foul on Ray Clemence and the goal was disallowed. City's game plan was to stifle Liverpool in midfield and try their luck from long range, but Francis Lee's and Colin Bell's efforts were easily held by Clemence. Foul play wasn't limited to who was on the ball, with Willie Donachie and Cormack being involved in an incident in the City half when play was going on at the other end of the pitch.

Such was the scrappy nature of the game that the Kop sang 'We want football'. A rare opportunity came when John Toshack missed a golden chance after 35 minutes, hesitating to confirm no offside flag was raised after a Keegan pass, meaning Corrigan was able to dive at his feet to gather the ball. But things soon returned to how they had been when Lee and Emlyn Hughes got involved in a tussle and had to be separated by referee Pat Partridge.

There was a chorus of boos as the teams left the pitch at half-time and City were jeered when they returned for the second half. They conceded a free-kick soon after the restart when Tommy Booth fouled Steve Heighway, but although Lindsay drove the set-piece dangerously across the box, Cormack, Keegan and Toshack all failed to connect. A few moments later Toshack crossed for Keegan but he blazed the ball wide from ten yards. The game was flowing far better now and was less bad-tempered, Booth heading just wide and Reds appeals for a penalty being turned down when Book slipped and fell on the ball, but Partridge ruled it hit his hand accidentally. However,

Larry Lloyd was unfortunate to end up in the referee's book for a mistimed challenge on Tony Towers, a caution that would potentially take him over the twelve disciplinary points that would trigger a suspension. City were winning the midfield battle and forced six corners during the second half to Liverpool's one, but clear-cut chances were still at a premium. The Reds had an almighty let off, though, five minutes from time when Donachie's free-kick was met by Summerbee, whose looping header bounced off the bar and into the crowd.

It meant the teams would have to do battle again at Maine Road the following Wednesday. Across Stanley Park, Everton's game with Second Division Millwall was little better as a spectacle, although at least there were two goals that would have made Kopites smile, as the Lions won 2-0.

Liverpool: Clemence, Lawler, Lindsay, Thompson, Lloyd, Hughes, Keegan, Cormack, Heighway, Toshack, Callaghan. Sub: Hall.

City: Corrigan, Book, Donachie, Doyle, Booth, Jeffries, Summerbee, Bell, Marsh, Lee, Towers. Sub: Mellor.

Referee: Mr P. Partridge (Middlesbrough).

Attendance: 56,296.

FA Cup 4th Round Replay: Manchester City 2 Liverpool 0
Wednesday 7th February 1973

It wasn't just the newspapers in Liverpool that were critical of City's tactics in the first game. *Match of the Day* gave a lot of emphasis to Tony Book's tackle on Steve Heighway that earned him a booking, which Book maintained looked worse on television than it actually was. City's assistant manager Ken Barnes used the match programme for the replay to respond to the criticism of his team:

> 'I thought the reports were more alarmist than they should have been. There was a lot more football than we were given credit for. There were some niggly fouls particularly during the tension of the last few minutes. There were few very bad fouls, I think the nastiness was blown out of all proportion. Nor were City entirely villains of the peace'.

Malcolm Allison predicted a 3-0 victory for City in the replay, the *Daily Post* reporting on the morning of the game that he had said: 'Liverpool are a beaten side, we've just got to finish them off'. His comments had certainly made their fans sit up and take notice, with queues of up to 400 yards forming for tickets the day before the game. On the other hand, City's tactics had certainly had an impact on Reds fans, many of whom didn't want to see more of the same in the replay and Liverpool's allocation of 6,000 stand tickets didn't sell out until the morning of the game. Although some Liverpool fans were expected to pay at the gate, the *Liverpool Echo* predicted that there would be less than 10,000 of them in the crowd, instead of the

15-20,000 that would normally be expected to travel to a tie of this nature.

Shankly announced the night before the tie that Tommy Smith would still be missing from the side and refused to be drawn on Allison's comments, instead simply stating that Liverpool could win. He told the *Post*: 'We created enough chances to have beaten City. That was satisfactory, all except our failure to put the ball into the net. At least we got ourselves into positions to score and our back division was very solid'.

The first chance of the game fell to John Toshack although his effort was well saved by Joe Corrigan, but Liverpool were being overpowered in midfield and were further hindered when Peter Cormack struggled to shake off an injury after a heavy tackle. After fourteen minutes City took the lead when Francis Lee unleashed a fierce shot from 25 yards which Ray Clemence couldn't hold and Colin Bell followed in to score from the rebound. With Cormack limping, it was too hard for Ian Callaghan and Phil Thompson to regain any control of the midfield and the Reds struggled to get back into the game.

In the 51st minute a disputed free-kick gave City their second goal. Lee had run the ball out of play and kicked it towards Clemence for a goal-kick, only for the linesman to flag for a foul on him by Emlyn Hughes. The kick was driven hard across the penalty area and turned into the net from close range by Tommy Booth, leaving Liverpool with a mountain to climb. After this the game threatened to return to the scrappiness that had been seen at Anfield, with Lee, Doyle and Larry Lloyd all being booked. Phil Boersma came off the bench to replace Cormack and Emlyn Hughes moved into midfield with Thompson dropping into defence. But despite their efforts the Reds couldn't find any way back into the game.

The exit was made even more disappointing for the Reds by the fact that had they won they would have been confident of making it to the quarter-finals, with City now facing Second Division Sunderland at home. Allison still wasn't finished and got in one last dig at the Reds. The *Liverpool Echo* reported the next evening that he had emerged from the dressing room after the game to say: 'Liverpool will not win the title, they are a very defensive side. Once Keegan was played out of the game they were not a striking force at all'. Allison did finally shut up after the fifth round when Sunderland beat them 3-1 in a Roker Park replay, leading to Wolves striker Derek Dougan to comment in his weekly syndicated column on 6th March: 'I can only assume that Malcolm was too stunned to articulate a reaction. Sunderland had shut him up good and proper, as they say in that part of the country'.

Liverpool: Clemence, Lawler, Lindsay, Thompson, Lloyd, Hughes, Keegan, Cormack (Boersma), Heighway, Toshack, Callaghan.

City: Corrigan, Book, Donachie, Doyle, Booth, Jeffries, Summerbee, Bell, Marsh, Lee, Towers. Sub: Mellor.

Referee: Mr P. Partridge (Middlesbrough).
Attendance: 49,572.

Football League Division One: Liverpool 0 Arsenal 2
Saturday 10th February 1973

For the second year in succession Liverpool had gone out of the FA Cup in a fourth round replay to a 2-0 scoreline. As with the previous season, the cup defeat had come amidst a slight dip in league form. Then, they responded magnificently to come within a whisker of winning the title and a response was needed this time. Bill Shankly's biggest task ahead of the forthcoming home game with Arsenal was to restore confidence and pride, as a win in that game would open up a three-point gap at the top over the Gunners, who had played a game more but were unbeaten in twelve matches. He had nothing more to say about the City game, preferring instead to look forward to what he described to the *Liverpool Echo* as a 'battle royal'.

The day before the game Shankly confirmed that Tommy Smith would be back in the side, the rest he had had having done him good and that Peter Cormack had failed to recover from the injury sustained at City. He would not be drawn on what his starting eleven would be and when it came to making the side public on matchday he had more than one surprise up his sleeve. As expected Smith slotted into defence with Hughes returning to midfield and Phil Thompson making way, but as well as Brian Hall replacing Cormack, Phil Boersma was recalled to the side and Steve Heighway dropped.

On a very heavy pitch, Boersma showed his worth early on when he went on a run down the left wing, beat Pat Rice and crossed for John Toshack who headed wide. Kicking into the Kop, Liverpool were winning the early midfield battles and, apart from John Radford, all Arsenal's men were behind the ball. Kevin Keegan was brought down a few times but the Reds weren't able to capitalise on the free-kicks that were awarded. On one occasion Boersma had a shot that beat Bob Wilson who was well off his line but it struck Hall and bounced away.

With Alan Ball outstanding, Arsenal managed to regain some control of the midfield and in the 25th minute the best chance of the game fell to Radford after a cross from the left, but as he tried to poke the ball past Ray Clemence the Reds keeper managed to stick a leg out and concede a corner. Arsenal were employing an offside trap to catch the Reds forwards out but twice Keegan was only marginally off and in the 34th minute he had Liverpool's best chance when his flicked header from a Boersma long-ball beat Wilson but went just wide of the post. As the half drew to a close Liverpool's pressure intensified, Alec Lindsay testing Wilson from 25 yards, but Arsenal did almost take the lead when Radford shot from outside the box, only for Clemence to fingertip it over.

It was clear that it would take something special to beat a well-drilled and efficient Arsenal defence and early in the second half the chance almost came when Toshack crossed to Keegan on the edge of the area. He laid the ball off to Ian Callaghan who fired a first-time shot but it went just wide. On the hour mark Keegan set up Hall and after he had rounded a defender he looked certain to score but Wilson threw himself down at his feet and managed to block the shot which then went over the bar.

Four minutes after Wilson had saved Arsenal, they went ahead after being awarded a penalty when Lindsay fouled George Armstrong. Despite the whistles of the Kop, Ball kept his nerve to stroke the ball beyond Clemence's right hand. Liverpool went straight back on the attack but, with Arsenal retreating even more into defence, they could find no way through and in the 70th minute Radford struck a decisive second goal, running onto a long clearance before rounding Clemence and rolling the ball into an empty net.

Callaghan came closest to pulling a goal back for Liverpool, but his shot from just outside the box was cleared off the line by Rice and in the last minute there were appeals for a penalty after Hughes went down under a challenge from Armstrong. Arsenal, though, were worthy of this victory which took them above the Reds, who were off the top for the first time since September. It was achieved in an efficient and organised manner, inflicting upon Liverpool their first home defeat since New Year's Day 1972, a run that had included 32 games in all competitions.

Tommy Smith felt that this Arsenal side was a very different proposition to the one that the Reds had faced at Highbury earlier in the season. In his *Liverpool Echo* column the following week he identified the forward partnership of John Radford and Ray Kennedy, which had played such a part in the double season of 1970-71, as a major factor, as well as the emergence of Alan Ball. The ex-Everton player had signed for £220,000 in the summer of 1971 but had a quiet first season; now he was prompting them in midfield.

Liverpool: Clemence, Lawler, Lindsay, Smith, Lloyd, Hughes, Keegan, Hall, Boersma, Toshack, Callaghan. Sub: Thompson.

Arsenal: Wilson, Rice, McNab, Storey, Blockley, Simpson, Armstrong, Ball, Radford (George), Kennedy, Kelly.

Referee: Mr J. Hunting (Leicester).

Attendance: 49,898.

Football League Division One: Manchester City 1 Liverpool 1
Saturday 17th February 1973

With Ray Clemence, Emlyn Hughes and Kevin Keegan going away with England, who were playing Scotland at Hampden Park in a game to mark the centenary of the Scottish FA, Bill Shankly took the opportunity to give the rest of the squad two extra days off so they would return fresher. Despite having fallen to second Shankly felt there had been signs of the old Liverpool in the first half against Arsenal and that the Reds could not have expected to have things go their way all season. He told the *Liverpool Echo* on the Monday after the defeat:

> 'We didn't expect to go through a season without setbacks. You don't expect to sail though a season and win the title without having to fight for it. We've got to fight now and come back from the setbacks we've had in the last few weeks. For half-an-hour on Saturday we were the old Liverpool, we pinned Arsenal back and might have scored a goal or two'.

As Liverpool sought to arrest the mini-slump, Maine Road, scene of the recent FA Cup exit, was probably the last place they wanted to go for their next league fixture. Larry Lloyd was due to start an automatic suspension in this game but this was put on hold as Shankly confirmed the two bookings picked up in the cup games would be appealed, with Lloyd particularly angry that Francis Lee had appeared to encourage the referee to book him in the replay. As Lloyd prepared his appeal, Lee was away in Blackpool with his team-mates, the City squad going for a three-day toning-up programme by the seaside.

On Valentine's Day help came from the skies as snow blanketed the North West, catching City unawares as they had not covered the pitch beforehand. Snow hadn't been the only thing that took the City groundsmen by surprise that week. A few days earlier, a floodlight pylon had been struck by lightning as they were working on draining the pitch, causing a plume of blue smoke and a large hole in the ground at its base.

As Liverpool were forced to train on their all-weather pitch, Shankly made no secret of the fact he wouldn't be unhappy to see the game called off, believing two whole weeks without a match was just what his side needed. He was also pleased to hear that Ray Clemence and Kevin Keegan had been left out of the England side that night, as Keegan especially had been looking jaded of late. Keegan may have been disappointed to have been only on the bench at Hampden Park but when he returned to Anfield on the Thursday he was presented with a cardboard box containing a mixture of both birthday and Valentine's Day cards, having just turned 22.

Despite Everton's game with Norwich being called off on the Friday, as well as Liverpool's reserve game against Wolves at Anfield, the snow had been cleared off the Maine Road pitch and with its drainage system having done its job, the game was given the go-ahead. The calling-off of the reserve game was the third time in succession the second string had seen a game fall foul of the weather and was especially unlucky for Jack Whitham. He had managed just sixteen minutes of first team football all season and was badly in need of competitive match practice, but now had to make do with an A

Team outing at Barrow.

Unlike with the FA Cup games, there were no noises coming out of Maine Road with Malclom Allison being surprisingly quiet. As Liverpool headed to Manchester minus Peter Cormack, who was still injured, Shankly kept his words simple by saying it was a vital game, as was every other before the end of the season, but one the Reds could win. In the end he would have to settle for a point, but can be pleased at the way Liverpool fought back to equalise in a game that saw Tommy Smith sent off for the only time in his career.

Shankly again made changes to the side, recalling Steve Heighway and Phil Thompson at the expense of Brian Hall and John Toshack. Given the team's recent slump in form, Thompson had been disappointed not to have got on during the Arsenal match a week earlier, the third successive league game in which he was an unused substitute. Reserve-team boss Ronnie Moran encouraged Thompson to go and see Bill Shankly to ask why he hadn't got a game and when he did so he was given a surprising response, recalling in *Stand Up Pinocchio*:

> 'Bill looked at me and rapped back. "Jesus Christ son you are asking me why you didn't play with that load of rubbish". He started to run through the names of the team and said "these are all has beens. You should be in here thanking me that I didn't play you with that load of crap. You are going to play for this club for years. You will captain this club one day. You will go on to play for England". I felt fantastic, I had gone in to complain and come out buzzing'.

Despite the weather conditions the pitch was in good shape, although soft, and the players had no difficulty in keeping their footing. Liverpool started the stronger, exploiting a number of mistakes to assert pressure but they had no clear-cut chances. The first shot was after about a quarter-of-an-hour when Emlyn Hughes tried an audacious volley from near the touchline after Mike Doyle had headed the ball clear, but it went well over the bar. The game was played very much in the middle of the park, with Kevin Keegan dropping back to help Liverpool stamp their authority, but the second Reds shot didn't come until the 27th minute when Hughes's thirty-yard effort went well wide. City were playing some neat football at times but couldn't penetrate a strong Liverpool defence with Larry Lloyd and Tommy Smith working well together.

City, whose minds may have been on the following week's FA Cup game with Sunderland, were not the ferocious team that Liverpool had faced earlier in the month and they didn't manage a shot until the 37th minute, Colin Bell's 25-yard attempt going well wide. Liverpool forced two quick corners but couldn't make anything out of them and then went behind two minutes before half-time. After Smith conceded a free-kick for a foul on Bell, Mike Summerbee floated it into the box and Tommy Booth rose unchallenged to head past Ray Clemence. The Reds were fortunate not to go 2-0 down before the break when, from another Summerbee free-kick, Francis Lee hit a stunning volley from the left-hand corner of the six-yard box but Clemence made a great diving save at the near post.

There were some signs of discontent as the teams left the field, as Smith and Hughes were having an argument, Hughes appearing to be blaming Smith for conceding the free-kick which led to the City goal. Liverpool started the second half strongly with Thompson, playing well as a sweeper in front of the back four, competently breaking up play and distributing the ball to others. Thompson remembers one moment in the game which made him realise how well he was performing:

> 'City used to like chipping the ball into the box towards Rodney Marsh and Francis Lee and my instructions were to get in the way of as many of these balls as possible. As the game went on I seemed to be intercepting everything and I could hear one of them getting some stick, only to respond "this skinny young b**tard isn't letting me have a kick". I grew inside immensely when I heard this from such a good player and knew I was doing an effective job'[52]

The first chance of the half came when Smith got forward to fire a shot just a few feet over the bar and Keegan put in a dangerous cross that was headed clear by Mike Doyle, but Boersma received a booking for fouling Lee as he tried to dispossess him. City nearly scored with their first attack which saw Rodney Marsh catch Clemence out with a lob which only just went over the bar.

With Liverpool pushing further forward they were getting more exposed at the back and after 65 minutes Lee broke clear after running onto a pass from Marsh and Clemence made a good save turning the ball away for a corner. From the corner there was an obstruction on the edge of the six-yard box, which led to Tommy Smith being booked for dissent. Every Reds player was on the goalline and they managed to block Marsh's kick with the rebound going wide. In the melee surrounding the free-kick there was a lot of pushing and shoving, leading to Smith and Tommy Booth being lectured by the referee, but Smith continued to argue and was sent off in the 70th minute. Smith was the third Reds player to be sent off that season and coincidentally one of the other two – Larry Lloyd's dismissal – had also been against City at Anfield.

With the Reds down to ten men Thompson moved back into defence and, with fifteen minutes remaining, Shankly replaced Heighway with Brian Hall, who took just two minutes to make an impact as he set up the Reds' equaliser. Taking a pass from Lindsay, he got to the byline and crossed for Boersma who had his back to goal. There didn't seem much of an opportunity to shoot but he swivelled round and hit a first-time shot into the top corner for a goal well deserved by a Reds team who had continued to play attractive

Match programmes from the first home game of the 1972-73 season against Manchester City, the first UEFA Cup game of the campaign at home to Eintracht Frankfurt and the away match at Arsenal when Jimmy Hill came out of the crowd to act as an emergency linesman
Author's collection

Emlyn Hughes in action for Liverpool against Derby County at the Baseball Ground on 2nd September 1972
© *Press Association*

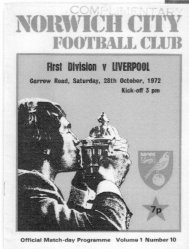

Programmes from the Stoke City home match on 21st October 1972 in what turned out to be Gordon Banks's last top class match due to an accident the next day; and from Norwich at Carrow Road a week later when 18 year old Phil Thompson made his first start for the Reds
Author's collection

Chris Lawler wins a header in Athens as Liverpool go through to the UEFA Cup 3rd round with a 6-1 aggregate victory
© *Press Association*

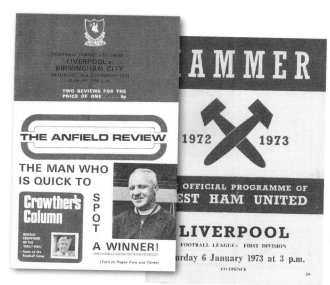

Programmes from the home match with Birmingham City on 2nd December 1972, Liverpool winning 4-3 after trailing 2-0 and 3-1; and from the away game at West Ham United on 6th January 1973, played the day after Bill Shankly was filmed as the subject of *This is Your Life*
Author's collection

Home match programmes from the games with Derby County on 20th January 1973 when the Reds failed to win a home league game for the first time in over a year; and from the match with Arsenal on 10th February 1973 when the Gunners' 2-0 victory blew the title race wide open
Author's collection

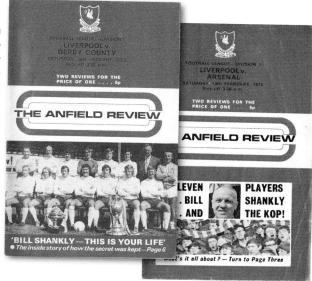

Tickets from the home legs of the UEFA Cup ties against Dynamo Berlin and Dynamo Dresden. For all games in the UEFA Cup, including the final, only the stands were ticketed
Courtesy Hyder Jawad

ITINERARY

Headquarters:—
Night of Monday, 19th March, 1973:
Berlin Hotel, Kurfurstenstrasse 62, West Berlin 30
(Telephone 0311/26-92-91).
Nights of Tuesday and Wednesday, 20th and 21st
March, 1973:
Newa Hotel, Christianstrasse, Dresden 801 (Tele-
phone Dresden 66-44-1).

Monday, 19th March, 1973   **Local Time**

Meet at Anfield Ground	15.00 hrs.
Motor Coach leaves Anfield Ground	15.15 hrs.
Arrives Manchester Airport	16.30 hrs.
Plane leaves Manchester Airport (B.E.A. Charter Flight)	17.00 hrs.
Dinner on Flight	
Arrives Tempelhof Airport (West Berlin)	19.00 hrs.
Motor Coach from Tempelhof Airport to the Berlin Hotel.	

Tuesday, 20th March, 1973

The players will train on the ground of
the Tennis Borussia F.C., West Berlin
at 10.30 hours.

Motor Coach leaves Berlin Hotel	13.45 hrs.

(The party will transfer from West Berlin
to East Berlin via the Friedrichstrasse
Border Point. It will be necessary to
change from one motor coach to
another at this point.)

Motor Coach arrives Newa Hotel, Dresden (approx.)	17.15 hrs.

Wednesday, 21st March, 1973

Motor Coach leaves Newa Hotel	18.40 hrs.
Arrives Dynamo Dresden F.C. Stadium	19.00 hrs.

KICK-OFF 20.00 Hours

Motor Coach from Dynamo Dresden
F.C. Stadium to Newa Hotel after
game.

Thursday, 21st March, 1973

Motor Coach leaves Newa Hotel	9.30 hrs.

(The party will transfer from East Berlin
to West Berlin via the Friedrichstrasse
Border Point. It will again be necessary to change motor coaches at this
point.)

Motor Coach arrives Tempelhof Airport	13.00 hrs.
Plane leaves Tempelhof Airport (B.E.A. Charter Flight)	13.30 hrs.
Lunch on Flight	
Arrives Manchester Airport	15.30 hrs.

Motor Coach from Manchester Airport
to Anfield Ground.

Itinerary for players and officials travelling on the club charter to Dresden, one of
their most gruelling European trips to date
Courtesy Rob Gowers

Tickets from the away legs of the
UEFA Cup ties against Dynamo
Berlin and Dynamo Dresden, both
matches cost 5.1 Marks
Courtesy Hyder Jawad

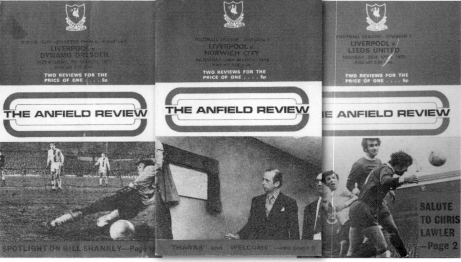

Programmes from the 1st leg of the UEFA Cup quarter final with Dynamo Dresden
which Liverpool won 2-0, the home game with Norwich City played on 24th March
1973 and the decisive match at home to Leeds United on Easter Monday
Author's collection

Kevin Keegan scores the second goal in a 2-0 win against Leeds on Easter
Monday to put the League title within Liverpool's grasp
© *Press Association*

Brian Hall, Larry Lloyd, Tommy Smith, Phil Boersma, Alec Lindsay and Ray
Clemence with the League Championship trophy after the Leicester game
© *Press Association*

Programme from the game
against Leicester that sealed
the championship
Author's collection

Bill Shankly with the League Championship trophy
in the dressing room after the Leicester match
© *Press Association*

Larry Lloyd and John Toshack jump for the ball in the UEFA Cup final 1st leg
against Borussia Mönchengladbach
© *Press Association*

Fans outside Mönchengladbach train station on the morning of the UEFA Cup final 2nd leg
© Chris Wood

Liverpool fans in the Bökelberg Stadium prior to the 2nd leg of the UEFA Cup final
© Chris Wood

Liverpool's players acknowledge the crowd in Mönchengladbach
© Chris Wood

Ian Callaghan on the ball in the 2nd leg of the UEFA Cup final
© Chris Wood

Liverpool fans celebrate on the pitch of the Bökelberg Stadium, in the middle of them is Tommy Smith with the trophy
© *Chris Wood*

Commemorative 1st Day Cover issued for the UEFA Cup final, signed by Tommy Smith and Chris Lawler
Courtesy Rob Gowers

Liverpool Football Club and Athletic Grounds Co. Ltd.

Champions English League Division One 1972-1973

Winners U.E.F.A. Cup 1972-1973

Celebration Dinner held at the Adelphi Hotel Liverpool

Friday, 20th July, 1973

Card from a celebration dinner held at the Adelphi Hotel on 20th July 1973 attended by players and coaching staff from the 1972-73 season
Courtesy Rob Gowers

football all game. City pressed forward to try to restore their lead but Bell headed over and Willie Donachie's 25-yard low shot was tipped round the post by Clemence. Smith, who had been taking a bath when Boersma's goal went in but returned to the bench for the last ten minutes, went on to praise Liverpool's fighting spirit, writing in his *Liverpool Echo* column the next week: 'What impressed me was the way the lads never gave up, they never lost their concentration for a minute and in those last twenty minutes brought all their old fighting spirit to bear on the situation'.

Liverpool: Clemence, Lawler, Lindsay, Smith, Lloyd, Hughes, Keegan, Thompson, Boersma, Heighway (Hall), Callaghan.

City: Corrigan, Book, Donachie, Doyle, Booth, Jeffries, Summerbee, Bell, Marsh, Lee, Towers. Sub: Hill.

Referee: Mr C. Thomas (South Wales).

Attendance: 40,528.

Football League Division One: Liverpool 2 Ipswich Town 1
Saturday 24th February 1973

The draw at Maine Road was a useful point for Liverpool but Arsenal's 1-0 win over Leicester meant that the Reds were now two points behind, although they did have a game in hand and better goal average. Leeds were two points behind the Reds with a game in hand themselves, so it was now extremely tight at the top and defeat for the Reds in their next match, at home to Ipswich, would turn the title chase into a four-horse race. The Suffolk side had won five of their last six games and were now four points behind Liverpool with a game in hand.

With Tommy Smith facing an automatic three-match ban for his sending-off, Liverpool looked certain to appeal, if only to buy time given there were just over two months of the season left and Larry Lloyd's whole appeal process had taken three months. Bill Shankly ordered Smith not to speak to the press about what had been said, meaning the following Saturday in his *Liverpool Echo* column the extent of Smith's comments on the matter were that having to leave the pitch with most of the crowd booing was the 'loneliest walk'. However, he found an unlikely ally in referee Clive Thomas who confirmed that no swear words had been used. The *Daily Post* reported on 20th February that Thomas had said of the incident:

'Smith did not use one swear word to me, either during the game or when I sent him off. There was never any indecent language. I have great admiration and respect for Tommy Smith but there are limits. What he told me on the field of play I would not take from anybody in the country. That is the reason he was sent off, I know and he knows what was said'.

As Liverpool battled to get Peter Cormack fit for the Ipswich game, the opposition had injury problems of their own with both central defenders, Allan Hunter and Kevin Beattie, struggling. Ipswich had the best away record in the First Division, having won six and lost just three of their fourteen games on the road so far. They had never won at Anfield in eleven visits but manager Bobby Robson was quoted in the *Echo* two days before the game as saying that history had to be defeated sooner or later and he would be looking to play positive football.

Striker David Johnson, who stood on the Kop as a kid but ended up signing for Everton, was relishing the prospect of his first game at Anfield since moving to Ipswich and believed his side were underrated, telling the *Daily Post* the day before the game:

'Tomorrow is a great opportunity to show that it is Ipswich and not Leeds or Arsenal that Liverpool need to beat. I get sick reading that Arsenal, Leeds and Liverpool are fighting it out. We never seem to get a mention at Ipswich. I suppose that's because we're "unfashionable", whatever that means. But I warn you, we're going to shock a few people before the season's over. We all agree that if we can win at Anfield we stand a great chance'

With Arsenal being involved in FA Cup action, victory in the game would take Liverpool back to the top of the table and Shankly had a selection poser as to whether or not to recall John Toshack and if he did, who should make way. It was confirmed on the Friday that Peter Cormack was still unfit and with Brian Hall having come off the bench to set up the equaliser at City, the *Echo* predicted on the Friday that it may well be Steve Heighway who made way. However, Shankly sprang a surprise when he dropped Phil Thompson to the bench instead and left Hall out of the twelve altogether. Bobby Robson was able to use Allan Hunter but with Beattie still injured, seventeen-year-old John Peddelty was given his league debut in defence.

Despite playing with four attacking players, Liverpool failed to exert any pressure from the start and had little spring in their step. The first chance fell to Ipswich after ten minutes but although Mick Lambert's cross evaded Ray Clemence there were no forwards in the centre to turn it in. Soon after, Liverpool did manage to force two corners in succession but nothing came of them and their first shot arrived after about a quarter of an hour but it was high and wide from Alec Lindsay. In the 21st minute the Reds finally created a meaningful chance. Phil Boersma beat Peddelty and hit a hard low shot but David Best got down to save. Two minutes later Steve Heighway was in full flow in the area and went down after being sandwiched between Hunter and Mick Mills but the referee refused to listen to appeals for a penalty.

These last few minutes had lifted the crowd and Ipswich were being restricted to breakaways, one of which almost brought a goal when Trevor Whymark hit a 25-yard shot that deflected off Tommy Smith and wrongfooted Clemence, but thankfully went over the bar. Ipswich's keeper Best had to be treated for some time after going down holding his stomach despite nobody being near him. After the game restarted Liverpool didn't test him as much as they should, as he didn't appear to be in great comfort, but the only time he was called into action for the rest of the half was when he had to save a shot from Emlyn Hughes that was straight at him.

Ten minutes after the restart, Ipswich had a strong appeal for a penalty when Whymark was sent clear and took the ball round Clemence on the edge of the area only to be tackled from behind by Smith and Chris Lawler. Despite the Ipswich players vehemently protesting, the referee was having none of it. Liverpool were struggling in midfield, with Hughes and Ian Callaghan playing nowhere near as well as they were capable, and only Keegan was providing any drive there. Ipswich were becoming more confident of getting forward and Lambert hit a shot from the edge of the area which went only just wide.

Liverpool's opening goal on 67 minutes was both unexpected and not necessarily deserved. Toshack hit a strong volley from the edge of the area which Best palmed onto the bar, but both Mills and Boersma missed the ball when it came back down and it fell to Heighway who had the simple job of tapping it into the net. Despite his part in the goal Toshack was substituted before the game re-started, an unpopular decision with the crowd who sang his name as he was replaced by Phil Thompson. Just two minutes later Ipswich were level, David Johnson holding off a challenge from Smith to score from a tight angle after a Colin Viljoen pass.

Keegan twice came close to restoring Liverpool's lead, first with a header from a Callaghan cross and then with a cheeky backheel, both efforts going wide. It was third-time-lucky for him, though, in the eightieth minute when Boersma crossed and he controlled the ball on his chest before firing a shot low into the bottom left corner of the net with the Ipswich defence static. Wary of leaving themselves too exposed, the Reds played keep-ball for the rest of the game, leading to some more booing from the crowd who wanted them to try for a third. Although it may not have been the most resounding of victories or a good performance, after six games without a win the Reds were just glad to have two points in the bag and return to the top of the table.

The booing of Toshack's substitution and when the play was slowed down for the last ten minutes upset some of the players, especially Hughes who told the *Daily Post:* 'We've come through a sticky patch. We've started winning again after six games yet we were getting booed'. Shankly explained to the *Post* that Toshack would have come off regardless of setting up the goal as he needed to push Keegan further forward, and although disappointed at the booing, understood that fans were so used to attacking football from the Reds at Anfield. David Johnson believed the win made Liverpool favourites for the title, telling the paper: 'Most teams that win the championship have a bad spell at some point and that's what Liverpool have been through'. Ipswich manager Bobby Robson acknowledged that it would now be very difficult to win the title but said that his side would keep on trying:

> 'We shan't drop our heads, of course, you never know what will happen in football. But this was a game we really had to win. We contributed to our own downfall, we had it in our own hands to win the match and I certainly felt we were worth a point. Mick Lambert had a gilt-edged chance when he was put through by Johnson. If we had scored first it might have been a different story. One of the Liverpool players bundled into Mick Mills back just as he was about to head the rebound off the crossbar away from the goalmouth. Mills couldn't clear it and they rushed in and scored'.[53]

Liverpool: Clemence, Lawler, Lindsay, Smith, Lloyd, Hughes, Keegan, Toshack (Thompson), Boersma, Heighway, Callaghan.

Ipswich: Best, Mills, Harper, Morris, Hunter, Peddelty, Hamilton, Viljoen, Johnson, Whymark, Lambert. Sub: Collard.

Referee: Mr P. Baldwin (Teesside).

Attendance: 43,875.

Top of the Division One Table

		Pl	W	D	L	F	A	GA	Pt
1	Liverpool	31	18	8	5	55	33	1,67	44
2	Arsenal	31	18	8	5	43	27	1.59	44
3	Leeds	29	16	8	5	51	30	1.78	40

13

The Berlin Wall

UEFA Cup 3rd Round 1st Leg Dynamo Berlin 0 Liverpool 0
Wednesday 29th November 1972

The impressive way that Liverpool disposed of AEK meant that William Hills installed the Reds 4/1 favourites to lift the UEFA Cup, with holders Tottenham Hotspur just behind at 5/1. The draw, made the following Friday, sent Liverpool behind the Iron Curtain to face Dynamo Berlin, the side of the East German army. Although these trips could be tricky, Bill Shankly was satisfied given the stage of the competition. The Reds had won four out of five previous ties against East European sides and they were at home in the second leg. Also, Berlin was not too far to travel compared to the likes of Romania and Hungary where they had played previously. Liverpool's request to play the games on their preferred day of Tuesday was denied by Dynamo, though, due to their league fixtures taking place on a Sunday.

Formed as recently as 1966, Dynamo had reached the semi-finals of the previous season's Cup Winners Cup in their first season in European competition, but their route to that stage had been straightforward and they had needed penalties to dispose of Welsh Cup holders Cardiff City. To reach the third round of the UEFA Cup, they had beaten French side Angers and Bulgarian's Levski Spartak, 3-2 on aggregate on both occasions. Dynamo's star man was powerful international forward Harold Schutze, while the side also contained midfield playmaker Manfred Becker who was now 32. Leeds had knocked fellow East Germans Carl Zeiss Jena out of the Cup Winners Cup in the previous round and the Reds had every reason to be confident of progress providing they applied themselves properly and stood up to Dynamo's physical challenge.

As usual, preparations for the away leg were meticulous, with Peter Robinson flying out to check hotel accommodation two weeks beforehand, at the same time as Shankly's assistant Bob Paisley took in a Dynamo match against Frankfurt Am Oder. Dynamo came on a spying mission to England, too, their coach Gunter Schröter watching the Reds' impressive 2-1 win at Tottenham and telling the *Liverpool Echo* afterwards: 'We were greatly impressed, English league football is the best in the world and the players are tremendously fit'.

Tommy Smith wrote in his *Liverpool Echo* column on 25th November that he was looking forward to seeing the contrast between the two halves of Berlin and that he was confident the Reds would be able to win the game over two legs. Unfortunately, Smith wouldn't get to see Berlin due to his car accident that happened that night, something that Bill Shankly refused to comment on as Trevor Storton was named as his replacement in the travelling party.

The Reds flew from Manchester to Tempelhof Airport in West Berlin on the afternoon before the game and enjoyed a short bus tour before having dinner at the Kempinksi Hotel. At around 7pm they set off for Checkpoint Charlie to cross into the eastern side, a procedure that involved plenty of paperwork and a change of buses and they arrived at their hotel just in time for bed. Phil Thompson recalls it being a particularly intimidating experience, with the kit skips checked, all passports being taken away and soldiers going along the bus checking under the seats with mirrors. Shankly wanted to spend as little time in East Berlin as possible and with the game kicking off at 1.30pm, it meant the players would be there for only about eighteen hours.

Due to visa restrictions only a handful of Reds fans made it to the game, a planned charter by Towns Travel not going ahead, meaning the players were up against it in the Friedrich Ludwig Jahn Sportpark, which was completely uncovered. There was great interest in the game in Berlin, where the press dubbed the match 'Beatleball', with all 20,000 tickets sold and many having to pay high black market prices.

Ray Clemence was in danger of missing the game due to a dose of flu which caused him to sleep through the sightseeing tour of West Berlin. But he had improved by matchday and was declared fit to play as the temperature hovered around freezing point, a far cry from the warm weather experienced in Athens three weeks earlier. Phil Thompson, who would be an unused substitute in the game, recalls how the backroom staff made sure the players didn't let the weather get to them, but Bob Paisley refused to let them have any tea to warm up:

'The club had supplies of Romika boots which had specially made grips for these conditions but we weren't allowed our own pairs, we were just given them at certain matches. Joe Fagan was a great psychologist when it came to making sure we would not be able to use the weather as an excuse. He told us that if we believed we would fall, then we would fall no matter what we were wearing, but with these Romika boots we could have the confidence that we could stay upright. When we went on the pitch to loosen up we were quite comfortable and the Berlin players were sliding around like ice skaters and looking at us wondering how we were managing not to fall. This was where Fagan and Paisley were years ahead of their time, being meticulously prepared for things and getting our minds right so we just had to concentrate on playing the game. We then went back to the dressing room and a tea urn had been placed on a table.

We all thought "great" and went over to it only for Bob Paisley to shoo us away, saying you don't know what may have been put in there. We were all freezing rubbing our hands together and staring and drooling over this lovely hot steaming teapot but there was no way we were allowed to have a drink from it!'[54]

Despite the capacity crowd, this didn't mean a hostile reception for Liverpool, with Emlyn Hughes describing it as just like a Sunday afternoon at the zoo, as they just stared and never chanted.[55] Storton came into the side for Smith and Dynamo started very strongly, Norbet Johannsen giving Alec Lindsay problems and Wolfgang Filohn hitting a shot across the face of goal. After riding out this early pressure the Reds did manage to create a chance when Peter Cormack fired over the bar, but on the whole their play was restricted to containing Dynamo and not leaving themselves exposed at the back. As expected, it was a physical game, Kevin Keegan being man-marked by Bernd Brillat and given some rough treatment, while Ian Callaghan was bundled over in the area but the referee declared it a fair challenge.

At half-time Keegan was taken off as he continued to struggle following a blow to his thigh, to be replaced by Brian Hall. It was a double frustration for Keegan, who had been disappointed that the game clashed with the testimonial of his childhood hero Alick Jeffrey in Doncaster, a game in which he had been invited to play.

In the second half there was a wind in the home side's favour, leading to Liverpool retreating even more into a defensive state, with Storton putting in a solid display and Lindsay also getting to grips with Johannsen. In a rare foray into the opposition half the Reds won a corner but it was wasted when John Toshack handled as he rose for a header. Dynamo's frustration at the steeliness of the Reds defence, which saw them caught offside eighteen times, was evident, though, as they resorted more and more to long shots. The game ended in the 0-0 draw that Liverpool appeared to have come for and it was clear that the return leg would be very different.

Despite being pleased with the result, Shankly was not happy with the fouls committed by Dynamo and the standard of refereeing. Speaking about the challenge that forced Keegan off at half-time, he told the *Liverpool Echo*: 'This would have been a sending-off offence in England, it was a very bad foul, it was the same player who later caught Steve Heighway'. The advantage of an afternoon kick-off meant that following the game they were able to head straight for Checkpoint Charlie and, after bureaucracies had been completed, their flight took off from Templehof at 6pm meaning they were back home at a reasonable hour as they looked ahead to their next league game.

Liverpool: Clemence, Lawler, Lindsay, Storton, Lloyd, Hughes, Keegan (Hall), Cormack, Heighway, Toshack, Callaghan. Subs: Lane, McLaughlin, Boersma,

Thompson.

Dynamo: Lihsa, Stumpf, Brillat, Filohn, Hübner, Rohde, Terletzki, Schutze, Schulenberg, Netz (Schwierske), Johannsen.

Referee: Mr M. Saridana (Turkey).

Attendance: 15,385.

UEFA Cup 3rd Round 2nd Leg Liverpool 3 Dynamo Berlin 1
Wednesday 13th December 1972

Although he knew he would be unavailable for the game, Tommy Smith believed the Reds would have no problems in the second leg, especially with the crowd on their side. He wrote in his *Liverpool Echo* column on 9th December:

> 'Just how are they going to react to the swaying, chanting Kop who are guaranteed to be at their best for this game. I think the noise and the tension will unsettle the Germans. They know that we have the beating of them, they will feel like lambs to the slaughter when they venture into that Anfield cauldron. It will be completely different from their normal surroundings. The lads feel they can gallop home with several goals to spare. I will be surprised and disappointed if they don't'.

Dynamo really didn't have a clue what awaited them at Anfield. Whereas in the previous round the whole AEK side had attended a game, not even coach Gunter Schröter had been to the ground, having watched the away game at Spurs as part of his spying mission. As well as having to contend with the Anfield atmosphere, Dynamo also had very little experience of playing under floodlights, as the East German FA didn't allow domestic games to be played under them. Only 45 minutes of their five European games to date that season had been played under lights, away to Angers in the first round, where Schröter felt that a handball that led to a penalty being awarded would not have happened in daylight. Schröter did not exude an air of confidence on arrival in Liverpool, telling journalists at Speke Airport:

> 'This being a night match will be a big disadvantage to us and a big help to Liverpool. It's no shame to lose against Liverpool, they are top class by European standards. But you have to be confident and if you are not, it's not worth playing".[56]

Schröter wouldn't give anything away about his tactics for the game, but this didn't bother Shankly who told the *Liverpool Echo* on the day of the game: 'The way they played the first leg gave us no real guide to their ability. But we are not worrying about them, it is they who have got the worrying to do, our only concern is how we play'.

Shankly's main concern was the fitness of his players, some of whom were carrying knocks after a bruising encounter at West Bromwich Albion the previous Saturday. As such he named a squad of nineteen for the game, including long-term injury victim Jack Whitham and youngsters Hugh McAuley and John Webb. Kevin Keegan failed a fitness test for the match, still suffering the effects of the thigh injury which forced him off at half-time in the first game. The other change to the line-up from the first leg was Phil Thompson being preferred to Trevor Storton as Tommy Smith's replacement, having performed well when selected for the West Bromwich game.

Prices for the home leg were the same as for the previous two rounds, the club adopting the usual practice of setting them higher than for league games to cover the extra costs involved of playing in Europe. By now UEFA had made a u-turn on their alcohol ban in grounds, allowing it to be sold at the discretion of the clubs and national associations themselves, but warning that any problems caused by it would lead to stringent sanctions. Peter Robinson had no doubts, however:

'We have no fears about our fans, they have never caused the slightest trouble. This is a service they greatly appreciate, they are hardly likely to abuse it. It is preferable that they should be catered for properly with orderly and controlled arrangements'.[57]

Kicking into the Anfield Road end, it took Liverpool less than a minute – 57 seconds to be precise – to get their noses in front. Steve Heighway powered forward from the halfway line, beating two men before unleashing his shot which was parried by Werner Lihsa but only into the path of Phil Boersma who had the simple task of slamming the ball into the net. However, after seven minutes Dynamo stunned the Reds with an equaliser, catching the defenders out of position as they swept forward after Peter Cormack had failed to connect with an Ian Callaghan cross. Although Larry Lloyd managed to get in a tackle on Wolfgang Filohn, the ball only ran to Ralf Schulenberg who evaded Alec Lindsay and rounded Ray Clemence before Wolf Rüdiger Netz took over and scored from two yards.

Dynamo then set out to frustrate Liverpool with a man-marking system, foulling and using the offside trap as much as possible. With 25 minutes gone, Heighway managed to restore the Reds' advantage, hitting a shot from outside the area that deflected off Bernd Brillat and wrongfooted the keeper, which led to the following evening's *Echo* headline of 'STEVE SHATTERS BERLIN WALL.' This time there was no quick fightback from Dynamo as the Reds maintained control of the midfield and, kicking into the Kop for the second half, they looked to finish the tie off as quickly as possible. After 56 minutes the third goal came when Cormack was impeded by Frank Terletzki and took a free-kick which John Toshack turned into the net.

Dynamo did nothing to try to rescue the tie, being content to continue frustrating Liverpool with offsides and the Reds coasted along, meaning there was little entertainment for the fans. One positive element was the confident display of Phil Thompson in midfield and appearance of Jack Whitham as a substitute after 74 minutes, returning to the first team after being out since January with knee and back problems.

Liverpool: Clemence, Lawler, Lindsay, Thompson, Lloyd, Hughes, Keegan, Cormack, Heighway, Thoshack (Whitham), Callaghan. Subs: Lane, McLaughlin, Webb, Hall.

Dynamo: Lihsa, Stumpf, Brillat, Filohn (Becker), Hübner, Rohde, Terletzki, Schutze, Schulenberg, Netz, Johannsen (Weber).

Referee: Mr P. Nikolov (Bulgaria).

Attendance: 34,140.

UEFA Cup Quarter Final 1st Leg Liverpool 2 Dynamo Dresden 0 Wednesday 7th March 1973

The day after their win over Dynamo Berlin, the *Liverpool Echo* reported that Liverpool's odds had been shortened to just 9/4 to win the UEFA Cup, although they would now have to wait until after Christmas to find out who their quarter-final opponents would be. The last eight consisted of two sides from England (Liverpool and Spurs), two from West Germany (Borussia Mönchengladbach and Kaiserslautern) and one each from Holland (Twente Enschede), Portugal (Vitoria Setubal), East Germany (Dynamo Dresden) and Yugoslavia (OFK Belgrade).

Writing in his *Liverpool Echo* column on 13th January, four days before the draw was to be made, Tommy Smith said that Liverpool feared nobody, although he was hoping to avoid trips to Dresden and Belgrade for logistical reasons and wanted to wait until the final before facing Spurs. Any team from Holland or West Germany would be welcome for travel reasons, but if he had to choose just one, he preferred Kaiserslautern, in order to gain some revenge on behalf of Stoke City, who had been beaten 5-3 on aggregate by them in the first round.

When the draw was made, on 17th January, it gave the Reds the tie they didn't want when they were sent back to East Germany to face Dynamo Dresden, this time the first leg taking place at home., Dresden, who became the first East German team to win the Double in 1971, were a far better side than Dynamo Berlin and were said to be the strongest team to come out of the country since it was formed in 1949. Their side, which contained six internationals, were the current unbeaten leaders of the Oberliga and had only lost on away goals to Leeds two years earlier.

However, with the Reds top of the First Division, they had every reason to believe they could progress. Bill Shankly admitted he would have preferred a western European team but in the quarter-finals they had to take who they were given. He told the *Daily Post* immediately after the draw was made:

'At this stage they are all difficult draws. They are top of the league, it's sure to be tough but we are not afraid of them in the least'. Tommy Smith was pleased to be at home first, writing in his next *Echo* column that if a healthy lead could be built-up at Anfield it would remove some of the tensions that would otherwise be present during the inevitable delays faced by travelling behind the Iron Curtain.

Difficulties were faced in scouting the opposition due to the winter shutdown of the Oberliga and the threat of industrial action at home. The only opportunity available for Reuben Bennett and Bob Paisley was on 28th February when Dresden were beaten 3-1 at home in a friendly against Polish side Zaglebie Sosnowiec, but with a threatened strike at airports it was decided not to go ahead with the trip. Liverpool weren't too worried by this, though, as it wasn't the first time they'd been unable to watch European opposition and they had still come out on the winning side on those occasions. Shankly was also able to call on Leeds boss Don Revie for advice on the basics while Larry Lloyd and Kevin Keegan had both played against members of the side in the England Under 23 friendly the previous summer. Ultimately, though, he put it simply by telling the *Liverpool Echo* on the day of the match: 'It is how we play that really matters; that is the whole essence of the game'.

The title may have been Liverpool's priority but by the time this tie came around the Reds had been knocked out of the FA Cup and Tommy Smith, writing in his *Echo* column on 3rd March, felt the UEFA Cup was a welcome diversion from the league programme. With Liverpool still to win a European trophy he believed it was time to set the record straight and also wanted to ensure the Reds were the side to keep the cup in England for the sixth successive year.

Dynamo played a final friendly against Halmstad on 4th March before flying to Liverpool the next day and staying at Southport as previous opponents had done, training at Haig Avenue on the day before the match and the day itself. They were joining up with coach Walter Fritzsch and one of his assistants, Dieter Fuchs, who had watched the derby game at Goodison the previous Saturday and told Shankly afterwards that they were impressed with Liverpool's speed. The *Daily Post* reported that they referred to Emlyn Hughes as 'Hooz' and also that they hadn't understood a word Shankly had said when they spoke to him.

Fritzsch admitted his side faced an uphill task as three of his international players would be missing. Siegmar Watzlich had a groin strain, Rainer Sachshe a bruised shin and Reinhard Hafner had been struck down with flu, but leading scorer Hans Jürgen Kreisch was available. The day before the game Fritzsch told the *Liverpool Echo*: 'This is a very big blow to us and we're very disappointed, we're playing at a great disadvantage'. He also had some criticism for the Anfield pitch, which he felt was too hard and didn't have enough grass.

Although John Toshack and Peter Cormack hadn't played against Everton, Shankly resisted the temptation to surprise Dresden by playing them in the first leg. Instead he opted for the side they had seen in action, knowing that the speed had concerned them.

Dresden opted for a man-to-man marking approach which stifled Liverpool and when they did venture forward, their finishing left a lot to be desired. It was clear that the game needed a special goal to break the deadlock and it came in the 24th minute. Steve Heighway released Phil Boersma and his cross was met at the near post by Brian Hall, the smallest man on the pitch, who nodded the ball home for his first headed goal. Hall almost had a second before half-time but his shot was cleared off the line by Hans Jürgen Dörner.

In the second half Dresden continued their man-marking approach, breaking out of their half only occasionally, and when they did, Larry Lloyd was equal to anything. Boersma turned from provider to scorer for the second which came on the hour, stopping a Heighway shot that was off target and beating a defender before smashing the ball into the roof of the net from ten yards. There was a blow, though, as Heighway, the Reds' most dangerous player, was forced off the field with a thigh injury after the goal and replaced by Toshack who rarely received the service he required. Dresden lost their captain Hans Jürgen Kreische but the Reds couldn't capitalise on this, although they did have a third goal ruled out for offside when Hall headed in Alec Lindsay's cross. To the dismay of the Reds' players the linesman flagged even though Lindsay appeared to have been onside when Hughes played the ball.

Liverpool: Clemence, Lawler, Lindsay, Smith, Lloyd, Hughes, Keegan, Hall, Heighway (Toshack), Boersma, Callaghan. Subs: Lane , Thompson, Brownbill, Webb.

Dresden: Boden, Ganzera, Dörner, Sammer, Geyer, Riedel, Rau, Kreische, Heidler, Richter, Lischke.

Referee: Mr P. Schiller (Austria).

Attendance: 33,270.

UEFA Cup Quarter Final 2nd Leg Dynamo Dresden 0 Liverpool 1 Wednesday 21st March 1973

The first leg 2-0 victory was satisfying for the Reds, knowing they had only twice lost by three goals in Europe, and Bill Shankly, angry at the offside goal, believed they had done enough. He told the *Liverpool Echo:* 'Why was Brian Hall's goal ruled out? It couldn't have been offside because Alec Lindsay came from behind. We have a good lead and I am happy with two goals. I'd say we were very likely to score over there'. Dresden's coach Walter Fritzsch believed his side's poor finishing in the first half cost them and Liverpool firmly had the upper hand now, the *Echo* quoting him as saying:

'We seemed to lose spirit after Kreische was injured. The big difference is that we had three chances and scored no goals but Liverpool had three chances and scored two goals. It's going to be tough now, for Liverpool are strong enough to score one goal in Dresden. It should have been better for us to have lost 3-1 than 2-0'.

Tommy Smith also felt that the Reds had done enough at Anfield to win the tie, writing in his *Echo* column the Saturday before the away leg that Dresden needed to be more adventurous and there was a good chance the Reds could find a goal. He believed if that did happen there was no chance that Dresden would score four, although the Reds had to be on their guard against conceding early, as that would really intensify the pressure.

Liverpool's visit to Dresden created unprecedented interest. All 32,000 tickets for the game, which at £1.25 and £1.50 were triple the normal prices, sold out within a couple of hours after lengthy queues had formed. Even Ajax, who had played in Dresden the previous season as reigning European Champions, hadn't generated such demand. A Dresden spokesman claimed that 100,000 tickets could have been sold and Liverpool's convincing victory over Dynamo Berlin in the previous round had been a key to so many people wanting to see the game.

However, the away leg did pose some logistical hurdles for Liverpool, with their normal preference for being out of the country for as little time as possible being thrown into chaos. With Dresden Airport being closed for runway resurfacing, the Reds asked if they could use a local military airfield instead but were refused. They were then left with no alternative but to fly to West Berlin and cross Checkpoint Charlie before taking a 120 mile coach trip to Dresden. This would entail spending three nights' away, leaving little time to prepare for the next league game against Norwich City, which thankfully was at Anfield.

The party flew out to West Berlin on the Monday morning minus Phil Boersma who had injured his shoulder in the previous Saturday's game with Stoke City. Also missing was reserve keeper Frank Lane who had an injured leg, and his place was taken by Grahame Lloyd. After spending a night there, they held a training session on the Tuesday morning at the ground of Tennis Borussia Berlin, before crossing Checkpoint Charlie for the two-hour coach journey to Dresden. Tommy Smith, who had been looking forward to seeing Berlin in the previous round but missed out through injury, couldn't believe the contrast, describing the western side as happy, bright and cheerful, but the eastern side as the opposite.[58]

The rain of Berlin gave way to drier conditions in Dresden and when the party arrived at the Newa Hotel they were met by around 1,000 locals packed onto the forecourt chanting 'Dynamo'. As police cleared the route for the players to make their way from the coach into the reception area the chanting continued and many tried to get autographs. It was apparent that the Reds were going to be up against a much more hostile crowd than they had been against Dynamo Berlin in the previous round. Due to the closure of Dresden Airport, no supporters' trip operated and only a very small number of Reds fans made it to the game.

At the Rudolf Harbig Stadium the Reds again put in a composed performance that matched any of their previous best on foreign soil. Yellow and black banners greeted the players onto the pitch but there was no onslaught from the Dresden players, in part due to the magnificent work of the Reds midfield who harried them all over the place. Tommy Smith and Larry Lloyd were solid when Dynamo did get further forward and Ray Clemence had very little to do. The goal that clinched the tie came on 33 minutes after a swift break out of defence as Kevin Keegan sent Steve Heighway racing clear but carried on running to goal himself. As Klaus Sammer caught up and was about to make a challenge, Heighway calmly laid the ball off for Keegan who smashed it past the keeper.

The goal clearly deflated Dresden and five minutes later Keegan had the ball in the net again when he volleyed in an Alec Lindsay free-kick only for it to be ruled out for offside. Dresden's solitary effort of note in the whole of the first half came just before the break from Hans Jurgen Dörner but his dipping shot from just outside the box went over the bar. Liverpool then cruised through the second half, Heighway and Alec Lindsay both having shots that were just inches wide as they reached a fourth semi-final in just nine years of European competition.

Such was the commanding nature of Liverpool's display that Ray Clemence said it was one of the quietest games he had ever had in Europe. Bill Shankly didn't underestimate the display, telling the *Liverpool Echo*: 'It was one of our finest ever performances in Europe, ranking with those against Standard Liege and Anderlecht. Naturally we fancy our chances of winning the competition now.' Dresden coach Walter Fritzsch admitted that the Reds were far better than he had believed possible. He was reported by the *Echo* as saying:

> 'They were so strong all the time and so cool. When they scored the goal we had no chance of equalising, we knew it and they knew it too. This is the first European game we have lost in Dresden in five years and we have beaten teams like Ajax and Leeds. But tonight Liverpool were the strongest of all.'

The coach left Dresden at 9.30am the day after the game and it was evening time before the players finally arrived back on Merseyside. Tommy Smith was glad to be home from the extended stay in Dresden, describing it in the *Liverpool Echo* the following Saturday as the one place he would never consider being transferred to, even if it were possible. He recalled that it was drab, looking like a vast estate as everyone seemed to live in flats and that the people were inhibited. He tried to find a present to bring home for his family but nothing he saw was of reasonable quality. Bob Paisley, though, did meet an English teacher called Wolfgang and would go on to keep in touch with him by letter, with Wolfgang eventually travelling to Liverpool in the early 1990s after the fall of the Berlin Wall to visit Bob and have a tour of Anfield.

Despite the difficulties encountered by this trip, which Shankly told the *Daily Post* was one of the worst they had faced in Europe, Liverpool will have been glad not to have faced the problems both on and off the pitch that Tottenham did in Portugal against Vitoria Setubal. Six players reported injuries after the game, including Pat Jennings who had sand thrown in his eye by a Setubal player. When the game ended in a 2-1 win for Setubal that meant Spurs went through on away goals, home fans invaded the area where Spurs supporters were gathered and set about kicking and punching them. One had £55 stolen from him, and another £50 and a waistcoat, as Spurs pondered making a formal complaint to UEFA about the matter.

Liverpool and Spurs were joined in the semi-finals by Dutch side Twente Enschede and West German's Borussia Mönchengladbach, who sent out an ominous warning when they thrashed compatriots Kaiserslautern 7-1 in their second leg to complete a 9-2 aggregate victory.

Liverpool: Clemence, Lawler, Lindsay, Smith, Lloyd, Hughes, Keegan (Toshack), Hall, Cormack, Heighway, Callaghan Subs: Lloyd, Storton, Webb, Thompson.

Dresden: Boden, Ganzera, Watzlich, Sammer, Geyer (Helm), Reidel, Rau, Dorner, Richter, Lichtenberger, Saches.

Referee: Mr Van Gemmert (Holland).

Attendance: 32,000.

14

Marching On

Going into the derby both sides needed the points for very different reasons. As Liverpool chased the title, Everton were in danger of getting dragged into a relegation scrap. After such a promising start to the season when they led the table early on, they had won just three league games since the beginning of October and were now in fourteenth place, just four points ahead of the relegation zone and nervously looking over their shoulders. Their plight was such that the *Daily Post's* Liverpool correspondent Horace Yates wrote on the morning of the game: 'Everton have been so disappointing that they could hardly win an argument'.

Despite what was riding on the game for both sides, it was one of the lowest key build-ups for many years with neither side saying anything to the press in the preceding week about what they were going to do. Ticket sales went slowly, not selling out until eight days beforehand when the last few ground tickets were snapped up at Goodison. However, this may have been down to the fact that for the first time Everton issued priority vouchers at an earlier league game, moving away from the usual system of putting the whole lot on sale in one go. Unsurprisingly, Liverpool's allocation of 5,000 sold out, but still not as quickly as expected and not all those who qualified appeared to take up their option.

Peter Cormack, out of the last three games through a knee ligament injury, was given a run-out in the reserve derby at Anfield on the Tuesday night, scoring Liverpool's goal past Gordon West in a fiercely-contested 1-1 draw. Although Cormack put in a decent performance, he did report some soreness after taking a knock in the first half but carrying on. There was worse news for Jack Whitham, whose return to fitness had attracted a number of scouts to the game only for him to be carried off with suspected cartilage damage.

With transfer deadline day a week away, Bill Shankly travelled to Glasgow the day after the mini-derby to take a look at Partick Thistle's eighteen-year-old forward Joe Craig in action against Dumbarton in a Scottish Cup tie. A mechanic by day, he was a tall bustling player in the John Toshack mould and had managed seven goals in his twenty Partick appearances so far, the latest coming in this 3-1 win that was also watched by Tottenham manager Bill Nicholson. If Shankly made a bid for Craig it would be as an investment for the future, although Partick, who had been drawn at home to Ayr United in the quarter-finals of the Scottish Cup and expected to progress, were unlikely to sell while they remained in the competition. In the end no bid was ever made by Liverpool and he stayed with Partick for three more years before joining Celtic in 1976.

As Shankly prepared to return to Liverpool from Firhill, he will no doubt have been given the good news that Arsenal had been surprisingly beaten by the First Division's bottom club West Bromwich Albion, meaning the Reds not only remained top of the table but also had a game in hand. Liverpool's win over Ipswich the previous week may have returned them to the summit, but it was only by a whisker, their goal average being 1.67 to Arsenal's 1.59. Goal average was worked out by simply dividing the number of goals scored by those conceded and this margin was extremely tight. Even if Liverpool were to beat Everton 1-0, a 3-0 victory for Arsenal over Sheffield United at Highbury would return the Gunners to the top of the table.

The day before the game Shankly decided not to risk Cormack and named the same squad as for the Ipswich clash. With John Toshack expected to be left out of the side, the *Liverpool Echo* predicted that it was a straight battle between Brian Hall and Phil Thompson for a place in the starting line-up. Thompson had watched the fixture from the Park End terraces just three seasons ago with his brother Owen when Sandy Brown's own-goal set Liverpool on the road to a 3-0 win. Owen still stood on the Kop cheering on Liverpool and his brother, and it had now become customary for him to receive a wave from Phil at their usual spot if he was playing. When Shankly announced his side, though, Thompson had to make do with a substitute role as Hall was preferred, with Toshack left out as the pace of Phil Boersma and Steve Heighway would be relied upon in breakaway attacks.

Although Everton were on a poor run of results, Steve Heighway felt this counted for nothing when it came to a derby. He wrote in his *Daily Post* column the day before the match: 'Nothing can be guaranteed about tomorrow's game. Past form can be ignored and the players know it. Their only attitude is to get into the thick of things and go at it as hard as they can'. One thing Heighway was grateful for was that, as he hadn't been born on Merseyside, he wasn't subject to the barrage of calls from family members for tickets to which some of the other players were subjected.

The match went on to become one of the great derbies from a Liverpool point of view as their title charge was well and truly put back on track. Two late goals from Emlyn Hughes won the game for the Reds, the first time a side had won both league derbies in a season since 1947-48. Breaking with normal tradition, Liverpool took the field first rather than the two teams run out together. This was nothing to do with a souring of relations between the two clubs, but because a slippy dressing room floor made it impossible for the Reds players to warm up properly. Shankly would go on to say afterwards that they had waited for Everton in the tunnel as soon as the referee's buzzer went, but when they didn't appear he felt it was important to get out and do a routine before kick-off.[59]

A draw was no good to either side and they both looked to attack from the start, Mick Lyons almost giving Everton the lead within seconds as he raced onto a brilliant through ball from Howard Kendall, only to shoot straight at Ray Clemence when he would have done better by squaring to Joe Harper. After this the Reds began to take control. Ian Callaghan, who was playing a record twentieth league derby moving ahead of Ted Sagar and Elisha Scott, controlled the midfield alongside Emlyn Hughes and Brian Hall, and Steve Heighway and Kevin Keegan were lively up front. John Hurst, though, was a rock in defence for Everton, but he could do nothing about a Heighway cross that found an unmarked Phil Boersma who headed over the bar from six yards.

Hall hit a shot from the edge of the box that went just over as Everton were forced to resort to long balls towards Lyons, Kendall showing some excellent precision. A great battle between Lyons and Larry Lloyd was developing and on one occasion Lyons got the better, making a snap-shot that led to a full-stretch save from Ray Clemence. Before this, though, Chris Lawler had tested David Lawson in the Everton goal with an overhead kick. The Blues keeper had come off his line to block a Keegan shot after he had run on to Hall's pass and Boersma had struck a volley inches wide. Everton finished the first half the strongest, Hurst having a header from a corner tipped over by Clemence and then John Connolly striking a shot from the edge of the box that hit the bar and bounced over.

Both sides missed great opportunities early in the second half. Boersma sent a shot well wide when Keegan was better placed to receive the pass and, from a free-kick after an obstruction by Tommy Smith, Kendall's ball into the box was headed over by Jones. Harper also had a swerving shot saved by Clemence as Everton began to get the upper hand, leading to increased noise from the home fans. Liverpool, though, kept their heads and began to re-assert their authority, the best chance of the game coming when Lawson got down to make a brilliant save from Boersma's downward header. The Everton keeper then made a great double save, blocking a Boersma shot with his body and, after Keegan had headed the rebound goalwards, he somehow got back to grab the ball on the line.

As Liverpool continued to press Tommy Smith brought the ball out of defence and exchanged passes with Keegan before hitting a shot that was held by Lawson, but Clemence had to be alert to save a Connolly effort that he only held at the second attempt. The breakthrough goal finally came with ten minutes remaining. Hughes strode forward with the ball and laid it off to Callaghan, continuing his run towards the box. Collecting Callaghan's return pass, Hughes rounded Lawson and calmly slid the ball into the net before going off on an arm-waving celebration that his team-mates couldn't keep up with. Everton didn't give up, Clemence doing well to save a header from Lyons but they were prone to the breakaway goal and so it proved two minutes from time. Alec Lindsay crossed from the left and although Lawson punched clear, the ball fell to Hughes who struck it first time on the volley, giving the keeper no chance.

It had been a magnificent game, both teams giving their all and tackling as if their lives depended on it, but never reducing it to a succession of fouls and it all meant no player was booked. Liverpool played with the confidence and authority of earlier in the season to come out on top, working better off the ball and with defenders getting forward. Although they had gained three points from the City and Ipswich games the performances hadn't been great, but that wasn't the case this time.

The day after the derby there was some small revenge for Evertonians as they won the Fans Challenge Match, played before a crowd of 1,000 spectators at Walton Hall Park. The Everton fans team, who were in the Eleventh Division of the Liverpool Sunday League, caused an upset by beating the Fourth Division Liverpool fans 5-4 on penalties after a 2-2 draw.

Liverpool: Clemence, Lawler, Lindsay, Smith, Lloyd, Hughes, Keegan, Hall, Boersma, Heighway, Callaghan. Sub: Thompson.

Everton: Lawson, Wright, Styles, Hurst, Kenyon, Darracott, Jones, Kendall, Harper, Lyons, Connolly. Sub: Belfitt.

Referee: Mr R. Matthewson (Worsley).

Attendance: 54,269.

Football League Division One: Liverpool 3 Southampton 2
Saturday 10th March 1973

Three days before playing Southampton the Reds returned to UEFA Cup action against Dynamo Dresden following the competition's winter break. The resumption of regular midweek fixtures meant Liverpool were looking ahead and doing all they could to avoid a major fixture pile-up in the last week of the season. In addition to a crucial game with Leeds on Easter Monday, the Reds were also scheduled to play Coventry City at Highfield Road the following night. This was well as having the prospect of a UEFA Cup semi-final on the Wednesday, leaving them with an impossible situation if they were to comply with UEFA's rules of the away team having to be in their destination country 24 hours before the game. Luckily, with the Football League's blessing, Coventry agreed to bring their fixture forward by a week, but there didn't seem any room for manoeuvre with the Leeds game, due to their continued involvement in the FA Cup.

With the transfer deadline occurring two days before the Reds were to face Southampton, an enquiry was made to Ipswich regarding the availability of David Johnson, but Liverpool were told he was not for sale at any price. There was one surprising arrival, though, as the day before the deadline Bill Shankly swooped to sign 21-year-old Bristol City striker Peter Spiring for £60,000. Spiring had only been a regular since the beginning of the season, taking over Chris Garland's striking role after he had moved to Chelsea, and was one for the future in Shankly's eyes. In total he had scored seventeen goals in 54 appearances for his previous club and Shankly told the *Liverpool Echo* on securing his signature: 'We have watched Peter a number of times and we decided we need extra strength'.

The move came as a shock to Spiring, who turned up for training to be told he was wanted by Liverpool. After a quick change, he was driven north by Reds assistant secretary Bill Barlow. Spiring took just half-an-hour to agree terms before Barlow travelled to Lytham St Annes to personally hand in transfer forms to the Football League to ensure there were no complications before the deadline. There was no chance of Spiring being involved against Southampton, though, as he was carrying a thigh injury that had kept him out of the last two games.

The Southampton game marked the official opening of the new main stand with the Duke of Kent, who was president of the FA, attending to unveil a plaque to mark the occasion. It was only the second time royalty had attended a match at Anfield, the other occasion being in 1921 when King George V and Queen Mary visited for an FA Cup semi-final between Cardiff and Wolves. The Duke, who surprisingly wore a blue-and-white shirt, flew into Speke Airport on the morning of the game where a crowd of several hundred had gathered. He was met by the Lord and Lady Mayoress before being driven to Anfield for a VIP lunch also attended by senior officials including Football League secretary Alan Hardaker and FIFA president Sir Stanley Rous. As the party made their way from the boardroom to the foyer for the plaque's unveiling, there was almost a nasty accident when Len Shipman, president of the Football League, took a tumble down the stairs and banged his head. After being helped to his feet and checked over, he was able to take his place with the rest of the party as the Duke pulled the cord to reveal the plaque which was made of Grecian white marble.

In the match programme, chairman Eric Roberts commented that the formal completion marked the end of a ten-year rebuilding programme at Anfield that had cost £1 million and seen the re-development of three sides of the ground. It was his belief that Anfield was among the best in Europe, but uppermost in the club's thoughts was that Bill Shankly should have all the support available to ensure the club remained at the forefront of league football.

Liverpool's midweek injury jinx struck again when Steve Heighway, who picked up a thigh strain in the UEFA Cup tie with Dynamo Dresden, failed to recover in time. It meant a chance for John Toshack, who had come off the bench for Heighway, to re-establish himself in the side and Peter Cormack also returned to the first team fold as substitute. Having recorded a second successive 2-0 win by beating Dresden, Shankly felt the bad patch was well and truly over as they prepared for the championship run-in. He described how the players were now smiling again and they were in just the mood they needed to be for this stage of the season. He was also glad to be facing a side that had nothing left to play for. [60]

Before the game Southampton manager Ted Bates described trying to win at Anfield as the hardest task in the world.[61] Their job was made even harder by a rail strike that meant they had to travel to the game by coach instead of train and they had a very small number of supporters inside the ground. However, Liverpool only managed to win the game by the skin of their teeth, Kevin Keegan scoring a winner three minutes from time after the Reds had thrown away a 2-0 lead.

Liverpool started well, moving the ball around quickly, and Phil Boersma justified his extended run in the side when he had a header well saved by Eric Martin and also put in a quick lob went just over the bar. Boersma was equally dangerous down the wing, on one occasion pulling a cross back into the area that was cleared for a corner from which Ian Callaghan's shot was well saved by Martin. In the 24th minute Brian Hall cut in from the left and had a low shot held by Martin, who then denied Keegan by blocking a one-on-one effort after Tommy Smith had played him in.

After 37 minutes Liverpool's dominance was finally rewarded when Smith crossed and Toshack headed across the face of goal. Nobody was there to meet it but the ball fell to Hall who chipped back into the danger area and Larry Lloyd was there to head home from close range. A minute later it was 2-0 after Callaghan had released Boersma with a defence-splitting pass. He drew the keeper and squared the ball to Toshack and, although his shot was blocked on the line by Paul Bennett, the ball fell to Hall. He passed to Keegan who made no mistake. Southampton's first real chance came a minute before half-time when Smith conceded a free-kick on the edge of the area but Jim Steele's effort was high and wide. However, before the referee blew for the interval Mick Channon pulled a goal back when a long punt downfield by Martin was left by the Reds defence and the Saints striker nipped in to head the ball past Ray Clemence.

Early in the second half Alec Lindsay almost made it 3-1 when he hit a shot just wide of the post after he had continued his run down the left to receive a Keegan pass after breaking up a Southampton attack. Callaghan also went close after 57 minutes when he fired just over the bar after Keegan had laid the ball off for him, but four minutes later another defensive error let

Southampton in to equalise. Slack marking allowed Brian O'Neil to find Terry Paine in the area and although Clemence rushed from his goal to gather the ball, he spilled it into the path of Paul Gilchrist who had the simple task of slotting the ball into the net from ten yards.

Despite the frustrations of losing the lead, Liverpool kept plugging away for a winning goal with Toshack and Emlyn Hughes both going close. After seventy minutes the Reds had a great chance when Hughes was fouled on the edge of the area but Lindsay wasted the free-kick, firing it well over the bar. Finally, with just three minutes remaining, Hughes released Boersma down the left and his run drew three defenders, allowing him to cross to Keegan who was unmarked at the far post and able to head the ball into the net.

The Southampton game may have contained plenty of mistakes by both sides but it was exciting to watch for the Duke of Kent and other guests, who were very impressed by the quality of the Reds support as well as how well behaved they were. The following Monday the *Liverpool Echo* reported how Eric Roberts had said afterwards:

> 'Their behaviour on the terraces with their chants was absolutely impeccable. Sir Stanley Rous, the President of FIFA said to me afterwards we were fortunate to have such supporters. The Duke of Kent also made a comment on what a wonderful repertoire the crowd have and how much he enjoyed seeing and hearing them'.

Although the crowd had been Liverpool's second lowest of the season, only the Coventry game on the Saturday before Christmas attracting less, Roberts felt it was reasonable in the circumstances of the rail strike which prevented many from outside the city attending.

Liverpool: Clemence, Lawler, Lindsay, Smith, Lloyd, Hughes, Keegan, Hall, Boersma, Toshack, Callaghan. Sub: Cormack.

Southampton: Martin, Kirkup, Burns, Fisher, Bennett, Paine, Steele, Channon, Gilchrist, O'Neil, Stokes. Sub: Walker.

Referee: Mr J. H. Yates (Redditch).

Attendance: 41,674.

Brian Labone Testimonial: Everton 2 Liverpool 1
Tuesday 13th March 1973

Despite the season nearing its crunch phase, Liverpool still volunteered to be the opposition for Brian Labone's testimonial match at Goodison Park the following Tuesday. Labone had been a solid centre half for Everton during the 1960s but his career had been curtailed by injury after the 1969-70 season and he played just sixteen more games in two years. He was so well respected that Bill Shankly had no hesitation in offering to play the game, telling the *Liverpool Echo* that day:

> 'He was a credit to the game and a grand servant to Everton. They thought him worthy of a testimonial and so do I. When Brian mentioned he was trying to get a team to play Everton I knew how much it might cost so I volunteered Liverpool for nothing as the opposition. I was pleased to do it as he was such a credit to the game'.

One set of extra games that Shankly didn't warm to, though, was a proposal that week by Southport for a Lancashire County Champions tournament, to be played the following summer between Southport, Liverpool, Bolton and Burnley who were all on course to finish the season as the county's highest teams in their respective divisions.

There is, and was, no such thing as a friendly where Everton are concerned and Shankly picked his strongest available side. He had hoped to include Peter Spiring but he was still carrying an injury that had forced him out of a reserve game against Leeds the previous evening, in which Peter Cormack played for 45 minutes. There were big cheers before the game during a legends' penalty shoot-out that saw veteran players Tommy Lawrence, Ian St John and Roger Hunt get beaten by a team of actors which included Richard O'Sullivan and Ken Cope.

Nearly 26,000 were there, more than had attended Goodison for some league games, to see Everton win 2-1 in a game that lacked any real competitive edge and saw only four fouls committed. John Toshack scored the Reds goal after 68 minutes, cancelling out Mick Lyons' opener which had come on the hour. However, with ten minutes left Jimmy Husband headed in Bill Kenyon's cross to give the home side a morale-boosting victory.

Liverpool: Clemence, Lawler, Lindsay, Smith, Lloyd, Hughes, Keegan, Hall, Cormack, Toshack, Callaghan. Sub: Thompson.

Attendance:25,779.

Referee: Mr J. Finney (Hereford)

Football League Division One: Stoke City 0 Liverpool 1
Saturday 17th March 1973

After Brian Labone's testimonial Liverpool turned their attentions to the trip to the Victoria Ground to face Stoke for a game in which they knew victory would see them move two points clear at the top of the table, as Arsenal and Leeds were in FA Cup sixth round action. Stoke were desperate for points as they were just one point above the relegation zone and their manager Tony Waddington knew his side had a tough job against a team that he believed would end the season as Champions:

> 'Liverpool don't rely purely on their defence to keep a point in the bag, they have a directness about them, they put in more shots at goal and

I think they've got better finishing power. They have a very positive approach in every match they play'.[62]

Despite their lowly league position Stoke had been beaten only once at home, drawing seven of their fourteen games. They had enjoyed a trip to the continent in the weeks before the game, taking advantage of a run of postponements and Tottenham being involved in the League Cup Final, to train in the sun and gain some match practice. The trip included matches in France against Nice and in Greece against Olympiakos, a game in which Gordon Banks made his first appearance since his car accident the day after he had faced Liverpool at Anfield. However, there was no chance that the World Cup-winning keeper would be able to face the Reds. Before the game, though, he did take to the pitch and was given warm applause as he presented a trophy to Stoke's ladies team.

Shankly opted to restore both Peter Cormack and Steve Heighway to his starting line-up, with Brian Hall on the bench and John Toshack again left out altogether for a drab game in which Liverpool needed an own goal to win 1-0. On a hard pitch which made it difficult to control the ball, the game started quietly with both sides packing their midfields and Ian Callaghan having the first shot on goal, an optimistic effort from forty yards that sailed well over. Heighway and Kevin Keegan were doing well down the flanks but when they crossed, Stoke's defence were easily available to clear, while the Reds were also often caught out by the offside trap. John Marsh in the Stoke defence was having trouble coping with the Reds attacking but Dennis Smith was able to cover for him on numerous occasions as no clear opportunities were created.

Midway through the half Stoke began to get into the game, winning a fortunate corner when Tommy Smith sliced a clearance behind the goal and from this Ray Clemence dropped the ball but it was scrambled clear. The best chance of the first half came on 26 minutes when Marsh chipped the ball into the box for Geoff Hurst to head down into the path of Jimmy Robertson and, as Clemence came out to narrow the angle, he tried a lob which cleared both Liverpool's keeper and the bar. This spurred Liverpool back into action and Marsh found the only way he could stop Heighway was to bring him down after half-an-hour, which led to a booking. The nearest the Reds came to scoring before half-time was when Heighway's long throw was flicked on by Keegan towards Chris Lawler, but John Farmer got down to gather the ball from his feet.

Jimmy Greenhoff went close to scoring early in the second half when he tried a shot from the edge of the area that went just wide. Stoke pressed more and pinned Liverpool back, forcing two quick corners, the second of which Larry Lloyd managed to clear. Keegan then had a run towards goal but was stopped in his tracks and brought down. Both sides made substitutions, the disappointing Hurst going off to be replaced by Terry Conroy, while Brian Hall came on for Phil Boersma who injured his shoulder in a collision with Dennis Smith. The winning goal came after 66 minutes when John Mahoney, under pressure from several Liverpool players, tried to turn the ball back to his keeper only to see it sail over him and under the bar.

Not long after the goal Cormack had a shot that went just over the bar and as Stoke pressed for an equaliser Clemence saved well from Greenhoff and Mahoney. Mindful of the forthcoming trip to Dresden in the UEFA Cup, Liverpool were happy to play out the game to keep hold of the two points and although they had been achieved in fortunate circumstances, at this stage of the season nobody was complaining.

Shankly was disappointed to lose Boersma to a similar injury that Roger Hunt had suffered at the same ground a few years before but he felt Liverpool were worthy of their victory given the circumstances. He told the *Daily Post*:

'It is not easy to win at Stoke, it is only the second time they have lost at home. We were causing them more trouble than they were causing our defence. Passing on a bumpy ground is never easy. Clemence only had one save to make, it was a hard shot but goalkeepers can decide championships and Clemence is a good goalkeeper'.

Liverpool: Clemence, Lawler, Lindsay, Smith, Lloyd, Hughes, Keegan, Cormack, Boersma (Hall), Heighway, Callaghan.

Stoke: Farmer, Marsh, Jump, Skeels, Smith, Bloor, Robertson, Mahoney, Hurst (Conroy), Greenhoff, Eastham.

Referee: Mr M. Sinclair (Guildford).

Attendance: 33,540

Football League Division One: Liverpool 3 Norwich City 1
Saturday 24th March 1973

The victory over Stoke meant that Liverpool were two points ahead of Arsenal, each side having eight games left to play. Leeds were third and could draw level with Liverpool if they won their three games in hand, but the Reds knew they had to play them at Anfield. With Leeds and Arsenal having to play each other at Elland Road, and Leeds also involved in both the FA Cup and European Cup Winners Cup, there was a real danger of the Yorkshire side burning out.

There was good news for Liverpool when Leeds and Arsenal were kept apart in the FA Cup semi-final draw, meaning there was a real prospect of them both reaching Wembley and taking their eye off the league. Tommy Smith wrote in his *Liverpool Echo* column on 17th March that if Liverpool could win their remaining home games and draw the away ones, which would leave them with 62 points, they would be Champions. The bookmakers certainly agreed with Smith as to where the title would end up, with Liverpool's odds after the Stoke game being slashed to 5/2 on.

The first of the remaining four home games was on 24th March against Norwich City, a side who had started the season well but hadn't won any of their last fifteen league games and were on a run of eight successive away defeats, failing to find the net in the last four. Given Liverpool had been away from Monday to Thursday on a gruelling trek to Dresden in the UEFA Cup, they couldn't have asked for a better fixture to return to, although nothing could be taken for granted. In a desperate bid to avoid relegation Norwich had made three new signings on transfer deadline day, bringing in Trevor Hockey from Sheffield United, Colin Suggett from West Bromwich Albion and Ian Mellor, father of future Liverpool player Neil, from Manchester City. One player who wouldn't be in their side was former Reds midfielder Doug Livermore, who failed to recover from a thigh strain that had forced him to miss the last three games.

In a game that saw the Reds triumph in the second half after a scrappy first period, the players were given a great reception when they took to the field following the midweek UEFA Cup win in Dresden. Despite recovering from the shoulder injury that had forced him off the field at Stoke the previous week Phil Boersma failed to force his way back in the side, Brian Hall keeping his place after a good display in East Germany. Hall had spoken with Shankly earlier in the week, expressing concern at his lack of first-team opportunities over the season since Peter Cormack's arrival. At the age of 26 he felt he needed regular first-team football but Shankly made it clear he was a vital member of the squad and wouldn't be sold.[63]

At the beginning the game the Reds showed no signs of tiredness after an exhausting trip and in the first minute Kevin Keegan, who had shaken off an ankle injury sustained in the Dresden game, sent Cormack clean through but Duncan Forbes managed to get back to clear the ball behind for a corner. From this Cormack headed the ball down into the goalmouth where Chris Lawler's shot was blocked at point-blank range by Kevin Keelan and Geoff Butler cleared the danger.

Norwich's first attempt on goal came in the tenth minute when they were awarded a free-kick forty yards out but this didn't stop Graham Paddon trying his luck and his hard low shot was well held by Ray Clemence. After a bright start Liverpool slacked off a little. Norwich gave them very little room in midfield and were always quick to pull eight men behind the ball whenever the Reds crossed the halfway line. Keegan was the biggest threat to Norwich, linking well with Cormack, and two minutes before half-time Liverpool had their best chance of the half when a Cormack shot hit the bar, and soon afterwards he had a shot well saved by Keelan.

Early in the second half the Reds were awarded a free-kick 25 yards out but Alec Lindsay's shot was well over the bar. The breakthrough did come in the fiftieth minute, though, Chris Lawler nipping in to intercept David Stringer's back-pass and score after the Norwich defender had broken-up an Emlyn Hughes-inspired attack. This was Lawler's fourth goal of the season, a good total for a full back although by his previous standards he was having a lean season. Four minutes later Hall crossed from the right and, after Heighway and Stringer had risen together for the ball, it bounced from them into the path of Hughes, who drove a low shot from the edge of the area into the corner of the net. Liverpool almost had a third soon afterwards when Keelan dropped Heighway's throw and, as Keegan got in to stab the ball goalwards, Alan Black managed to get it clear.

To their credit Norwich had no intention of going for damage limitation and made a substitution, bringing on forward Paul Cheesley for midfielder Trevor Howard. But Liverpool were playing with confidence and rhythm now and City hardly got a look in. Keelan saved a glancing header from Keegan after a free-kick by Hall, then Callaghan had a shot go just wide. Norwich pulled a goal back out of nowhere in the 73rd minute and Liverpool could only have themselves to blame. Cheesley played a ball over the top towards Ian Mellor and the Reds defence collectively appealed for offside. By the time it was clear no flag was going to be raised, Mellor had controlled the ball and fired it past Clemence from near the penalty spot.

Norwich sensed they could get an unlikely draw and Paddon tried his luck again from a long-range free-kick, this time his shot being headed clear by Tommy Smith. Liverpool's nerves were finally settled two minutes from time when Hall scored with a fine shot from 25 yards. Norwich boss Ron Saunders was disappointed at the way the Reds had scored their two goals, telling the *Daily Post*: 'Honestly, we made it easy for Liverpool, we gave away two ridiculous goals'. Given the disruption to Liverpool's build up to the game, Shankly was glad to get the two points and was pleased at the way the players had played a good passing game despite the ground being dry and hard.

Liverpool: Clemence, Lawler, Lindsay, Smith, Lloyd, Hughes, Keegan, Cormack, Hall, Heighway, Callaghan. Sub: Toshack.

Norwich: Keelan, Butler, Black, Stringer, Forbes, Hockey, Howard (Cheesley), Suggett, Briggs, Paddon, Mellor.

Referee: Mr H. G. New (Bristol).

Attendance: 42,995.

Football League Division One: Liverpool 1 Tottenham Hotspur 1 Saturday 31st March 1973

On the Monday after the Stoke match, Larry Lloyd travelled to London with Bill Shankly and youth development officer Tom Saunders to appeal against bookings he had accumulated that had taken him over the twelve points that triggered a ban. Both his bookings that were picked up against Manchester City in the league and FA Cup matches at Maine Road were overturned, meaning the threat of a two-match suspension was gone. Lloyd was relieved at the outcome, telling the *Liverpool Echo:* 'I felt all along that neither incident was a bookable offence. It was a really fair commission and I feel a lot better now'. On the Thursday Tommy Smith was to appeal against his sending-off against City but that hearing was postponed due to the linesman involved being out of the country.

On the evening that Lloyd had pleaded his case to the FA panel, Arsenal beat Crystal Palace 1-0 at Highbury to draw level on points with the Reds, although the Gunners had now played a game more. Two days later Leeds dropped a point when they could only draw 1-1 at West Bromwich Albion. As Leeds were dropping points, latest signing Peter Spiring put himself into contention for a call-up to the first team picture, scoring for the reserves in a 2-0 win over Preston North End in the Lancashire Senior Cup.

The Reds' fixture the following Saturday against Tottenham Hotspur at Anfield was kicking off at 11.30am due to the Grand National, meaning they could really increase the pressure on Arsenal and Leeds by extending their lead before their rivals had even kicked off. Tommy Smith, though, wasn't keen on the morning kick-off due to the disruption it caused to the normal match-day routine and believed a Friday night game would have been better. In his *Liverpool Echo* column published on the evening of the Spurs game he wrote that he would normally only be getting up at that time but now everything had to be done at least two hours earlier than normal, although he acknowledged that there was the advantage of having the chance to increase the lead on Arsenal and Leeds in advance.

Before thinking of Spurs, Shankly had to keep an eye on his players who were involved in international action. John Toshack was away in Cardiff for the Wales v Poland World Cup qualifier at Ninian Park, a game the Welsh won 2-0 to give England a helping hand in qualification. Unfortunately for Toshack and Liverpool, he returned to Melwood with an ankle injury that meant he faced a spell on the sidelines. Ray Clemence was another player who was called up for international duty, selected for a Football League XI playing the Scottish League at Hampden Park. However, the Reds keeper pulled out of the game with a back injury, although it was not thought serious enough to keep him out of the Spurs game.

Clemence was told to rest at home but Phil Boersma, Steve Heighway and Kevin Keegan were guests of honour that week at The Everyman Theatre for the opening of a play called *When The Reds,* a look at Liverpool heroes of the last 25 years through the eyes of a supporter named Ray. Based on an original story by Alan Plater, it was adapted by Willy Russell and contained a number of supporters' songs. The starring role was played by Bernard Hill, who would later achieve fame as Yosser Hughes in *Boys FromThe Black Stuff.*

When the weekend came Toshack was Shankly's only injury worry. Peter Spiring was included in the squad and he was given a place on the bench ahead of Phil Boersma, who was instead included in the reserve side to face Burnley at Turf Moor. Spurs, seeking their first win at Anfield in sixty years, looked set to be returning to North London with both points at half-time only for Kevin Keegan to equalise in the second period in a thrilling game that saw Pat Jennings save two penalties.

Liverpool took the game to Spurs from the start, forcing three quick throw-ins near the corner flag although nothing came from them. Phil Beal then fouled Keegan on the right edge of the penalty area and from Brian Hall's free-kick Larry Lloyd headed the ball goalwards but Jennings managed to palm it away. The Reds tried sending a lot of long balls forward hoping to expose Ray Evans, who was usually a right back but was now playing in the unaccustomed position of centre back in place of the injured Mike England, but they didn't present him with any difficulty.

After fourteen minutes Steve Heighway came close to giving Liverpool the lead when he collected a pass from Tommy Smith just inside the Spurs half, beat Evans and Joe Kinnear before unleashing a fierce shot that Jennings didn't just turn away but was able to hold-on to. Just after this, Spurs nearly took the lead after an error by Peter Cormack. His poor pass was intercepted by Alan Gilzean who played the ball into the penalty area towards John Pratt, but Emlyn Hughes had been alert to the danger and got back to make a great tackle as the shot was being lined up. Cormack suffered an injury scare when he required treatment to his hip after a collision, but he was fit to carry on and soon afterwards had an angled header well saved by Jennings. During the stoppage in the game Peter Spiring began to warm up on the touchline and was given a good reception by the Kop.

In the 21st minute Spurs took the lead against the run of play, Gilzean smashing Ralph Coates's low cross into the net. There were protests from Smith and Lloyd who felt that Martin Peters, who had initially failed to connect with the centre, had strayed into an offside position but they were waved away. Liverpool responded and Chris Lawler drove the ball over from just outside the box, but Spurs' well-organised midfield was preventing them from developing any rhythm and they were restricted mainly to long shots. One of these from Ian Callaghan nearly shaved the post and another was sliced high and wide by Hall. Despite having the lead the visitors didn't sit back on it and still got forward, Clemence being forced into a diving save after a volley by Peters. Liverpool managed to assert more authority in the closing stages of the first half which became mainly one way traffic. In the 39th minute Cormack was brought down in the area by Cyril Knowles and a penalty awarded, but Keegan's low kick to Jennings's right was saved and then scrambled away by defenders. Before half-time the Spurs keeper denied

Liverpool again, scrambling backwards to tip a Keegan header over the bar, and on another occasion he raced out of his area to put the ball out for a throw-in as Cormack raced onto a long punt by Clemence.

The onslaught continued in the second half, with Cormack and Lawler both having efforts go narrowly over and Jennings diving to save a dipping Alec Lindsay shot which was just creeping in. Spurs were by now pulling nine men back behind the ball and applying offside tactics and back-passes to hang on to their lead, which was not appreciated by a jeering Kop. In the 57th minute Hall beat the offside trap but his centre, which was meant for the onrushing Hughes, was misplaced and Jennings came out of his goal to gather the ball safely. Jennings continued to thwart Liverpool almost single-handed, in the 67th minute somehow managing to turn a Peter Cormack volley from inside the six-yard box around the post.

In the seventieth minute Jennings was finally beaten by a mishit shot by Keegan. Callaghan crossed from the right and Hughes stepped over the ball to tee-up Keegan, whose effort hit the ground and bounced over the deceived Jennings. The atmosphere in the ground was now at fever pitch as Liverpool continued to pour forward in search of a winner, forcing a series of corners that were desperately cleared by the Spurs defence. In the 74th minute Heighway crossed from the left and it was flicked on by Cormack to Hall at the far post but Jennings, who had been covering the near post, somehow got across his goal to push Hall's header away. With five minutes to go Lloyd had a shot which beat Jennings, only for Kinnear to punch it off the line leading to a penalty being awarded. Smith stepped up to take the kick but this time Jennings dived to his left and caught it at the foot of the post. Smith sank to his knees and beat the turf with his fists in frustration and, as Jennings stood and punched the air, the referee waved play on and laughed, saying 'this is wonderful stuff', leading even the dejected Smith to raise a smile.[64]

Despite this frustration Liverpool still weren't finished and with two minutes left Hughes hit a shot from outside the area that beat Jennings, only to rebound off the post. The Reds certainly couldn't be accused of not giving their all in search of victory but they were denied by world class goalkeeping, described in that evening's *Liverpool Echo* as 'one of the most amazing exhibitions of goalkeeping Anfield has ever seen, it was utterly breathtaking'.

Bill Shankly said it was the best goalkeeping performance he had seen in forty years in the game but, typical of him, claimed the one he saved from Hall's header was luck. Jennings himself was extremely modest, saying he had been lucky to have guessed right for the penalties. Regarding the point-blank save from Cormack, he said: 'There was only one yard of the goal he could have shot at so I covered it'. Of the goal he conceded, Jennings said he believed he'd have saved it if Keegan had struck the shot as he intended. 'I anticipated a ground shot and dived to my right accordingly but he didn't hit it right," said Jennings. 'He hit it into the ground and it bounced over my head'.[65] His opposite number Ray Clemence, though, was having none of Jennings's modesty, telling the *Daily Post* reporter the following Monday that he felt that the display was the best he had ever seen and as good as Gordon Banks at his best.

Just like at Anfield, there had been an exciting finish at Aintree that afternoon, as Southport-trained horse Red Rum came from fifteen lengths behind at the final fence to claim what would be the first of three Grand National wins.

Smith's day wasn't helped by having the second penalty saved, which he admitted in his column the following week almost drove him to tears and played on his mind for several hours in the afternoon. He only felt better when news came through that Arsenal and Leeds both lost, meaning the 1-1 draw had been a point gained. It left the Reds a point clear of Arsenal with a game in hand. Leeds were seven points behind with two games in hand, leaving Liverpool as firm favourites for the title. Their position was much more favourable than when they had lost out by one point a year earlier, now having 53 points compared to 48 at this stage in 1971-72.

Liverpool: Clemence, Lawler, Lindsay, Smith, Lloyd, Hughes, Keegan, Cormack, Heighway, Hall, Callaghan. Sub: Spiring.

Spurs: Jennings, Kinnear, Knowles, Coates, Evans, Beal, Gilzean, Perryman, Chivers, Peters, Pratt. Sub: Pearce.

Referee: Mr R. E. Raby (Leeds).

Attendance: 48,477.

Top of the Division One Table

		Pl	W	D	L	F	A	GA	Pt
1	Liverpool	36	22	9	5	65	37	1,76	53
2	Arsenal	37	22	8	7	51	33	1,54	52
3	Leeds	34	18	10	6	57	35	1.63	46

15

Knocked Down then Back Up Again in the West Midlands

**Football League Division One: Birmingham City 2 Liverpool 1
Saturday 7th April 1973**

Bill Shankly believed that six points from their remaining six games would be enough to bring the title to Anfield. He told Chris James of the *Liverpool Echo* on 2nd April: 'We would then have a terrific number of points and Arsenal would have to get eight from five games to catch us and only one of these matches is at home'. Leeds would need to win seven of their eight remaining games to overhaul Shankly's target and with them also being involved in the FA Cup and European Cup Winners Cup, it was hard to see how they would not run out of steam at some stage.

It may have been nearly three weeks away and there were four games to play beforehand, but the Easter Monday match with Leeds was clearly on the mind of many. The *Daily Post* reported on 5th April that postal applications for stand tickets had been oversubscribed by thousands, with Peter Robinson commenting: 'It is sad to disappoint so many people and turn good money away and I can only stress that it is a waste of time for anybody else to apply'. Although the match was due to take place just two days before the second leg of the UEFA Cup semi-final, it had been impossible to find an alternative date due to Leeds's fixture backlog. Bill Shankly, however, felt that neither side would be at a disadvantage as they both had European ties, in Leeds's case a Cup Winners Cup semi-final with Hajduk Split.[66]

As Shankly's new team closed in on the title, a third player who had been in both his 1964 and 1966 title-winning sides was moving into management. That week it was announced that Ian St John, who was playing at Tranmere Rovers, would take over as manager of his first club, Motherwell, when his contract expired on 1st July. St John followed Ron Yeats (Tranmere) and Gordon Milne (Coventry) into management. Jimmy Melia, who had played 24 games in 1963-64 before losing his place to Alf Arrowsmith but still qualified for a medal, was manager of Crewe Alexandra and Shankly was extremely proud of how many of his former players were progressing into management. He told the *Liverpool Echo* on 5th April: 'They are all studious chaps and know the game'. It was clear Shankly's own enthusiasm was rubbing off on them and it can be further demonstrated from the 1972-73 side, with Peter Cormack, Emlyn Hughes, Kevin Keegan, Chris Lawler, Trevor Storton and John Toshack all managing at some point in the future.

Liverpool's next game was away to a Birmingham City side who had been promoted the previous season. Only a dramatic slump on their part and a revival of the teams below could see them relegated, but, there was no way they would be taking it easy against the Reds. Their manager Freddie Goodwin said on the Tuesday before the game:

> 'This match is a great opportunity for us to measure the progress we've made against a side which is proven to be of top First Division class. Victory would be a big boost for it would confirm to my players and football in general that we are a good team, and being a young team, one which can develop into a very big side in the years ahead'. [67]

That young side he was referring to included players such as Bob Latchford and Trevor Francis, who would go on to command large transfer fees later in the decade. The day before the game Shankly announced on departure for the West Midlands that the starting eleven would be unchanged, the only decision to make being whether to use Phil Boersma or Phil Thompson as substitute. Peter Spiring was named in the reserve side to face West Bromwich Albion at Anfield alongside a local seventeen-year-old amateur who had been promoted from the A Team after a number of impressive displays. His name was Jimmy Case.

John Toshack had also been hoping to play for the reserves but, after he admitted he had been struggling with mystery pain in his left leg for the past four months that was affecting his form, Shankly withdrew him from the side so he could be seen by a specialist. Toshack had played for Wales against Poland in midweek and could hardly walk by the end of the game, such was the pain in his left leg. This prompted him to accept that the pain, which was sometimes in his thigh but at other times in his knee or Achilles tendon, wouldn't simply go away and he had to see Shankly. The boss told the *Daily Post*:

> 'We don't know ourselves whether they are all connected with the same injury, that's what the specialist will tell us. John was in fantastic form earlier in the season, he looked like a world beater. But after the Carlisle injury, although he kept scoring he wasn't as fast or as dangerous as he was in those earlier games. We could tell something was wrong but because John didn't say anything we didn't connect it with an injury of any kind'.

With Leeds and Arsenal both involved in FA Cup semi-final action it was a great opportunity for Liverpool to extend their lead at the top. On the morning of the game the *Post* reported that Shankly was aware of Birmingham's revival. He said: 'If we can win at Birmingham we will be in a very strong position.

Birmingham have improved tremendously now that they have got a lot of their injuries cleared up'. Unfortunately, Shankly's caution turned out to be right as the Reds went down 2-1, Birmingham continuing their recent revival as they picked up their fourteenth point out of the last twenty available.

There was a swirling wind at St Andrews which, allied to a hard pitch, made it very difficult to judge the bounce of the ball and to control it. Liverpool started the better of the two sides and Emlyn Hughes had the first chance of the game, shooting just wide from the edge of the area after eight minutes. Shortly after this the Reds were awarded a free-kick by the right corner flag which was taken by Steve Heighway, but Larry Lloyd was unable to get any power behind his header. Ray Clemence wasn't called into action until the twelfth minute, when he touched a drive from Alan Campbell over the bar. The Reds continued to have the better of the play, however, Keegan creating a shooting chance for himself which was well saved by Dave Latchford and Brian Hall volleying just over the bar.

Birmingham began getting back into the game, Alec Lindsay having to be alert to intercept a pass that would have sent Trevor Francis clear. Tempers then became frayed when Clemence was knocked to the ground by Bob Hatton after he had caught the ball, leading to a booking for the Birmingham player which was not appreciated by the large and vociferous home crowd. After a period of treatment Clemence was able to continue, and at the other end there was a similar incident when Peter Cormack challenged Latchford, forcing him to drop the ball at the feet of Keegan who stabbed it home, but the goal was ruled out for a foul.

A minute before half-time Birmingham took the lead when Bob Latchford rose above Lloyd to meet Malcolm Page's cross with a powerful downward header into the corner of the goal after Clemence was left stranded, having hesitated after at first coming for the cross. The home side continued their momentum at the start of the second half, Francis having a 25-yard shot that went just wide. Liverpool tried to get back into the game but the Birmingham defence were solid and their luck was summed up when a Chris Lawler header was deflected wide off Keegan. With a quick counter attack Birmingham almost doubled their lead after 57 minutes, Clemence saving Hatton's shot and from a tight angle Latchford striking the rebound against the post with the ball bouncing out of play. Just a minute later, though, it was 2-0 with another break-away goal, the ball being cleared to Latchford on the halfway line. He laid the ball off to Hatton who went on a fifty-yard run towards goal. Despite the best efforts of Tommy Smith to catch him he held the Reds defender off and slid the ball past Clemence.

Liverpool were undaunted by being 2-0 down and Keegan's volley was well saved at point-blank range by Latchford. Just two minutes after Birmingham's second goal the deficit was reduced when Smith hit a powerful free-kick into the net after a handball. In the 66th minute Keegan missed a brilliant chance to level the scores when he was clean through, only to miss his kick and see the ball bobble into the arms of a grateful Latchford. Birmingham were not prepared to sit back and defend their lead. The slackening wind allowed them to play some skilful and entertaining football, and Hatton should have done better when a Francis cross found him unmarked, only for him to head the ball wide.

When they needed to defend, Birmingham did so gallantly and in numbers as they packed the box whenever Liverpool's pressure intensified, Hughes and Heighway both having shots blocked by the sheer numbers of players in there. Keegan had a powerful eighteen-yard header go narrowly wide but the Reds just couldn't find a way through. Latchford had the ball in the net for Birmingham again with two minutes left as they exposed gaps in the Reds defence, but it was disallowed due to him having committed a foul on Lloyd. As frustration set in, Hughes was sent off in injury time after he was adjudged to have elbowed Francis, who stayed on the ground for some time.

There were kind words from Tommy Smith for Bob Latchford, scorer of Birmingham's opening goal. In his *Liverpool Echo* column the following Saturday he described him as a good old-fashioned centre forward who may have lacked ball skills but had plenty in other areas, including the ability to get back up again after being knocked down and the determination and belief to win the ball even if it doesn't look possible. Smith was unsure of their other starlet Trevor Francis, though, saying: 'He didn't do anything which particularly struck me'.

Shankly was livid with the refereeing. In addition to being angry at the Hughes sending-off, he believed the Reds should have been awarded two penalties for fouls on Cormack and Heighway. The Reds winger was later angry at suggestions Liverpool were feeling the pressure, believing that it didn't do a good Birmingham side justice. He wrote in his *Daily Post* column the following Saturday:

'We weren't pleased after our defeat at Birmingham but I don't go along with those who claim that the tension of the battle for points had given us a neurosis. Birmingham have been doing well lately and they had something to prove to themselves for they came as close to anyone else to licking us at Anfield. If there is pressure upon Liverpool there is also pressure upon the Gunners and Leeds'.

Liverpool: Clemence, Lawler, Lindsay, Smith, Lloyd, Hughes, Keegan, Cormack, Heighway, Hall, Callaghan. Sub: Boersma.

Birmingham: Latchford D, Martin, Pendrey, Page, Hynd, Roberts, Campbell, Francis, Latchford B, Hatton, Taylor. Sub: Want.

Referee: Mr R. C. Challis (Tonbridge).

Attendance: 48,114.

Football League Division One: Liverpool 1 West Bromwich Albion 0
Saturday 14th April 1973

Although it was disappointing to lose at St Andrews, there was no time for moping about. Liverpool had to remember they were still in pole position, put things behind them and pick themselves up that week for the first leg of the UEFA Cup semi-final with Tottenham Hotspur, which they won 1-0. With five games to play the Reds were still a point ahead, had the best goal average, easiest run-in and also knew that Leeds and Arsenal still had to face each other. Arsenal were now deflated after a shock FA Cup semi-final defeat to Sunderland and had a derby with Spurs looming. Leeds, who did manage to reach Wembley, also had the European Cup Winners Cup to contend with as well as their games in hand, and something was likely to give.

Liverpool stated their intention to appeal against the sending-off of Emlyn Hughes against Birmingham, believing that the elbow had been accidental. They were also informed that Tommy Smith's appeal against his dismissal at Manchester City would finally be heard in Easter week. This meant there was the possibility of Smith's appeal being thrown out and him being banned for the last three games of the season, although there was the safety net of the independent panel, the process of which would delay the suspension into the next season.

The situation contrasted greatly with that across the park at Goodison, where Harry Catterick was sacked from his role as team manager, although he would remain at the club in an executive position. Derby's Brian Clough and Woverhampton's Bill McGarry were the early front-runners to take over the managerial role, which attracted a salary of £12,000 plus 20% in bonuses. The *Daily Post* suggested on 12th April that McGarry was preferred due to his less abrasive style, although Clough had a chance as the Everton board were after somebody who could capture the media in the way Shankly did. The previous evening McGarry had been in the crowd when Everton lost 4-1 at West Bromwich Albion and he refused to rule himself out of the running when *Post* reporter Michael Charters questioned him, saying: 'Of course any manager must be interested because Everton is one of the great jobs in the game'.

Also in the crowd at The Hawthorns was Bill Shankly, making a final check on Liverpool's next opponents, Albion being due to visit Anfield the forthcoming Saturday. The game looked a certain two points for the Reds on paper, but Albion had managed to get results against Arsenal and Leeds in recent weeks. Liverpool were well aware of Albion's fighting qualities as, in a League Cup tie earlier in the season, the Reds had needed a winner in the last minute of extra-time in a replay to progress.

Two days before the Reds were due to face Albion, Emlyn Hughes was pipped for the Football Writers' Player of the Year award by Pat Jennings.

The Northern Ireland keeper's two penalty saves against Liverpool two weeks earlier seemed to have swung the vote, with him gaining twice as many as Leeds's Paul Madeley. Hughes had to settle for equal-third with Jennings's Spurs teammate Alan Gilzean.

As April meant the start of a new tax year, this was the first league game at Anfield that was subject to VAT which was now chargeable on admission to all football matches, although Liverpool had decided to absorb this until the end of the season. They had warned, however, that for 1973-74 stand tickets would go up 10p to 95p while prices for the Paddock, Anfield Road and Kop would remain unchanged. Such a move was a further blow to a game which was already reeling from falling attendances, with crowds at Anfield holding up quite well compared to so many other clubs.

Liverpool's side for the match was the same that had lost at Birmingham for what turned out to be a dire game, Albion making it quite clear from the start that they were after a 0-0 draw and showing little effort to get back into it even after Kevin Keegan had scored a fourteenth minute penalty.

With Albion packing the middle of the field, Liverpool used the flanks to try to find an opportunity and the first chance they created, following a cross by Brian Hall, was turned away for a corner. This was taken by Steve Heighway but Peter Cormack's shot was blocked and Albion scrambled the ball clear. When Heighway was brought down in the area by Roger Minton the referee had no hesitation in pointing to the spot and Keegan confidently made no mistake in tucking the kick away to the keeper's right despite an Albion player trying to put him off before his run-up. It was a huge relief for the crowd who had seen five penalties missed at Anfield so far during the season.

Albion had a chance to get back into it when Len Cantello dispossessed Tommy Smith, but Emlyn Hughes was on hand to get back quickly to make a tackle and play the ball back to Ray Clemence. On the whole Liverpool kept the upper hand, though, with Albion resorting to aggressive tactics to stop them in their tracks. Cormack was extremely unlucky not to double the lead in the 25th minute when his shot hit the post and rebounded against keeper John Osborne before bouncing to safety. There were strong appeals shortly afterwards when Cormack tried his luck again and, in making the save, Osborne was believed to have stepped back over his line, but the linesman was level and didn't raise his flag.

Liverpool were kicking into the Kop for the second half but this didn't make the game any more exciting or lead to any clearer chances as it remained a midfield battle. For the first fifteen minutes neither keeper was called into action, with the only attempt on goal being a long-range effort from Ian Callaghan that went wide. The Reds continued to press down the flanks, a ploy that forced twenty corners during the course of the game but very few chances were created from them. Osborne did make a good save from a dipping volley from Hughes that had a swerve on it as well, but the only thing of note the Albion keeper did was two minutes from time when he fingertipped away a Keegan shot after he had been set up by Heighway. The game ended with a hard challenge on Heighway and as the final whistle blew he had to be helped off the pitch, as did Alec Lindsay who had taken a knock a few minutes before.

Albion's unwillingness to make a competitive game of it had made for a dour encounter, which fan Chris Wood recalls as 'absolutely awful' to watch, but the Reds were relieved to have got the two points. There was good news from Highbury, too, where Arsenal had been held to a 1-1 draw by Tottenham in their final home game of the season. Shankly wasn't bothered about the quality of the football at such a crucial stage, telling the *Daily Post* afterwards:

> 'Anything we get now can win us the league, the toughest title in the world to win. It was a difficult game and the opposition didn't contribute much to make the game any better to watch. But there was a lot at stake for both sides, they were fighting to survive and we were fighting to win the league, so they were two very good points'.

Never one to mince his words, Tommy Smith, writing in his *Liverpool Echo* column the following Saturday, branded Albion's tactics as ridiculous in their quest to stay up. He said: 'They were probably the worst team to come to Anfield in the league this season and even if they do manage to stay up they will have to pull their socks up if they are to avoid the same problems next season'.

Liverpool: Clemence, Lawler, Lindsay, Smith, Lloyd, Hughes, Keegan, Cormack, Heighway, Hall, Callaghan.

WBA: Osborne, Minton, Wilson, Cantello, Wile, Merrick, Brown, Shaw, Astle, Hartford, Johnston. Sub: Robertson.

Referee: Mr J. D. Williams (Wrexham).

Attendance: 43,853.

Football League Division One: Coventry City 1 Liverpool 2
Tuesday 17th April 1973

Arsenal's dropped point the previous Saturday meant that three wins from the last four would be enough to win the league for Liverpool given the superior goal average, and the *Daily Post* reported on the following Monday morning that their title odds were now down to 7/2 on. Leeds were quoted at 6/1 and Arsenal were out to 10/1 as they faced four tough away trips to Everton, Southampton, West Ham and Leeds. Arsenal's Alan Ball refused to give up, though, pointing to his side's excellent away record:

'So the league title race is all over bar the shouting is it, well I wouldn't be so sure about that. Anyone who has written off Arsenal's chances should have a careful look at our away record. Since 9th December we have played eight away league games, winning five of them at Tottenham, Liverpool, Chelsea, Ipswich and Manchester City, drawn two and lost one. I must be realistic and admit that the odds are against us at the moment after dropping a home point against Spurs on Saturday. But we won't be prepared to concede anything until it is mathematically impossible for us to overhaul Liverpool. Bill Shankly's boys are due to play Coventry. On form they should win but if they slip up that would put a very different complexion on things and Arsenal would be right back in the reckoning. I think we are capable of winning all of our remaining four games, including the last one at Elland Road because if we play to our best form I don't think anyone can stop us'.[68]

The Reds now prepared for their third successive league game against a West Midlands side, a Tuesday night trip to Coventry City as they looked to end a hoodoo that had seen them pick up just one point in three away games in that region. Liverpool had lost only once at Highfield Road since Coventry's promotion in 1967, winning two and drawing two. The Sky Blues were comfortably placed in mid-table with nothing to play for and had lost five of the last six games, so nothing short of victory was the target for the Reds. However, Coventry's joint-boss Gordon Milne had a warning that this was a game his players would be up for as they sought to arrest their slump. He told the *Liverpool Echo:* 'In the last six matches we played very well in two or three of them but got nothing. The fact that this is a vital match for Liverpool might well help motivate us and break the spell'

Alec Lindsay and Steve Heighway were the biggest doubts for the trip to Coventry, having both had to be helped off the pitch after the Albion game, but this posed no great concerns as Phil Boersma and Phil Thompson were available to play in midfield with Emlyn Hughes slotting into left back if need be. The Reds stayed in a hotel in Shakespeare country at Stratford-on-Avon although there would be no going to the theatre as Shankly called for plenty of rest and quipped of the bard: 'Och he learned it all from Burns'[69].

Lindsay was ruled out of the game early in the day but there were still hopes for Heighway, although in the end his knee failed to stand up to a fitness test. Boersma came into the side for the first time since injuring his shoulder against Stoke a month earlier and stole the headlines, scoring twice to put Liverpool within touching distance of the title.

The Reds were well organised, gave nothing away and controlled the game from the start, but there was very little goalmouth action for the first half-an-hour. In the 37th minute, though, the Reds took the lead after winning a corner that was met by Kevin Keegan with an overhead kick. This dropped at the feet of Boersma whose shot was too powerful for Neil Ramsbottom to hold and he could only help it into the net. A mistake by Alan Dugdale almost let Keegan in before half-time but he shot straight at Ramsbottom.

In the 61st minute Boersma got Liverpool's second when he headed in Peter Cormack's cross after Ramsbottom had let it slip through his hands. The Reds could have had a third six minutes later when Keegan tapped home after Ramsbottom had parried Cormack's header but it was ruled out for offside. Coventry tried their best to make a game of it and Chris Lawler headed a Chris Cattlin header off the line two minutes after the Reds had scored their second goal. But Liverpool were in no mood to give anything away, Chris Lawler totally nullifying the threat of Tommy Hutchison down the left and Emlyn Hughes being faultless at left back. The home side's cause had not been helped in the first half when Scottish international midfielder Willie Carr was forced off with a leg injury, but they did manage a consolation with five minutes remaining through Brian Alderson. Despite pulling a goal back there was no late rally and Coventry never looked like snatching an unlikely draw.

Liverpool: Clemence, Lawler, Thompson, Smith, Lloyd, Hughes, Keegan, Cormack, Boersma, Hall, Callaghan. Sub: Spiring

Coventry: Ramsbottom, Coop, Cattlin, Smith, Barry, Dugdale, Mortimer, Alderson, Stein, Carr (Green), Hutchison.

Referee: Mr D. J. Biddle (Bristol).

Attendance: 27,280.

Top of the Division One Table

		Pl	W	D	L	F	A	GA	Pt
1	Liverpool	39	24	9	6	69	40	1.73	57
2	Arsenal	38	22	9	7	52	34	1.53	53
3	Leeds	36	19	11	6	59	36	1.64	49

16

Easter Extravaganza

Football League Division One: Newcastle United 2 Liverpool 1
Saturday 21st April 1973

Bill Shankly was naturally delighted with the result at Coventry, telling the *Liverpool Echo*:

'Tonight's win put us in a tremendously strong position considering the respective programmes of the teams involved. It has helped remove some of the pressure. If we win at Newcastle we will take an awful lot of catching'.

Rather than return to Liverpool from the Midlands, Shankly went to London with Tommy Smith for his appeal against his sending-off against Manchester City. The FA upheld the decision, but the Reds immediately lodged an appeal to the independent tribunal to ensure that their captain would not be suspended for the last three games of the season.

With the title now Liverpool's to lose they were given another boost from the most unlikely source the following night when Leeds were surprisingly beaten 1-0 at Elland Road by Manchester United, who were enjoying a revival under Tommy Docherty and were now twelfth in the table. That result meant that even if Leeds won their two games in hand and beat Liverpool on Easter Monday, they would still be two points behind the Reds with an inferior goal average. Shankly was jubilant at the Leeds slip up, telling Roger Kelly of the *Daily Post* after he had heard it:

'This means we can win the championship on Saturday. If we win and Arsenal lose at Everton we could make sure of the championship on goal average. Leeds have had it now, I think they'll probably lose at home on Saturday as well against Crystal Palace'.

In a show of support that is hard to imagine now, Docherty said he was delighted the title would be heading to the other end of the M62, saying: 'I am sorry for Don Revie but it looks like Bill Shankly's boys are now going to take the title. They must have the best chance and I'll be delighted for Bill'.[70]

On Good Friday Liverpool headed to the North East in preparation for their last away game of the season against Newcastle United which was to take place the following day. Alec Lindsay was left behind in the hope he could build up his fitness in time for the Leeds game on Easter Monday but Steve Heighway was fit again and travelled. John Toshack, after being given an injection by the specialist, was included in the reserve side to face Blackburn at Ewood Park. Bill Shankly had a swagger about him before the squad set off, telling the press: 'If we win and Arsenal lose that's it. If we play as well as we did at Coventry Newcastle won't stand a chance'.[71] However, any favours from Everton would have to be done without the aid of a manager, Ipswich's Bobby Robson turning down the chance to manage them that week in what was becoming quite a saga.

As it was, things didn't go to plan after everything looked on track midway through the first half when Kevin Keegan gave Liverpool the lead. John Tudor struck twice to give the home side the two points, although as Arsenal managed a 0-0 draw at Goodison the title couldn't have been secured anyway. Steve Heighway had recovered from his knee injury but he had to make do with a substitute role as Phil Boersma kept his place in the side. A pre-match downfall and blustery conditions made playing conditions difficult but the Reds almost took a first-minute lead when Phil Thompson hit the post with a 25-yard volley. In the seventh minute Boersma took a pass from Ian Callaghan and shot across the face of goal but nobody was on hand to turn the ball in. Newcastle's first chance came from Jimmy Smith but his shot was too weak to trouble Ray Clemence.

It was a solid midfield battle which the Reds were just about sneaking and, after a free-kick was awarded for a foul on Keegan, Brian Hall should have done better when Thompson found him on the edge of the box, but his shot was well over the bar. The goal Liverpool craved came in the 24th minute when Peter Cormack's ball into the goalmouth was headed by Bobby Moncur straight into the path of Keegan who had the simple task of nodding it past Willie McFaul into the net.

Newcastle fought back with Terry McDermott having a low drive well saved by Clemence as crowd trouble started to break out behind both goals, with one fan running the length of the pitch while play went on around him. In the 33rd minute Clemence made a great save from a Tudor volley and by now most of the play was taking place in the Reds half as Newcastle fought desperately to get back in the game. After 42 minutes they got their equaliser when Malcolm Macdonald nodded a Terry Hibbitt centre across the face of goal and Tudor sneaked in to to head the ball home before Clemence could get to it. Liverpool responded and Thompson went close just before half-time with another volley which this time went wide.

Fan Peter Etherington had travelled to the game on the special train and after going in the Strawberry pub near the ground stood on the Gallowgate End. Looking towards the Leazes Terrace, he recalls in *One Boy and His Kop* how everybody seemed to have a Newcastle shirt on, an unusual sight as this was some twenty years before the Premiership and such shirts being marketed as a fashionable item.

In driving rain, Liverpool started the second half brightly, McFaul diving at

Cormack's feet to make a brave save after Chris Lawler had knocked down a Thompson cross. Liverpool then had a let-off when Larry Lloyd misjudged a bounce allowing Macdonald to have a run on goal, but Tommy Smith got across to make a fine tackle. Liverpool's failure to play to the whistle then almost cost them when Tudor collected a shot that had been mishit by Moncur and, as the defenders appealed, he shot straight at Clemence, who managed to make a save with his legs and Smith got in to hook the ball to safety. Liverpool were not prepared to settle for a point, however, with Emlyn Hughes, who was filling in for Alec Lindsay at left back, getting forward and seeing two long-range efforts go over the bar.

Newcastle took the lead after a terrible mistake by the otherwise faultless Smith, who miskicked a cross from Macdonald straight to the feet of Tudor, who had the simple task of stabbing the ball home with Clemence stranded. Cormack and Brian Hall both went close to an equaliser but with gaps being left at the back, Newcastle could easily have found a third goal themselves. Macdonald had a shot saved by Clemence and another blocked by Smith, while Hughes got in the way of a McDermott effort. As play drew to a close, Liverpool threw everyone except Thompson forward in a search for the equaliser but McFaul made a gravity-defying save from Lawler in injury time, blocking his shot from four yards out and then getting back to scoop the ball into his arms before it crossed the line. The Reds players stood and shook their heads as it was obvious it wasn't to be their day.

Liverpool: Clemence, Lawler, Thompson, Smith, Lloyd, Hughes, Keegan, Cormack, Boersma, Hall, Callaghan. Sub: Heighway.

Newcastle: McFaul, Craig, Clark, McDermott, Howard, Moncur, Barrowclough, Smith, MacDonald, Tudor, Hibbitt. Sub: Nattrass.

Referee: Mr N. Burtenshaw (Great Yarmouth).

Attendance: 37,240.

Football League Division One: Liverpool 2 Leeds United 0
Monday 23rd April 1973

To avoid a long tiring journey home, the team flew from Newcastle to Speke on the Saturday evening to allow extra time to rest before the crucial Easter Monday game against Leeds. Tommy Smith blamed the defeat to Newcastle on thinking the game was too easy and the players relaxing too much after taking the lead[72].

Bill Shankly felt the timing of Newcastle's equaliser changed the course of the game completely, telling the *Daily Post*: 'They scored on the stroke of half-time. Psychologically that's bad. It meant we went in feeling down and they went in on top of the world. Although they'd never looked like scoring until then'. The defeat was a blow but it didn't change the bare facts of the matter, that if Liverpool could beat Leeds then the title was theirs unless a freak combination of results followed. The bookmakers certainly didn't believe a collapse of Devon Loch proportions was on the cards, the *Post* reporting on the morning of the game that the Reds were 7/1 on for the title.

The Reds hadn't beaten Leeds at Anfield since December 1967, when their keeper Gary Sprake famously threw the ball into his own goal. Since then Leeds had avoided defeat in four league games and two cup ties, which included a 0-0 draw in 1968-69 that confirmed them as champions, drawing an extremely sporting response from the Kop. It gave added bite to the game as Liverpool were determined to secure the title at the expense of their great rivals. Interest was inevitably huge in the game, with Roger Kelly writing in the *Daily Post* that morning that it was impossible to say if there had ever been a more important game between the two sides. 'How do you compare today's game with the 1965 cup final, countless other cup games and dozens of thrilling league matches?' he commented.

The gates were locked just over an hour before kick-off with thousands outside for a game for which Leeds were beset with injuries, those missing including Eddie Gray and Johnny Giles. Steve Heighway returned to the Reds side and nearly scored after just two minutes, his drive going agonisingly wide. But the game then evolved into a tense affair, Leeds aiming to frustrate in midfield and absorb pressure, hoping to catch Liverpool on the break as they sought a win that would give them a title lifeline. Their tactics worked and a nervous-looking Liverpool couldn't find a way through in the first half as Paul Madeley and Paul Reaney were outstanding at the back. The best chance of the half came on 24 minutes when Leeds broke away and Peter Lorimer blazed wide, and they also came close when Joe Jordan had a close-range shot blocked by Ray Clemence.

After a frustrating first half Liverpool had the perfect start to the second, going ahead within two minutes. Leeds failed to clear a corner properly and Chris Lawler kicked it over his head into the box where Kevin Keegan rose to nod it down for Peter Cormack to score from twelve yards and send the Kop wild. Leeds were deflated now, managing just one attempt on goal for the rest of the game, an Allan Clarke effort that went well over. The Reds were in total control and only the composure of Madeley and Billy Bremner prevented a rout, limiting the home side to half-chances.

With five minutes to go the second goal came. Cormack crossed and keeper David Harvey and Roy Ellam had a misunderstanding over who should clear, allowing Keegan to nip in and score his twentieth goal of the season. It was one of easiest of the lot and he recalled afterwards: 'When my shot went into the net I felt like jumping right over the Kop. It wasn't a good goal but I was looking for a goal and it served its purpose by increasing the gap and taking any pressure off the lads'.[73]

Keegan didn't jump into the fans as he wished, instead he stood in front of the Kop with his arms raised soaking up the adulation as his team-mates rushed towards him, while Leeds defender Norman Hunter, lucky not to have been booked after two earlier fouls, picked the ball out of the net. The roars got even greater when news came though that Arsenal could only draw at Southampton. The title was now Liverpool's and both fans and players knew it. So much so that when the Reds players left the field, Don Revie's side sportingly lined up to applaud them off, a magnificent gesture demonstrating the respect the two clubs held for each other. With a UEFA Cup semi-final second-leg just two days away, though, there were no champagne celebrations, the players drinking lemonade and tea in the dressing room.

Despite calls from the Kop for him to do so, Bill Shankly did not go back onto the pitch to greet the Kop but he did say afterwards that they had excelled themselves with their backing for the team. One man who wasn't at Anfield was Gerry Marsden, whose number one hit was the Kop's anthem. He was performing at a Christian folk concert at Chester Cathedral and, on hearing the result, played *You'll Never Walk Alone* to the packed congregation of 2,000 people.

Chris James wrote in the following day's *Liverpool Echo*: 'Only freak results, that are best left to mathematicians and computers can stop Liverpool winning the championship now. And in the eyes of the football world – both at home and abroad – they are the new champions'. Such a view was echoed by Revie who said: 'If we haven't won it ourselves then I am delighted the championship has gone to Anfield'. Leeds captain Billy Bremner admitted: 'Liverpool deserve it, they are so consistent. I am delighted for them, I don't begrudge them anything'. Arsenal boss Bertie Mee, whose side had drawn 2-2 at Southampton, didn't go as far as conceding the title but said: 'I wish my name was Bill Shankly'.[74] To put it simply, the only way Liverpool could miss out on the title was if they lost against Leicester and Arsenal won their remaining two games, both away at fifth-placed West Ham and third-placed Leeds, by a combined total of seven goals. Even the most pessimistic Kopite didn't believe that could happen.

Liverpool: Clemence, Lawler, Thompson, Smith, Lloyd, Hughes, Keegan Cormack, Hall, Heighway, Callaghan. Sub: Boersma.

Leeds: Harvey, Heaney, Cherry, Bremner, Ellam, Hunter, Lorimer, Clarke, Jordan, Yorath, Madeley. Sub: Jones.

Referee: Mr G. Hill (Leicestershire).

Attendance: 55,738.

Top of the Division One Table

		Pl	W	D	L	F	A	GA	Pt
1	Liverpool	41	25	9	7	72	42	1.71	59
2	Arsenal	40	22	11	7	54	36	1.50	55
3	Leeds	39	20	11	8	63	39	1.61	51

17

London Calling

UEFA Cup Semi Final 1st Leg Liverpool 1 Tottenham Hotspur 0
Tuesday 10th April 1973

At the semi-final stage of the UEFA Cup, Twente Enschede would have appeared to be the weakest team left in the competition and the side the Reds would have preferred to face, but when the draw was made in Zurich two days after the second leg of the quarter-final the Reds were paired with Tottenham. Tommy Smith felt there was some inevitability that the Reds would be drawn against Spurs and wrote in his *Liverpool Echo* column on 31st March that it was a case of better the devil you know than the devil you don't.

With the 2nd leg due to take place on 25th April, just two days after Liverpool's crunch title clash with Leeds, the Reds appealed to Spurs to bring the games forward, suggesting that the first leg be at Anfield on 4th April and second leg at White Hart Lane on the 11th. However, the suggestion was rejected as Spurs had provisionally arranged to play an outstanding league game with Chelsea on 4th April and they also did not appear keen to lose the advantage of having a second leg on the 25th, knowing the importance of Liverpool's game two days earlier.

Entrance prices for the home leg were set at the same as for previous rounds, with seats costing £1. Sales went slowly, with 400 remaining the day before the game, which were on sale along with 800 that were sent back by Spurs. The justification for raising prices in earlier rounds was to cover the cost of the away leg and, although these were considerably reduced due to it being in England, Liverpool still had to meet the expenses of match officials. For the Anfield leg they were from Sweden, while the White Hart Lane game would be officiated by Italians. In the *Liverpool Echo* on 31st March, Reds correspondent Chris James queried why Scots, Irish or Welsh officials couldn't be used in order to cut down on costs and also reduce the language barrier. UEFA did show some commonsense, though, in the appointment of their official observer, the duty going to Football League president Len Shipman.

Ten days before the first leg Spurs keeper Pat Jennings had put in an unbelievable performance as his side held Liverpool to a 1-1 draw at Anfield, after which Bill Shankly had told the *Echo*: 'The only consolation is that he can't play like that again in the UEFA Cup'. Tommy Smith also felt that

Jennings couldn't possibly be as good again, believing that the Reds had created enough chances to win by three or four goals in that game.[75]

Although the Reds were on the brink of their first European trophy, the league remained the priority and the *Daily Post* reported on the morning of the game that Shankly's main concern was not getting any injuries that would affect the title run-in. As such, John Toshack, who had been troubled with leg pains for four months, was not risked as he continued to seek specialist advice. Shankly believed a two-goal lead at Anfield would be enough to win the tie but, as it was, the Reds would have to be content with a 1-0 victory as they failed to capitalise on a blistering spell of pressure either side of half time.

Despite it being a game between two English sides it started off at a continental pace, Spurs bringing everybody back behind the ball and Liverpool not risking too many men forward for fear of conceding a counter-attacking away goal. Midway through the first half the Reds upped the pace and the onslaught began. Steve Heighway took a long throw which Kevin Keegan struck fiercely towards goal but Mike England blocked the shot.

The goal came in the 27th minute when the Reds were awarded a free-kick after Steve Perryman had fouled Brian Hall. Smith's kick beat the wall but was cleared off the line and Alec Lindsay pounced to hammer the ball into the net. Spurs tried to respond. Martin Chivers shot just wide and Ralph Coates over the bar, but the Reds soon managed to regain control in the run-up to half-time. Heighway had a shot saved at the foot of the post by Pat Jennings and Keegan saw two efforts blocked in the six-yard box. Jennings then saved well from Smith, Ian Callaghan had a shot blocked by England and Brian Hall hit the bar as Spurs were glad to make it to half-time with the score at just 1-0.

Liverpool continued to pound the Spurs goal at the start of the second half, Heighway shooting just wide and Lindsay and Peter Cormack both having shots saved. Hall, Heighway and Callaghan were dominant in midfield and Keegan lively, but the Reds couldn't find a way past the Spurs defence. The visitors seemed content to sit on a one-goal deficit, rarely testing the Reds defence, and Larry Lloyd comfortably dealt with things on the rare occasions the ball was played forward to the ineffective Martin Chivers. As the half wore on the Reds ran out of steam somewhat, before engaging in a late surge to try to find the second goal, Heighway shooting over when clean through and Keegan frantically appealing for a penalty after appearing to be felled by England.

With the Reds having to settle for just 1-0, Shankly expressed some satisfaction that they hadn't conceded a goal. He felt the tackle on Keegan was a blatant penalty, but believed that the continental referee was reluctant to give it due to the amount of play-acting he witnessed when he refereed domestic games. Spurs boss Bill Nicholson was furious at the performance of his side, who he felt did nothing to try to find a vital away goal and were lucky to have got away with a 1-0 defeat. It was apparent that the tactics they employed in the game had not come from him. The players were locked in the dressing room for an hour after the game and arguing was heard to come from inside. He told reporters that Chivers had not been taken off for an injury or to add an extra defender, but because he could not see him getting a goal.[76]

Liverpool: Clemence, Lawler, Lindsay, Smith, Lloyd, Hughes, Keegan, Cormack, Heighway, Hall, Callaghan. Subs: Lane, Thompson, Storton, Boersma, Brownbill.

Spurs: Jennings, Kinnear, Knowles, Coates (Pearce), England, Beal, Pratt, Perryman, Chivers (Evans), Peters, Gilzean. Subs: Baines, Collins, Neighbour.

Referee: Mr B. Loow (Sweden).

Attendance: 42,174.

UEFA Cup Semi Final 2nd Leg Tottenham Hotspur 2 Liverpool 1 Wednesday 25th April 1973

While Liverpool were going into this game just 48 hours after virtually clinching the title against Leeds, Spurs hadn't played since the previous Saturday. They had been granted a lucky reprieve, though, as up to a fortnight earlier they had been due to face Sheffield United at Bramall Lane the night before the second leg. The Football League had refused to authorise the postponement of the fixture without both clubs' consent and only a late change of heart by the Blades led to that game being re-arranged.

Tommy Smith felt Liverpool would be through to the final if they could find a goal. He wrote in his *Liverpool Echo* column the preceding Saturday: 'We will set out to contain Spurs but if we get an attacking opportunity you can bet we'll be up there looking for that vital goal'. He also dismissed the Reds' League Cup defeat at White Hart Lane earlier in the season as having no bearing, pointing out that all three Spurs goals had come during a tropical-style downpour in the first twenty minutes.

Having played Leeds on the Monday, Liverpool's players were excused training on the Tuesday and flew to London in the evening in preparation for the game on the Wednesday. With Alec Lindsay and Peter Cormack injured it was clear Phil Thompson would play but Cormack's replacement was less obvious. On the evening of the game the *Echo* speculated that perhaps Trevor Storton or John Webb might wear the number eight shirt to do a shadowing job on Martin Peters. Spurs would be at full strength after the doubtful Martin Chivers and Cyril Knowles were declared fit, and their assistant manager Eddie Bailey predicted a good contest saying: 'We must be careful not to concede goals whilst trying to score ourselves. It promises to be a great game which is usual when we play Liverpool'.[77]

Shankly opted for Phil Boersma as Cormack's replacement, indicating that he was planning to attack and seek an away goal rather than sit on the lead. After a brief Spurs onslaught at the start of the game Liverpool took command, giving Spurs no time on the ball and looking nothing like a side who'd played in a demanding encounter just over 48 hours earlier. The Reds won eight corners in the first period to Spurs none and at half-time were in total control with one foot in the final. But the game was turned on its head three minutes into the second half when Alan Gilzean's throw long was headed on by Chivers and Peters came in unnoticed to stab the ball into the net. Liverpool didn't panic and just seven minutes later the crucial away goal came with a classic counter-attacking strike. Emlyn Hughes, playing at left back, cleared upfield where Kevin Keegan and Mike England rose to meet the ball. Under pressure, England's header went backwards and Keegan was on to it in no time, homing in on goal. As Pat Jennings advanced, Keegan squared to Steve Heighway who had the simple task of rolling the ball into an empty net, which Peter Etherington recalls sparked scenes of 'pandemonium' in the Paxton Road end where most of the Reds support was gathered.

Although they needed two goals to go through, Spurs were not going to let their grip on the trophy go without a fight. Peters fired against the bar, then John Pratt hit the rebound wide and in the 71st minute they got a second goal, Peters firing Larry Lloyd's headed clearance through a crowded area into the net. Spurs poured everyone forward in search of the winning goal, but Liverpool dug deep into their last reserves of sapped energy. The midfield was immense and the back four solid as a rock, Lloyd winning a series of challenges against Chivers. When the Reds did manage to get forward, Keegan gave England the runaround but on the whole the second half was the total opposite of the first, with most of it being played in the Reds' half. At times the defensive clearances were ones of sheer panic rather than control but Liverpool did all they could to hold on and disappoint the majority of the near 47,000 crowd.

Spurs manager Bill Nicholson went into the Reds dressing room afterwards to offer his congratulations on reaching the final and even had time for a joke as Tommy Smith recalls:

'After the game Nicholson came into our dressing room to offer his congratulations, which was typical of the man. "Have you heard who you'll be playing in the final Bill?" Nicholson asked Shanks. "Aye, Borussia Mönchengladbach" replied Shanks. "Yes, well just as well you went through and not us" said Nicholson wistfully. "I can't pronounce it"'.[78]

As the players changed and got ready for their flight home, Peter Etherington was hotfooting it down the Seven Sisters Road, in his words, getting 'pummelled all the way by Spurs supporters' on the way to the tube station. He remembers his feelings when he finally arrived back at Lime Street Station at 4am, writing in *One Boy and His Kop:* 'I arrived back a bit battered and bruised, tired, but extremely happy. This football club of mine could make me forget almost anything. I was certainly prepared to put up with almost anything for them'. When the Reds players arrived back at Speke Airport in the early hours, Bill Shankly told the *Liverpool Echo*:

> 'The game was a credit to both teams. They are always tremendous games between Liverpool and Spurs. The goals sparked off the match, before then we were very composed. But when the goals came the game burst into flames which made it good for the fans'.

Keegan said of his role in the tie-clinching goal:

> 'I couldn't put the ball across to Steve too quickly because Jennings would have been able to cut it off. I had to take the ball on another yard or so to make Jennings think I was going to shoot and cover the shot and that left the space to get the ball across'.

Liverpool: Clemence, Lawler, Thompson, Smith, Lloyd, Hughes, Keegan, Boersma, Heighway, Hall, Callaghan. Subs: Lane, Webb, Brownbill, Toshack, Storton.

Spurs: Jennings, Kinnear, Coates, England, Knowles, Perryman, Beal, Peters, Gilzean, Chivers, Pratt.

Referee: Mr A. Angonese (Italy).

Attendance: 46,919

18

Coronation Day

Football League Division One: Liverpool 0 Leicester City 0
Saturday 28th April 1973

Peter Cormack's goal against Leeds had been his eighth in the league, a respectable total from thirty games for a midfielder and a key factor in the Reds' success. His form for Liverpool had attracted the attention of Scotland manager Willie Ormond, who watched him play against Leeds with a view to including him in the squad for the Home International Championships. However, Liverpool's qualification for the UEFA Cup final ended his hopes of a recall, as Ormond was insistent that any player selected must report for duty on 7th May, two days before the first leg against Borussia Mönchengladbach.

After arriving back from London following the second leg of the UEFA Cup semi-final in the early hours of 26th April, most of the players attended the wedding of reserve defender Roy Evans at Liverpool's Metropolitan Cathedral later that day. The wedding had been brought forward due to Evans being offered a contract to play for Philadelphia Fury in the North American Soccer League for the summer, which required him to fly out to the States on 1st May. Evans, who had played twice in 1970-71 but not featured at all for the past two seasons, would go on to have a far more successful coaching and management than playing career and joked thirty years afterwards: 'I asked Tommy Smith to be my best man so I wouldn't look too bad in the wedding photos. Mind you if you look back at the pictures now Smithy looks far better than I do'.[79]

Although it seemed a foregone conclusion that the Reds would clinch the title, no chances were taken in the preparations. Normally the players would spend the night before games at Anfield in their own homes but on this occasion they were taken to a hotel. With no other teams able to clinch the championship that day, the *Liverpool Echo* speculated the evening before that the trophy might well be presented at Anfield assuming Liverpool secured the point required. With Leicester's chairman Len Shipman also being president of the Football League, it seemed natural that he would be able to make the presentation afterwards. This was confirmed by the *Daily Post* on the day of the game and there were appeals for fans to keep off the pitch at the end with the club concerned about damage ahead of the UEFA Cup final.

Sadly, one of Liverpool's best known fans, Ted Forshaw, would not be able to see his beloved Reds clinch an eighth league title, having recently died in Broadgreen hospital aged 68. The brother of Dick Forshaw, a member of the 1922 and 1923 title-winning sides, Ted had attended Liverpool matches home, away and abroad in a red coat and top hat covered in badges and decorated with a miniature FA Cup. He had also gone to watch England in the World Cup in Mexico three years earlier and even lent his support to Manchester United in their European Cup-winning season.

Cormack was missing from the side after injuring his ankle against Leeds, but Alec Lindsay returned after regaining his fitness. Cormack was replaced by Boersma but Phil Thompson's recent form made it impossible to leave him out and it was Brian Hall who made way for Lindsay. Shankly, who admitted to having lain awake half the night worrying about who to leave out before finally making his decision at 5am, had believed Thompson played in the Leeds game like a seasoned pro. Describing him as having match-stick legs, he told the *Echo*:

'It is not what size you are that matters, it is how strong you are, how strong willed. He is a great player, so composed. He knows where he is all the time and is aware of those around him. He was not only winning the ball for us but laying it off well also'.

His captain was full of praise for him as well, Tommy Smith writing in his *Echo* column that day that Thompson had turned from an outstanding prospect into a fully-fledged First Division player. Thompson himself remembers that game as being a key point in his Reds career but also knew there was still much more to be done:

'I felt this was the game that I had arrived. I can remember doing a tackle on Allan Clarke near the half way line and then continuing with the ball past another player. The Kop started singing my name and it felt fantastic. It was the moment I knew that I had really arrived as a Liverpool player. However, I knew there was still more to do. I may have arrived but now it was up to me to really establish myself, something which I believe needed to be done over three seasons. When I was first at the club in the late 1960s we had a youth coach called Tony Waiters. He was very ahead of his time and gave me a plan of how I should be looking for my career to turn out. He said that at eighteen I should be getting ten starts a season, at nineteen or twenty be figuring in half the games and after that being a regular. As it was, it turned out exactly that way'.[80]

Playing against Leicester was Thompson's twelfth league start of the season and, as he had also figured twice as a substitute, he would qualify for a championship medal having passed the league threshold of fourteen appearances. However, he knew that despite the performance against Leeds, nothing could be taken for granted:

'I felt I may be left out if Alec was fit. Before the game I found out that I was in the team and that Brian had been dropped and not even made the bench. I pulled him aside to apologise that he had been left out at my expense but he was very understanding, saying that it had nothing to do with me and any anger he had was with the boss'.[81]

The gates were shut half-an-hour before kick-off leaving many in tears outside and the Kop gave the players a tremendous reception as they took the field with Leicester – seemingly sacrificial lambs to the slaughter – forming a guard of honour. One absentee from their line-up was defender Alan Woollett, who was too distraught to play after the death of his dog, much to the amusement of most of his team-mates when they found out on the previous day's train journey to Liverpool. A little boy, two-year-old Michael Briscoe from Cantril Farm, was led out of the terrace by a policeman and onto the pitch where he presented Tommy Smith with a replica of the league trophy made from silver foil. Yet lifelong Reds fan and journalist Brian Reade, who was in the Anfield Road end, recalls the atmosphere was extremely tense. He wrote in *43 Years With The Same Bird*, published by MacMillan in 2008:

'Not an inch of concrete lay empty in Anfield's standing areas but the atmosphere was far from carnival. Most fans had waited six years to see the league trophy shine at Anfield – some of us had waited all of our lives. We were sick with fear and anticipation. There was a feeling we'd celebrated prematurely after the Leeds game and we'd get our comeuppance. After all, hadn't history taught us that's what Leicester were for?'

Smith then won the toss meaning the Reds were kicking towards the Anfield Road end for the first half but they struggled to get any real rhythm going, perhaps not surprisingly given they had played the second leg of the UEFA Cup semi-final since the Leeds game. Leicester had the first chances but Ray Clemence dealt easily with a low Alan Birchenall shot and Frank Worthington's header from a Keith Weller cross was weak and off target.

Midway through the half Liverpool began to get going and Kevin Keegan hit a fierce shot that was parried by Peter Shilton and turned away for a corner by Steve Whitworth. Ian Callaghan then saw Shilton make a fine fingertip save from a 25-yard drive and Keegan went close again, having a header saved. At the other end Worthington did much better with a shot that went only just wide as Leicester began getting back into the game again with Weller and Worthington linking well. When Chris Lawler gave away a free-kick 25 yards from goal, Worthington tried a curling effort but it was comfortably saved by Clemence. There was a sense of nervousness from the Kop, especially when Denis Rofe shot well over the bar when he should have done far better. But the last action of the half almost saw the Reds take the lead from a free-kick just outside the area, which Smith hit fiercely and only fractionally wide. Things were extremely tense, with Brian Reade writing:

'I didn't want to see the match, I wanted the referee to blow his whistle after two seconds. I couldn't take the thrills and spills, the ooohs and aaahs, the possibility that we'd have "one of those days" while plucky opponents with nothing to lose rose to the occasion, writing themselves into the history books. And guess what, our fears were fully justified. Maybe the fears of the crowd got through to the players, maybe the Leicester team remembered their destiny in life was to be Liverpool's bogey team, maybe there is something in the finest of humans that makes them question themselves as they are about to be bathed in glory. Who knows. But we were dire, and never looked like scoring'.

Early in the second half Callaghan shot just wide and Shilton made a point-blank save from Keegan after he had tried to turn in an Emlyn Hughes volley from just five yards. In the 52nd minute Mike Stringfellow, scorer of the Leicester goal that beat Liverpool in the 1963 FA Cup semi-final, almost broke Reds hearts again when he found himself clean through. Clemence, though, managed to block his shot and, although the rebound fell back at his feet, the angle was now tight and the second effort was easily saved. Stringfellow then had the ball in the net in the seventieth minute but his header was ruled out for offside, ironic in the circumstances given that such a decision had cost the Reds the title a year earlier. Liverpool's only chance of note in the latter stages of the game came soon after this when they were awarded a free-kick after Rofe obstructed Keegan, but from this substitute Brian Hall, who had just come on for Phil Boersma, failed to control the ball and it was cleared.

The game began to peter out but it wasn't until there was a minute remaining that the Kop were confident enough to begin chanting 'Champions', 'ee aye adio we won the league' and then a moving *You'll Never Walk Alone*. As the final whistle blew on what had been an anti-climactic end to the league season, a huge roar from the Kop caused a row of pigeons on the roof to scatter away and the celebrations began. Brian Reade described how they went:

'The release was a collective scream from every pore of the club. We hugged, we kissed, we pogoed, we joined in with any one of the six different songs that were going on at any given moment. We sighed, we inhaled, we looked up to the blue skies and gave our thanks'.

As the players gathered near the centre of the pitch the league championship trophy was brought out, quickly followed by Bill Shankly who came down from the directors' box. He took off his overcoat, revealing that he was wearing a bright red shirt, and the noise of the crowd reached a crescendo. Liverpool had used only sixteen players in the league during the season, two of whom, Trevor Storton and Frank Lane, had played only a handful of games and were away with the reserves at Nottingham Forest. The fourteen who had featured predominantly were all present for the presentation of the trophy, Liverpool's eighth title, which brought them level with Arsenal. Some youngsters ran onto the pitch but the Kop soon chanted 'off, off, off' and they left.

The players and Bill Shankly set off on a lap of honour, with the trophy at first being carried by Tommy Smith and Phil Thompson. First they ran alongside the Paddock and Main Stand where club president Tom Williams, who had seen the first title triumph in 1901, watched from the directors box. Although he had seen all eight titles he said 'there's a new thrill in every one of them'.[82] With many fans now on the pitch, they ran towards the Anfield Road end, then down the Kemlyn Road side towards the Kop, where 22,000 adoring fans were gathered waving flags and scarves, a spectacle normally barred but not on this occasion. It seemed the players would never be allowed to leave as for several moments they stood in front of the Kop soaking up the adulation, with some more fans managing to break through the police cordon to hug them. It was an outpouring of emotion as seven years of pent-up frustration at winning nothing was unleashed. The crowning of a new side, one which was capable of going on to win more glories in the future. Fan Chris Wood still remembers how emotional he felt:

> 'It was the first time I had been present to witness the club win something. Thousands had that "seven year itch" completely exorcised on this afternoon. All the banter (not always friendly) from work-colleagues and school-friends could be put away for good. All those who gloated when we lost at Watford in 1970 and just missed out in 1971 and 1972 had nothing to say now. This was our moment and it felt so damn good I am getting emotional just thinking about it'.

Towards the end of the lap, Shankly, who already had one scarf around his neck, picked up another that had been thrown onto the pitch and kicked aside by a policeman. He said that nobody could do that to something that was somebody's life and Chris Wood says of this moment:

> 'If I shut my eyes, I can still see Bill Shankly picking up that scarf in the corner of the Kop and the Main Stand only a few yards from where I was standing at the back of the Paddock. I can see the pride in his eyes and the smile on his face. He/we shared many great moments together but this was special, as he said afterwards, because it was with a new team'.

Leicester's players remained on the pitch for the whole time to take in the scenes, everybody bar one of them standing up. The one who squatted down was Frank Worthington and he must have looked on wondering just what might have been had he taken a little extra care of himself the previous summer. They again formed a guard of honour as the players finally left the pitch before the champagne started to flow in the home dressing room.

Having at one point stood in front of the Kop with his hands clasped together as if giving a prayer of thanks, Shankly seemed totally overawed by it all as he walked slowly towards the tunnel, the *Liverpool Echo* describing him as 'looking like a man who has won the pools but can't think of anything to spend the money on'. The Kop chanted for the players to return to the pitch but by now they were engaging in their own private party and eventually the crowd began to trudge out of the ground chanting 'Super Reds' as they did so. In a nice gesture Shankly and the players autographed the match ball and presented it to the referee before they went to the players' lounge.

Smith said afterwards that the Reds were deservedly champions and since the start of the season he had never doubted that they would win the title, even when they were struggling in January and February. He wrote in his *Liverpool Echo* column that evening:

'We thoroughly deserve the honour because throughout the season we have been the best and most consistent side. I never doubted right from the moment that we started the season in such fine style that we would be champions in the end. Even when we had that lapse just after Christmas I wasn't worried and knew we would pull out of it. We had a similar lapse the year before only it took us longer to get out of and left us just a fraction too much to do. This year we have pulled out of that slump quicker and since we picked up a point in that game at Manchester City we have dropped only five points before today's game since mid-February. In my long-term consideration of a season I always take some sort of mid-term slump into account, because it invariably becomes a fact. Arsenal and Leeds suffer differently, however. Instead of having a really bad time for a month they drop the odd point here and there whereas outside our lapse period we tend to win regularly home and away'.

After the game Ian Callaghan and Chris Lawler took their wives for a meal but soon re-joined their team-mates for further drinks. There was not even time for cola or lemonade for the teetotal Shankly, though, as he travelled to Manchester to appear on *Match of the Day*. The following morning, as players nursed hangovers, Shankly went to Anfield to see how the staff were getting on before returning home to spend the afternoon with his grandchildren. Reflecting, Shankly said the occasion had been the happiest day of his life. Comparing it to other successes he told the *Daily Post*:

'I have known nothing like it as a player or manager. This title gave me greater pleasure than the previous two, simply because here we had a rebuilt side, some of them only two or three seasons in first team football and they stayed the course like veterans. I am delighted'.

Ray Clemence recalls how it's hard to express what it means to be champions due to the consistency required. He says of the triumph:

'You've got to be consistent over 42 games: On the nice grass pitches of August and September; on the mud and rubbish and snow and ice of November, December, January, February; and also to be able to play your football on the bobbly, windy pitches of March and April. You've got to have a team for all seasons and to go through a whole season and to finish top of the pile is an incredible feeling'.[83]

Telegrams flowed into Anfield, including ones from rivals Everton and Leeds, while Bobby Charlton, who was retiring from football, found time to send a message. Liverpool, in turn, dispatched telegrams to Scottish champions Celtic and the winners of the other three divisions of the Football League. For the first time in league history, the winners of all four divisions had come from the same county as Burnley, Bolton and Southport made it a Lancashire clean sweep. It led to a motion being tabled in the House of Commons calling for the Minister of Sport to personally congratulate the clubs and county. In another motion, tabled by Bob Parry, MP for Liverpool Exchange, he called for the Commons to 'congratulate the management, players and staff of Liverpool FC for winning the First Division Championship for a record-equalling eighth time'. Parry's motion also mentioned the fans, stating that they had displayed 'sportsmanship, good humour and behaviour which should serve as an example to football fans everywhere in the United Kingdom'.[84] Although an Evertonian, Parry said that he had tabled the motion on behalf of all his constituents who were Liverpool supporters, including his own father.

Liverpool: Clemence, Lawler, Lindsay, Smith, Lloyd, Hughes, Keegan, Boersma (Hall), Thompson, Heighway, Callaghan.

Leicester: Shilton, Whitworth, Rofe, Stringfellow, Manley, Cross, Sammels, Birchenall, Weller, Worthington, Glover. Sub: Farrington.

Referee: Mr I.P. Jones (Glamorgan).

Attendance: 56,202.

Top of the Division One Table

		Pl	W	D	L	F	A	GA	Pt
1	Liverpool	42	25	10	7	72	42	1.71	60
2	Arsenal	41	23	11	7	56	37	1.57	57
3	Leeds	40	20	11	9	64	42	1.52	51

Ian St John Testimonial: Liverpool 4 Chelsea 2 Monday 30th April 1973

The plaudits for Liverpool continued well into the next week. Wolves striker Derek Dougan felt they were the best side and had special praise for Bill

Shankly, writing in his weekly newspaper column:

> 'Poetic justice has been done, Liverpool have set a fine example and proved that attacking football can pay dividends. Liverpool have done football in England a service by winning the championship and I trust the effects will be felt throughout the league next season, revealed in sharp, co-ordinated attacking football. You have to meet Bill Shankly before you really get the measure of the man as manager. Whether he's talking about football or boxing his enthusiasm is infectious. He talks in a way that makes you passionately interested. He talks about football in a way that makes it the most exciting game in the world. Hence his success. The players respond with all their energy, pride and enthusiasm. This is something you've got or haven't and it can't be contrived. Bill Shankly radiates the very spirit that has led Liverpool to the championship'.

Coventry's joint manager Joe Mercer said: 'It's a popular win, nobody begrudges Liverpool the championship. They still play their football in a way that is so uncomplicated and so free'. Stoke's Tony Waddington echoed: 'I'm certain they deserved the championship, there's no question about it in my mind. Liverpool are like a tank that goes steamrollering over everything, they are relentless'.[85]

Just 48 hours after being crowned champions the fans had the opportunity to pay homage again – as well as to stars of the past when the Reds were back at Anfield for Ian St John's testimonial against Chelsea, a game which would see several former players make guest appearances. They had been chosen as opposition due to a friendship that had developed between St John and their manager Dave Sexton when they were staying at the same hotel in Spain for a fortnight. Delighted to have Chelsea as opposition, St John said: 'I think this will help to make it a game that people enjoy, plenty of football from players who possess a great deal of skill'. Looking forward to being at Anfield again after two years away, he said:

> 'I am grateful to the club for making these facilities available and to the members of my testimonial committee who have put in so much work. Above all I am looking forward to this last reunion with manager Bill Shankly and my old team-mates and with the fans who also gave me endless encouragement during my time as a Liverpool player. In many ways it will be a sad moment when I say goodbye, the end of an era for me. You can't turn back the clock, but the memory of the good times will never dim. I hope the fans feel the same way as I do for they were fantastic for me'.[86]

It was Anfield protocol at the time that players due a testimonial did not get one until their playing careers had finished. St John had since been in South Africa with Hellenic, then back home with Coventry and Tranmere, playing under ex-team mate Ron Yeats at Prenton Park. However, he had decided to hang up his boots and go into management following a broken leg suffered earlier in the season after being tackled on the training ground.

The testimonial committee had hoped to apply an experimental offside rule that was being tried in the Watney Cup, in which a dotted line ran from the edge of the penalty area to the touchline and players could only be offside between there and the goalline. The FA, however, denied them permission to play by these rules, meaning there was no danger of players hovering just outside the box waiting for the ball to come their way.

St John hadn't played since breaking his leg and admitted that, although he would have loved to have played the whole game, only a substitute appearance was feasible. He recalls in his autobiography *The Saint*, published by Hodder and Stoughton in 2005: 'I trained hard because I wanted to go out with a touch of style, but it was an ordeal, the worst I'd experienced in all my career of fighting injury. The worst thing was trying to get full weight on the broken leg'. As such, the newly crowned champions were given centre stage for the first half, which was preceded by St John's nine-year-old son helping Tommy Smith carry the championship trophy onto the pitch amid a rousing rendition of *You'll Never Walk Alone*. St John then took to the pitch with both sides forming a guard of honour before taking a seat in the dugout.

The first half was rather uneventful but there was a huge cheer after 27 minutes when Kevin Keegan made way for St John. At half-time the Reds made five more substitutions as the past and future combined on the field. Phil Thompson, by now acknowledged as a future star at Anfield, came off the bench along with old favourites Gerry Byrne, Roger Hunt and Willie Stevenson, as well as Peter Thompson who was still at the club but hadn't featured for the first team in 1972-73. In the 63rd minute Phil Thompson played a through ball to St John and although the offside flag was raised, the referee ignored it and St John opened the scoring. Although Tommy Baldwin equalised in the 67th minute the years were rolled back in the 70th when Roger Hunt headed in a Peter Thompson cross. After 75 minutes Hunt added another when he lobbed Peter Bonetti and, although Steve Kember pulled another back for Chelsea, St John made it 4-2 before full time.

As he prepared to hang up his boots for good, St John was extremely thankful to the Liverpool supporters and a little sorry he hadn't managed a hat-trick, as he had done in his first game for the club, a Liverpool Senior Cup final against Everton in 1961:

'If only I could take them all up to Scotland with me. These are the people who helped my career more than I can say and although I have played in front of bigger crowds at Anfield it was wonderful of them to turn up on such a wet day to make the night so memorable. What a thrill it was to put two goals into the Kop net. I did my best to get a hat-trick so I could have begun and ended my career here with three goals. I thought I had done it when the ball hit the post but back it came'[87]

St John's testimonial was not quite the last action at Anfield that season, though. There was still one more game to be played on the hallowed turf, the first leg of the UEFA Cup final against Borussia Mönchengladbach!

Liverpool: Clemence, Lawler, Lindsay (Byrne), Smith (Thompson), Lloyd, Hughes (Stevenson), Keegan (St John), Cormack, Hall (Hunt), Toshack, Callaghan (Thompson Peter).

Referee: Mr N.Batty (Helsby).

Attendance 29,808.

19

The Best Supporters in the Land

The capacity crowd against Leicester meant that attendances at Anfield had topped the million mark for the second successive season and that the average of 48,078 was the highest the club had ever recorded.

It had been touch and go that the figure would be reached, though, as crowds had dipped at times during the season, which was played against the background of increasing economic hardship. Although on the whole Liverpool's gates held up well, it had been a different story around the country, with the Football League being worried enough in December to unveil a blueprint for the future and invite the opinions of club chairmen. At many clubs the trend was worrying with once-proud Lancashire town clubs such as Blackburn and Bolton averaging less than 10,000.

Although Liverpool hit the top of the league table at the end of September, continuing a remarkable run of home wins in the league stretching back to January, gates at Anfield were falling as they were across the country. The gate against Sheffield United on 23rd September was the first sub-43,000 league crowd since 41,627 turned out for a game against Huddersfield in October 1971 and the fifth successive game at Anfield in which the attendance was down on the previous one. Gates also dropped in January and February after parking restrictions were imposed in the streets around Anfield.

Many reasons were put forward for the decline in gates such as increased hooliganism and rising prices. It wasn't just the increased price of admission to Anfield that had to be taken into account, but also the rise in bus fares and fact prices were rising against a backdrop of increasing industrial disputes that saw many fans having no income at all due to strikes.

Arthur Mercer of the Liverpool Supporters Club pointed out the higher costs of travel in the *Daily Post* on 25th September 1972 in addition to the hooligan problem. He recalled how in the 1960s it was possible to get a train ticket to London and one night's accommodation for £2.50, but now it was £5.20 just for a return on the train and meeting other supporters was now out of the question. He spoke of 'grand nights out drinking and swapping stories' in the 1960s, but now there was little sense of brotherhood and vicious things were happening to supporters at other grounds, with little concern being shown for the welfare of the travelling fan.

Mercer also raised the issue of players becoming more detached from the fans, with the club not allowing anyone to attend supporters' club functions due to the smoky atmosphere. At the end of 1971-72, the supporters' player of the year trophy had to be delivered to Anfield, rather than be presented to the winner in person at the club. This was a far cry from the 1964 title-winning season when Ian St John and Ron Yeats drank with fans in the Maid of Erin pub on Scotland Road after the 5-0 win against Arsenal that clinched the championship.

Worrying, too, was the increase in hooliganism. At the end of November FA secretary Denis Fellows, in response to rising incidents of hooliganism and pitch invasions, called for anybody under eighteen to be refused admission to terraced areas of the ground. He also called for more to be done by clubs to refuse known trouble-makers entry to the ground rather than just take their gate money, writing in *FA News*:

> 'We may, by this very act, bring back the decent people who tell us they are staying away because of the threats of young hooligans. I feel almost ashamed to put forward such a suggestion but we are not living in the old days of good order and respect for authority'.

However, Football League secretary Alan Hardaker didn't believe there was a rise in hooliganism at grounds, it was just a case of morbid publicity being given to it by tabloids. Writing in *League Football* on 2nd December, he said:

> 'The time has now come to ask Parliament what they are doing about the increasing violence which is appearing in all walks of life, in relation to which football's problems are just the tip of an offensive iceberg. I would suggest that some authority is immediately restored to the schools and that Members of Parliament should concern themselves with a campaign to back schoolteachers to the hilt in instilling in the young a vital need for self discipline'.

The Football League, though, did go to the extreme length of spending £250,000 on buying and fitting out a train especially for football fans, which could be leased by individual clubs. The first 'league liner' went from Burnley to London Euston on 27th January, taking 490 fans to a game at Queens Park Rangers and the first-class carriages were equipped with headphones, a disco, television and refreshment bar.

Liverpool fans themselves did not have a reputation for looking for trouble, with a league table compiled by police chiefs and unveiled at the beginning of October putting fans of the Reds and Southampton joint-bottom of a worst hooligans list that was topped by Chelsea and West Ham. George Forsythe, a superintendent from Coventry, told the *Liverpool Echo* on 2nd October: 'We've never had any trouble with Liverpool supporters, they've always been more interested in football than the aggro'. Peter Etherington sums up the general attitude of Liverpool fans at the time, which ties in with what Forsythe had said, saying in March 2012 that the main priority was to go for a day out and watch the football. He recalls that during 1972-73 in particular things seemed to get worse with trouble, at West Ham, for instance, where he 'got legged to the tube when there'd been no problems the previous year'. On the whole, though, Etherington remembers that if Liverpool fans got attacked, they would give it back but they never went looking for a fight, they were much more interested in watching the game.[88]

20

European Glory

UEFA Cup Final 1st Leg Liverpool v Borussia Mönchengladbach
Wednesday 9th May 1973 (abandoned)

Liverpool's opponents in the final would be Borussia Mönchengladbach, who had comfortably disposed of Twente Enschede in the other semi-final, 5-1 on aggregate, with Günter Netzer outstanding in both legs.

There was a word of warning, too, from Aberdeen manager Jimmy Bonthrone, whose side had been beaten by them in the first round, 3-2 at Pittodrie and 6-3 in West Germany, although the Dons had led 3-2 at one stage of the second leg. Warning of their attacking qualities he did save some optimistic words about their defending, saying:

> 'They are probably the most skilled attacking side I have ever seen and I think they're certainly the best Aberdeen have ever played. The whole side are geared for attacking and in this respect there is not a dud in the side. They are like Ajax or Celtic at their best. I don't see them changing their tactics to face Liverpool so they'll be two first rate games at least. They are not unbeatable. The defence, when you force them into defence, was not as well organised as Juventus for example'.[89]

Reds fan Chris Wood, a close observer of European club football, admitted he was nervous about the match, describing Borussia as an 'outstanding team bristling with players with talent of an international standard'. Borussia were third in the Bundesliga (although would eventually finish fifth) and despite the ominous signs Tommy Smith wasn't too concerned about their threat. He wrote in his column in the *Liverpool Echo* on 28th April that they had not had too difficult a route to the final and that Liverpool had shown their capabilities against Bundesliga opposition by eliminating Eintracht Frankfurt and also beating Bochum in a friendly. Netzer was also aware of the threat Liverpool posed, saying 'I consider Liverpool extraordinarily strong both physically and in the arts of the game'[90].

Despite the magnitude of the match it was not made all-ticket, with admission to the terraces being pay on the night. Eyebrows were raised, though, at the cost of seats, which rose to £2 as opposed to just £1 in previous rounds. The *Echo* reported on 30th April that this was down to additional levies that were being imposed. UEFA, who usually took 3% of gate receipts, were entitled to 10% for the final, while the Football League were allowed 4%. Since the beginning of April the government had also been taking 10% in VAT, which the club had been absorbing into their existing pricing structure. Despite the much higher cost of stand tickets, prices for terrace admission rose only slightly, up to 50p in the Kop and Anfield Road and 60p in the Paddock, a rise of 5p on earlier rounds and 10p on normal league prices. These still compared favourably, though, to what fans would be paying in the away leg, where the most expensive seat would cost £4.50 and the terraces £1.50. As well as having to deal with the applications for stand tickets, which were limited to shareholders and season-ticket holders, Liverpool were deluged with worldwide press interest. Requests for press box tickets were received from as far afield as Brazil, Japan and Kenya, with Australasia the only continent that would not be represented.

There were ten days between the last league match and the first leg of the final and after the euphoria of the title success had died down much of the *Liverpool Echo's* sports coverage was about the ongoing Everton managerial saga, with Bolton's Jimmy Armfield emerging as a frontrunner as soon as the season ended. However, he opted to remain with Bolton, whom he had just steered to the Third Division championship.

In the FA Cup final there was a shock as Sunderland beat Leeds 1-0, which Chris James described in the *Echo* as a shot in the arm for football, as their victory captured the imagination of families up and down the country. Liverpool confirmed, though, that they would not be accepting an invitation to face the Wearsiders in the Charity Shield. Bill Shankly explained that the club's training was geared to being in peak condition on the first day of the season, not a week before. This led to accusations that the Reds may have felt differently if Leeds would be the opposition and that they were being disrespectful to Sunderland, who relished the chance of facing the league champions. However, the *Daily Post* reported on 7th May that Peter Robinson had informed the FA before the final was played that Liverpool would not be taking part.

Borussia coach Hennes Weisweller's only chance to watch the Reds had been in the Leicester game, at which he would have seen a far different performance than they were capable of. He knew, though, that that hadn't been a true reflection of Liverpool's qualities and admitted he would have preferred to have faced Tottenham. Weisweller hinted that he would be looking to attack in the first leg and that his side needed to take a goal back to West Germany. Their route to the final had certainly indicated that they didn't like to sit back in the away leg, having only failed to win once en route to the final, when they drew 0-0 in the first leg of the third round in Cologne. However, Shankly said two days beforehand that he was taking no notice of what they said and it would have no bearing on what team he selected, remembering the Fairs Cup tie in 1969-70 when Vitoria Setubal threatened to build a defensive wall at Anfield, only to go on the attack and score two early goals.

Liverpool's spies Bob Paisley and Reuben Bennett had seen their attacking qualities at first hand on 2nd May, when they saw Borussia win 3-1 at Werder Bremen in the first leg of the West German cup semi-final, a trip that also saw them check out training facilities ahead of the second leg. As well as Netzer, they had other outstanding players in forward Josef Heynckes and defender Berti Vogts. These players were among nine who had been capped by West Germany and they also had Henning Jensen, a Danish international forward who had played alongside Emlyn Hughes in the Three v Six match in January to celebrate the expansion of the Common Market.

The day before the first leg Shanky had to interrupt his preparations when Emlyn Hughes's appeal against the sending-off he received against Birmingham in April was heard. Liverpool were livid at the timing of this but appeals to the FA by Peter Robinson and Eric Roberts fell on deaf ears. When it was pointed out that Shankly needed to be making last-minute preparations with his players and had arranged a press conference with attendees from fourteen countries, they simply suggested that Shankly wasn't compelled to attend the hearing. However, the thought of one of his players being unrepresented was one that the Reds boss wouldn't entertain. Writing in the *Daily Post* on 7th May Reds correspondent Horace Yates pulled no punches in a damning assessment of the situation:

> 'All this means nothing to the FA as they stubbornly dig in their heels. Doesn't it matter to them whether they win this final and bring further laurels to the sport? Would they rather have their pound of flesh and make things as awkward as they can? Seemingly so. The FA have the rest of the summer to find a suitable date to dispose of the Hughes case without upsetting anybody. Surely between now and August they can find a mutually acceptable date? The answer of course is that they could quite easily, if only they would. Not only are the FA refusing to be helpful, but they are determined to be just as unhelpful as they possibly can. What a contrast from the continental position. There, authority bends over backwards in its efforts to assist teams engaged in prestigious continental matches'.

At the appeal the sending-off was upheld, but there was a victory of sorts when the FA ruled that no three-match ban would have to be served. Shankly and Hughes then went straight to a country hotel for some rest, the manager revealing that he wasn't afraid to use a substitute if necessary. Whereas in league games he was wary of making a tactical substitution in case a player got injured, in European games two were allowed and he was happy to make use of the system if it could help win the tie. The ten days' recuperation since the last league game meant niggling injuries to Peter Cormack and Steve Heighway had cleared up and Shankly had a full complement of players to choose from.

Unlike previous opponents, Borussia declined the use of Southport's facilities and opted to stay in Liverpool city centre, where Weisweller acknowledged that he hadn't seen the real Reds against Leicester. He told the *Liverpool Echo* on the afternoon of the game:

'Their players were a little nervous knowing that they only needed one point to win the title. I expect Liverpool will be a more attacking side tonight than they were that day. It will be a good game and goals are going to be scored, we will attack – there will be no defensive stuff from us'.

As Shankly had earlier intimated, though, Weisweller was bluffing. In torrential rain Borussia sat back from the start, employing a man-marking system and with Günter Netzer playing as a sweeper rather than in his normal midfield role. In incredibly slippery conditions Kevin Keegan still managed to evade his marker Ulrich Surau on a number of occasions and Emlyn Hughes and Tommy Smith both had shots wide having been able to get forward due to Borussia's unwillingness to move out of their own half. Larry Lloyd had a header saved by the keeper who needed to dive at full flight and Peter Cormack headed wide from a tight angle after a cross by Steve Heighway. The Reds also had two strong penalty appeals, one when Keegan was felled by Rainer Bonhoff and another when Berti Vogts appeared to handle the ball.

However, with the rain continuing to lash down puddles soon started merging into small lakes and the wings looked like they had rivers flowing down them. With the ball constantly stopping dead in the water, it was clear the game couldn't continue and the Austrian referee Erich Linemayr took the teams off after 28 minutes to see if the rain would ease and give the groundsmen a chance to drain some of the water. The Kop chanted 'we want football' and 'ee aye adio we're not going home' but even they would have to admit that with no let-up in the rain, continuing with the game was impossible and twenty minutes later it was formally abandoned. It was not surprising the Kop were so desperate for football again, as announcer George Sephton remembers the first record he had to hand when the referee took the teams off didn't go down too well:

'When the referee took the teams off there was no way of telling if they were going off for two minutes or sixty. I remember saying to the crowd "I'll let you know as soon as I know what's happening and all I can do for now is play you some music." For some reason the first disc I grabbed was *Une Banc, Une Arbre Une Rue* by Severine which had won the Eurovision Song Contest a couple of years previously. That was one of the few times I was actually booed by the Anfield crowd![91]'

Tommy Smith believes the referee had no option but to do what he did. He remembered that it was akin to trying to play football in a two-inch deep paddling pool[92] and that it would have been more appropriate to wear flippers than football boots.[93] Even Bill Shankly, who would be up for a game of football anywhere, agreed there was no choice. He told the *Daily Post*:

> 'It was terribly unfortunate but inevitable just the same. Nobody could play football in those conditions. It was absolutely farcical and the referee was right to abandon the game. There were fifty yards of water along the pitch, I have never seen anything like it'.

However, Shankly did make sure he didn't let on to the referee that he wanted the game to be abandoned, in case it made him decide to play on. He wrote in his autobiography *Shankly My Story*, published in 1976:

> 'I had been down to see him and he said "if it doesn't get any better we will have to stop". I said "it's not too bad" because I knew these continentals. If I'd have said "oh yes put it off" he might have thought "oh, oh – he wants it off". So I said "it's not too bad really, I've seen worse grounds than that". He said "No, I was on it. I know. I'll go out and try to kick the ball on it". So he went out and when he came back he said "No the game is off until tomorrow". Boy, was I glad to hear that!'

It later transpired that the torrential nature of the downpour had damaged a drain, causing a piece of it to be wedged in a release, leading to the huge amount of surface water. Amazingly, given the time of year, it was the second time in three years that the first leg of the final had been abandoned. In 1971 when the competition was known as the Fairs Cup the match between Juventus and Leeds United in Turin was called to a halt after 51 minutes for the same reasons with the sides level at 0-0.

Liverpool: Clemence, Lawler, Lindsay, Smith, Lloyd, Hughes, Keegan, Cormack, Hall, Heighway, Callaghan. Subs: Lane, Storton, Toshack, Boersma, Thompson.

Borussia: Kleff, Danner, Surau, Vogts, Bonhoff, Kulik, Jensen, Wimmer, Rupp, Netzer, Heynckes.

Referee: Mr E. Linemayr (Austria).

Attendance: 44,967.

UEFA Cup Final 1st Leg Liverpool 3 Borussia Mönchengladbach 0 Thursday 10th May 1973

It was hastily arranged to replay the match the following night, with admission prices being fixed at 10p for all parts of the ground, although only holders of ticket stubs from the 9th May could enter the stands. Admission was set so low as the club did not want to be accused of cashing in by charging full-price two nights running, especially given the receipts of £40,000 had dwarfed the previous Anfield record takings of £28,500, set for a Fairs Cup semi-final against Leeds two years earlier. As such, a figure was arrived at that would just cover the costs of staging the game. Amongst the additional expenses incurred were £1,500 for police and stewards and £500 for an extra nights' hotel accommodation for the Borussia party.

However, the low admission price caused a worry for those who'd been on the terraces, as a rush of people looking to take advantage of the low price was predicted and many feared being locked out. The downpour had caught Anfield officials by surprise and, unlike when a European Cup game with Cologne was called off in 1965 and vouchers handed out as fans left, on this occasion no contingency plans had been made. Nobody had foreseen the severity of the storm and even half-an-hour before kick-off, there was never any doubt about the game taking place. When the rain did eventually stop it was followed by heavy wind which meant all surface water had gone from the pitch the following morning.

Despite the admission for the rearranged game being just 10p, it still posed problems for fan Phil Rimmer, who was a student in Wrexham at the time. He recalls:

'It certainly was the right decision as the ball was floating on the puddles when it passed along the ground. But I was now in a dilemma as I had already spent what money I had for the week. There were no debit cards and ATM machines then and my bank account was back home in Bolton! Fortunately a college friend who had no particular interest in football came to the rescue and offered to go to the game. Three of us went in a van and for two of them it was their first visit to Anfield'.

Another fan faced with travel problems was Chris Wood, who was due at work in London the next morning, but he recalls:

'My twin brother was in his final year at Liverpool University so I contacted him and was allocated a spare room in Rathbone Hall which did at least give me a bed for the night and the opportunity to ring work the next morning to take the day off'.

Both sides made a change for the re-match. For Borussia, Ulrich Surau, who had unsuccessfully tried to man-mark Kevin Keegan, was replaced by Heinz Michallik. For Liverpool, having seen that Borussia were weak in the air, Bill Shankly decided to exploit this and recalled John Toshack to the side at the expense of Brian Hall. In his autobiography *Tosh*, published in 1982 by Arthur Baker Ltd, Toshack claimed to have confronted Shankly at Anfield on the morning of re-arranged game, telling him: 'You've gone out at home in a European final playing with two men up because the Germans kidded you into believing they would attack. You can stuff your team, you'll be lucky to get a corner tonight.' Toshack then claims to have returned to his Formby home only to receive a call from Shankly who told him: 'Get to your bed, there is a good chance you'll be playing tonight'. Shankly, though, made no mention of any row in his own autobiography, stating that he had made the decision immediately after the abandonment, writing: 'I said to big John Toshack "Get away home to your bed son and get a rest for God's sake – you are playing tomorrow night"'.

Whatever the truth of the matter, Shankly's decision to play Toshack was a masterstroke as the big striker, starting his first game for two months, made two goals for Kevin Keegan as the Reds built up a resounding 3-0 lead to take to West Germany. Borussia were undone during a blistering twelve-minute spell around the midway point of the first half. In the 21st minute Toshack headed the ball across the goalmouth and Keegan dived in to score with a header from twelve yards that went into the corner of the net. Soon afterwards the Reds were awarded a penalty after a handball but Keegan's kick was saved by Wolfgang Kleff. However, in the 33rd minute he scored with a volley from ten yards, again after a knockdown by Toshack.

In the 62nd minute the Reds were awarded a corner taken by Keegan from the left, which Larry Lloyd rose to head powerfully into the net. Lloyd, who was more renowned for saving goals than scoring them, recalls the euphoria in his autobiography *Hard Man Hard Game*, published in 2008 by John Blake Publishing:

'This was an out of body experience, I nearly died on the spot. I've never known anything like it and doubt I will again. But that once in a lifetime moment is good enough for me. If I could have changed anything about that goal it would have been to score it at the Liverpool supporters' end. I headed the ball into the net from Keegan's corner. Oh I jumped and hugged and if I could have sprinted to the other end to leap about with those fabulous Liverpool supporters I would have – but I was a big f*cker and could leg it nowhere! As someone who has been dubbed the most under-estimated player of his time, I think of this mind blowing moment with pride. Sh*t I was f*cking good that day'.

It was only at 3-0 down that Borussia began attacking with any note, Netzer getting forward more and just three minutes after Lloyd's goal they were awarded a penalty, but Ray Clemence dived to his right to push the ball away and send the Kop wild. For the rest of the game the Reds defence didn't give an inch and contained them mainly to passing the ball around without being able to break through.

With the game being on a Thursday, an unheard of night for football at the time, there were strange scenes at the Liverpool Supporters Club in Lower Breck Road afterwards, as Chris Wood remembers:

'The BBC had planned to show the first leg highlights on the Wednesday evening and at short notice announced that they would show the highlights on the Thursday evening. So we trooped back to the supporters' club happy and excited at the thought of watching highlights of a most impressive victory against a very good team. However, on arrival inside the club, it was clear that Thursday Night was Bingo Night and nothing was going to change that. We were told that the television did not go on when it was Bingo Night. In the end a compromise was reached. We were allowed to gather around the television set in a corner of the room as long as we did not have the sound on. So that's what we did, trying to enjoy the highlights of the cup final while some men, but mainly women, of different ages were scrutinising their bloody bingo cards'.

As the supporters watched Ray Clemence's excellent penalty save again, the Reds keeper admitted he had done his homework on Josef Heynckes's penalty technique before the game, watching him take a kick against Kaiserslautern in the quarter-final. Shankly was full of praise for his players. Knowing they had beaten a top-class side, he told the *Liverpool Echo*:

'It was a fantastic performance by us, it was a high-class game, an international-class game. Both teams did well and it wasn't a case of what Borussia did wrong, it was what we did right. If we can sneak one in over there, they will have to score five to win'.

Liverpool: Clemence, Lawler, Lindsay, Smith, Lloyd, Hughes, Keegan, Cormack, Toshack, Heighway (Hall), Callaghan. Subs: Lane, Storton, Thompson, Boersma.

Borussia: Kleff, Danner, Michallik, Vogts, Bonhof, Kulik, Jensen, Wimmer, Rupp, Netzer, Heynckes.

Referee: Mr E. Linemayr (Austria).

Attendance: 41,169.

UEFA Cup Final 2nd Leg Borussia Mönchengladbach 2 Liverpool 0 Wednesday 23rd May 1973

Between the two games there was little time to rest for some of Liverpool's players with the Home International Championships starting less than 48 hours later. The tournament, which saw four of Liverpool's players away for over a week, was not how Bill Shankly would have liked to have seen his players spending their time between the two legs. But at least Ray Clemence, Emlyn Hughes, Kevin Keegan and John Toshack would be remaining in the British Isles and Shankly put his foot down when it came to the Republic of Ireland's plans, refusing to allow Steve Heighway to join their squad for away games with the USSR, Poland and France.

Two days after the final England manager Sir Alf Ramsey applied common sense and chose not to play any of the Reds three England players against Northern Ireland at Goodison Park. The game was switched there from Belfast for security reasons and the lack of any Liverpool players is likely to have been a factor in keeping the attendance down to 29,865.

The most ardent of Reds, though, would have said the most important game in the city that day was across Stanley Park at Anfield where Liverpool's reserves were parading the Central League trophy around the time the teams were kicking off at Goodison. The Reds second string, coached by Ronnie Moran, had kicked off at 1pm against Wolves and John McLaughlin scored twice in a 2-0 win that clinched their fourth title in five seasons. It bode well for the future, with many of the players in the side having been part of the team that reached the FA Youth Cup final the previous season. They included Brian Kettle, Derek Brownbill, Tommy Tynan and Dave Rylands. They were unable to make it a double two days later, though, when they lost the Liverpool Senior Cup final 2-1 against a strong Tranmere Rovers side at Prenton Park.

With the league season over, speculation was already starting about who would be arriving at Anfield for the following campaign. Shankly was angry, though, at reports linking the Reds with a £250,000 bid for Derby County's Colin Todd, telling the *Liverpool Echo* on 14th May: 'If you want to talk about another club's players I suggest you talk to the club concerned'. When the paper contacted the Baseball Ground manager Brian Clough was unavailable but a spokesperson described the Reds chances of securing their central defender as less than acquiring the Crown Jewels. Four full-time players were released from the club, though, the most well-known being midfielder Steven Arnold who had played twice for the first team in 1970-71. There was better news, though, for junior players Brian Kettle – who was given a full-time contract after being an apprentice – and Jimmy Case, who was upgraded from amateur to part-time status as he continued his electrical apprenticeship.

As Shankly worked with what players he did have available to train, it was frustrating that of the trio on England duty only Emlyn Hughes saw any action, playing for England against Wales on 15th May. There was bad news from this game for the Reds, though, as John Toshack, playing in opposition, strained his Achilles tendon to give the Reds boss a big injury headache ahead of the return leg of the final which was now just a week away. Toshack was immediately withdrawn from the Welsh squad due to play Northern Ireland on the following Saturday and returned to Anfield for treatment.

Shankly's mood was made better on the 18th, though, when he was named Manager of the Year, picking up a cheque for £1,000. Shankly had been the clear favourite, his only serious competition coming from Sunderland's Bob Stokoe who had steered his side away from the Second Division relegation zone and to FA Cup glory. The *Echo* revealed that Shankly had received a telegram from rival Don Revie, who had emerged as a candidate for the Everton job, which read: 'Sorry I can't be with you but my warmest congratulations to a great manager and a great friend'. While he was in

London for the awards, Shankly attended the independent tribunal against Tommy Smith's sending-off and finally had a disciplinary process go against him as Smith's ban was upheld. It meant the Reds captain would miss the first three games of the new season which Shankly described as a blow, telling the *Echo*: 'From a fitness point of view it is a bad time for Tommy to be out because you need the first two or three games to get your legs running again'.

Shankly's determination to keep the Reds machine rolling meant that rather than stay in London for the England v Scotland international, he returned to Merseyside to take in Northern Ireland v Wales at Goodison Park, watched by a pitifully low crowd of less than 3,000. Although he refused to say who he was going to watch, it was suspected that his target was Oxford United's Dave Roberts, but afterwards he said nobody had caught his eye and he may have been better off staying at Wembley.

It was only two days before the second leg that Shankly had his full squad together again for training, but there was a boost when John Toshack, the man Mönchengladbach feared most, passed a fitness test to secure his place in the sixteen. This didn't mean that their big Welshman was guaranteed a spot in the team, however, as there was every possibility that Shankly would adopt a change of tactics when defending a 3-0 lead. The day before the game Chris James speculated in the *Liverpool Echo* that Brian Hall might be used for his speed in counter attacks, or Phil Thompson could instead be brought in to shore up the midfield. For Borussia, their hopes of overturning the deficit were not helped by the fact Günter Netzer was struggling to shake-off a foot injury.

The match was to be played in the 35,000 Bökelberg Stadium, which contained only 2,000 seats. The home side knew it was inadequate for a game of this magnitude, especially as there were 10,000 British troops stationed in the town. However, negotiations about switching the game to Fortuna Dusseldorf's 70,000 capacity Rheinstadion twelve miles away broke down due to what Borussia perceived as unreasonable demands for a 25% portion of gate receipts.

Liverpool flew out the day before the game, taking the UEFA Cup with them on behalf of deposed holders Tottenham. After landing at Dusseldorf they stopped off to take a look at the ground on the way to the hotel and saw that what it lacked in capacity it certainly made up for in pitch quality. The grass was lush green all over, a stark contrast from the muddy pitches and dust bowls they had been playing on in England during the last few months. After an hour's training session at a local army camp, where Shankly gave an officer a tongue-lashing for initially only providing one ball, the players returned to their hotel. From there Shankly sent a 'good luck' telegram to Kirkby boxer John Conteh, who was fighting to become British and Commonwealth Light Heavyweight Champion at Wembley Arena.

Conteh went on to defeat defending champion Chris Finnegan on points and as he sat in his dressing room with an icepack afterwards, joked that he may perhaps send Shankly the longest cable he had ever received in return.[94]

The ground's low capacity meant that Liverpool's ticket allocation was just over 1,000, with the majority of fans being airlifted to West Germany on one of ten charter flights operating from Speke on the morning of the game at the cost of £26 for a daytrip and £36 for an overnight stay. It was the biggest Merseyside football airlift to date, beating the 800 fans who had travelled to Milan for the European Cup semi-final eight years earlier. Those travelling were given a boost by customs officials, who agreed to waive the rule on duty-free only being allowed back into the country if the traveller had been abroad for 24 hours or more.

Not everyone took the easy route, however, and despite not having tickets, eight intrepid fans set off at 7.30pm the night before from Dale Street in an old ambulance. Their journey was almost over before it began when the exhaust nearly fell off, but they were able to make a repair and set off on the journey to Dover, where they were catching a ferry at 5.30am. Chris Wood was another fan who travelled by ferry without a ticket, sailing overnight from Harwich to Hook of Holland and then by train to Mönchengladbach. Arriving at about 10am he took a bus to the ground where he was able to secure one of a small number tickets that had just gone on sale for the away terrace.

For Peter Etherington, though, he had had to forego the chance to watch the Reds claim their first European trophy thanks to the efficiency of the Skelmersdale housing department. Back living with his mum at the time, he had agreed that if they could find a place of their own, he and his wife would get back together. But he was absolutely gutted at having to miss out on a place on one of the charter flights. He recalls:

'Only three weeks after going on the housing list in Skem they came up with the goods for us. We went to look at a three bedroomed house. This was our chance to get back together and I was missing little Stevie so much we jumped at it. There's always a snag. This was that, we would have to move in on 21st May – two days before I was due to fly to West Germany for the second leg of the final. Of course I had to put my wife and child first so there was no way I could go. It was with a heavy heart I went to Towns to cancel the flight. They kept my five pounds deposit for my trouble, which was nice of them!'

Despite trailing 3-0, Hennes Weisweiler still believed it was possible to overturn the deficit. They had twice managed to score four goals in domestic games since the first leg and the Borussia manager was brief but to the point beforehand, saying: 'We are still in this tie with a chance, I believe we can still win'. Shankly was certainly not seeing the second leg as a formality, telling reporters 'We are under no illusions, this game is not over'. Tommy Smith, a veteran of European heartbreaks against Inter Milan in the 1965 European Cup semi-final and Borussia Dortmund in the Cup Winners Cup final a year later, made it clear he had no intention of being on the losing side this time. 'Who would not be confident with a three-goal start', he said, 'I'll bet the Germans would like to be in our shoes. I have been in two big European games before when we lost, I don't intend to see another prize slip away from us'. [95]

After the gates opened, the home supporters packed almost every inch of terracing in the tiny ground and greeted the teams with a wall of noise, blowing horns and chanting their side's name. Behind one goal, Liverpool's fans, who numbered about 4,000 when local soldiers and those travelling independently were taken into account, did their best to turn the terrace into a mini-Kop, waving red and white flags and chanting as loudly as they could. The Reds' contingent did see their side achieve European glory, but it was a far closer call than they would have liked, as Borussia stormed into a 2-0 lead within half-an-hour thanks to a fantastic display of fast-passing football only for the Reds to hang on in the second half.

On a stormy night it wasn't just in the distance that thunder clapped and lightning struck, as Borussia tore into the Reds from the kick-off. Günter Netzer had shaken off his foot injury and was pulling the strings in midfield, pinging passes around with supreme accuracy. Behind him Berti Vogts was calm and composed building moves out of defence, and up front Bernd Rupp and Jupp Heynckes were a constant threat. Whether it was in trying to combat long passes or short bursting one-twos, Liverpool had no answer to Borussia in the first half. The inevitable first goal came on the half-hour when Rupp got to the byline and crossed for Heynckes to score from close range. In the 39th minute it was 2-0 with Heynckes again the scorer, this time hitting a beautiful curling shot from the left corner of the penalty area.

Half-time couldn't come quickly enough for the Reds players so they were able to receive instructions from Shankly and re-group. They did so in supreme fashion. Tommy Smith made countless interceptions and tackles, putting in a tremendous captain's performance and organising the rest of the side, keeping up their morale. Chris Lawler was faultless and Larry Lloyd commanding over Rupp, while Alec Lindsay was much more confident after half-time, and when the Reds rearguard was breached, Ray Clemence was alert to the danger and quick to get off his line and handle the ball well. Peter Cormack, Emlyn Hughes and Ian Callaghan spent most of the game helping the defence out, with even Kevin Keegan dropping back on numerous occasions. Chris Wood remembers that Mönchengladbach had blown the Reds away in the first half but were a different and more tired team in the second. However, as the half wore on and with no away goal forthcoming, he recalls sitting on the terrace with about ten minutes to go, only to be asked if he was alright by a fellow supporter. He then realised that if he had travelled all that way he was going to make sure he saw Liverpool win the cup so stood back up, just as Ian Callaghan tangled with a Borussia forward and there were big shouts for a penalty. Phil Thompson recalls being sat on the bench as the minutes ticked away:

> 'Our bench was quite a way down the touchline, near the edge of the penalty area. Netzer and Heynckes were knocking the ball around unbelievably in the first half but the game eventually petered out. For most of the second half Shanks was pacing up and down pointing at our fans, as if to say "don't worry". Sometimes he didn't seem to be watching, maybe because he was so nervous'.[96]

As the half wore on Liverpool managed to gain control, Borussia having run themselves into the ground, and although Heighway, Toshack and Boersma (who came on for Heighway after 77 minutes and operated as a lone striker) all missed chances, it wasn't to matter as the Reds held on to claim the cup. Finally, as Alec Lindsay hit a ball clear upfield, the whistle blew and Liverpool's UEFA Cup journey, which had taken them a total of 8,000 miles had now come full circle and ended in glory just 120 miles from Frankfurt, their first destination back in September.

For the presentation, UEFA officials carried a large table onto the pitch. Tommy Smith recalls in *Anfield Iron:*

> 'I did wonder why two UEFA officials handed it to me. When I took hold of it I found out. The UEFA Cup must be the largest major trophy in world football; what's more it has a heavy marble base. I was exhausted after the sheer effort of the match but I felt I had no option but to lead the lads on the traditional lap of honour. The UEFA Cup has no handles either so it is difficult to hold at the best of times. We hadn't gone far when I turned to Cally so he could brandish it for all of our supporters to see. Cally carried it for about six yards then handed it back saying "I can't carry this it weighs a ton!" No one else fancied carrying it either so I held it aloft for the duration of the lap. When I entered our dressing room still carrying the UEFA Cup I saw Shanks sitting down mulling over his first major European trophy. "Here you are boss", I said handing him the cup, "It's all yours". To be honest I was glad to be rid of the thing, I don't think I could have carried it another yard'.

During the lap of honour, many Liverpool fans had managed to get onto the pitch but it was all good-natured, although when one jumped on Smith's back the Reds captain turned round and warned him he may end up with the cup over his head if he didn't get off. Chris Wood remembers that as soon as the whistle went the Liverpool end was 'bouncing', with the Reds having lots more fans in the ground than initially anticipated. After following the lead set by others and climbing over the fence, he recalls running alongside Emlyn Hughes for several seconds. Phil Thompson's brother Owen was one of the fans on the pitch, having taken his UEFA flag that had been brought home from the previous summer's Mini World Cup in Spain as a momento. Although an unused substitute in both legs of the final, Thompson still felt very much involved and acknowledges that at the age he was he couldn't expect to play every week. By adding a UEFA Cup winning medal to his league championship medal he had now secured a personal treble, as he also had also played enough reserve games to qualify for a Central League medal as well.

Revealing the secret of his half-time team talk that galvanised the players, Shankly told the *Liverpool Echo* afterwards:

'I told the players not to panic because the Germans still had to score two more goals if they were to win the cup. I told the defence to make the pitch shorter by pushing up out of the penalty area in support of the attack instead of sitting on top of the goalkeeper. We did this and after ten more minutes Borussia had run themselves out. Once they began to tire I knew that we would win the cup'.

Skipper Tommy Smith admitted to the *Echo* that he had been worried at half time:

'I was worried, who wouldn't be, when our lead was suddenly one. But they blew up after ten minutes of the second half. They had no strength left after they had put so much into the first half. We lasted the better towards the end and we had a couple of chances'

Borussia coach Hennes Weisweiler was naturally disappointed not to overturn the deficit but acknowledged Liverpool's qualities, telling the press: 'We were unlucky not to get at least a third goal. I thought we had earned it but Liverpool were a far different side in the second half. They are very strong and one of the best teams in Europe without a doubt'.[97]

After a brief and private celebration in Mönchengladbach's clubhouse, the players went to Cologne Airport where they took off for Speke on a BAC 1-11 plane and even at 28,000 feet Shankly was already turning his thoughts to an assault on Europe's greatest prize the next season. He told journalists 'The people on the continent are beginning to get frightened of Liverpool, Günter Netzer told me so tonight. Next season we're playing in Europe again, playing in the number one competition – the European Cup'.[98] While he plotted more European domination, the players were taking it in turns to sing songs over the microphone before Shankly himself took centre stage not to sing, but to pay tribute to all those who had made the season such a successful one. Their aircraft landed at Speke at 2.16am, where 3,000 fans had gathered to greet them. As well as the fans on the viewing balcony, several hundred more were on the tarmac, having just got off supporters' flights and they mobbed the players as they came down the steps and went through customs.

Back in Mönchengladbach Chris Wood, who had missed an important exam to attend this game, had returned to the city centre and was drinking in a bar near the station run by two Englishmen that stayed open until 3am, before finally finding a quiet corner to grab some sleep. As fans who had travelled independently started to board trains during the morning rush hour, they made the locals fully aware of who they were and why they were there. On the train back to Holland, one of Wood's companions would shout of the window at every station 'Wir haben den pokal gewonnen', translated simply as 'we won the cup'. On the North Sea crossing, an Ajax fan congratulated him on Liverpool's triumph, but said that he'd see the real champions of Europe the following week, referring to his club's forthcoming European Cup final with Juventus in Belgrade. That didn't detract, though, from what he remembers as 'about the highest high we felt we could experience', knowing that the Reds, along with being league champions for the first time in seven years, had finally won a European trophy after the near-misses of 1965 and 1966.

On the Friday night the triumphant squad, minus Ray Clemence and Emlyn Hughes, who were in Czechoslovakia with England, and Steve Heighway, who was on holiday, undertook a bus tour of the city. They departed from Anfield at 6.15pm, although only after John Toshack and Alec Lindsay had rushed back into the ground to retrieve the trophies – which none of the party had taken onto the Southport corporation bus. Once the League Championship, Central League and UEFA Cup trophies were safely aboard, they headed down Arkles Lane and Utting Avenue to Queens Drive, along there to Allerton Road and back towards the city centre via Smithdown Road, Ullett Road, Park Road and Great George Street. Once in the city centre, they went down Berry Street, Renshaw Street, Ranelagh Street, Church Street and Lord Street (neither of which were pedestrianised then), North John Street, Dale Street, Exchange Street East, Tithebarn Street, Great Crosshall Street and Byrom Street eventually ending up at the Picton Library.

An estimated 250,000 lined the route, with around 20,000 being in the vicinity of Picton Library. There was a huge cheer when Shankly stepped off the bus outside the library and onto a dais, followed by Tommy Smith who was carrying the UEFA Cup. After a rousing chorus of *You'll Never Walk Alone* and chant of 'Champions' Shankly told those who had gathered:

'This is the greatest day of my career, if there is any doubt that you are the greatest fans in the world this is the night to prove it. We have won something for you and that's all we are interested in, winning for you. The reason we have won is because we believe and you believe. Thank God you are all here, you don't know how proud we are, you don't know how much we love you'.

There were also cheers for John Conteh, who displayed his championship belt, having been invited to join the team on the bus and he admitted getting on it was more nerve-wracking than entering the boxing ring. As the crowds finally began to disperse, the players and Conteh joined Lord Mayor Frank Burke for a civic reception in the Walker Art Gallery.

As the majority of Liverpool's players went for a well-earned holiday in Majorca, Shankly remained at his desk for another week to tie-up some loose ends. As he looked forward to taking part in the following season's European Cup, he was unimpressed by the quality of that year's final, in which Ajax beat Juventus 1-0 in Belgrade to secure a third successive triumph. Describing Johnny Rep's winning goal as one that any English First Division keeper should have saved, he told the *Liverpool Echo:* 'There's no doubt about the quality of the teams but the way they played last night, the way they strolled about, maybe would have got the bird over here.'

Despite the European glory, though, the league championship was the one that mattered most to Shankly. Sat beside the championship trophy in a television interview, he jabbed it and said: 'The main thing in our bread and butter is this, that's what we want to win all the time and this is the one that we want'.

Liverpool: Clemence, Lawler, Lindsay, Smith, Hughes, Keegan, Cormack, Toshack, Heighway (Boersma), Callaghan. Subs: Lane, Hall, Storton, Thompson.

Borussia: Kleff, Surau, Netzer, Bonhof, Vogts, Wimmer, Danner, Kulik Jensen, Rupp, Heynckes. Subs: Simonsen, Michallik, Sielof,Schrege.

Referee: Mr P. Kazakov (Soviet Union).

Attendance: 34,905.

21

The Legacy of 1972-73

On reflection, Bill Shankly believed 1972-73 was Liverpool's greatest season, telling the *Liverpool Echo* on the day of the victory parade:

'There's no doubt about it, we've achieved so much this season especially when you consider the games we've played. It's definitely been my greatest year with Liverpool and the side will get better yet, we can still achieve much more'.

Shankly's prediction was not wrong. The 1972-73 side that became the first English team to win the championship and a European trophy in the same season set the foundations for the glory that followed.

Unbelievably, Bill Shankly's achievements that year went unnoticed and he was overlooked in the Honours List, while Bobby Charlton, who announced his retirement from playing, had his OBE upgraded to a CBE. Fans were furious and campaigned on his behalf, but the following year, after Shankly had added another FA Cup to the trophy cabinet and retired himself, the situation was finally rectified when a new government, led by Huyton MP Harold Wilson, awarded him the OBE. Brian Reade was one of those furious fans, but Shankly was typically modest and nonplussed by the snub. Reade recalls in *43 Years With The Same Bird* that when he sent Shankly his reply from then Leader of the Opposition Harold Wilson stating there was nothing he could do, Shanks' letter back simply said 'The people who dish out honours are not my kind of people, my people go to Anfield. If I can make you all happy, then that is my greatest ambition'.

There was no doubt that Shankly had succeeded in his ambition of making the people happy and started a process that ensured they would be for many years more. After the win against Leeds, chairman Eric Roberts had made a bold prediction that 'Mr Shankly has welded a tremendous side together and the future could hardly be brighter. We have the makings of another five years' glory side here'.[99] He was only half right, as Liverpool went on to dominate football for the next two decades. Even though Shankly would retire little more than a year later, Bob Paisley seamlessly took over the managerial reins and led the club to even greater success. In the next twenty seasons, only in 1975, 1985, 1987, 1991 and 1993 did silverware fail to end up in the Anfield trophy room.

Shankly had proved that you don't need to spend big to win the title.

Whereas the likes of Arsenal and Manchester United had spent £200,000-plus on players, Liverpool's side had been put together by carefully scouring the lower divisions and blending players with potential into great ones.

Phil Thompson recalls how well the side gelled together and how the younger players were aided by the older ones, an essential part of a winning team:

> 'It was nice to come into the side at that time. With Smithy, Cally and Chris Lawler we had a Scouse heart. Tommy Smith was great to me when I forced my way into contention, as was Emlyn. They really looked after me, there was a peer thing in the dressing room with the older more experienced players showing the younger ones the ropes. It was like I was just coming out of junior school into senior school and getting shown how things were done by the prefects. We were all taught to enjoy it and also to have the nights out but there was a time when you stopped drinking and prepared for the game in a professional manner. At Liverpool you had to get 8, 9 or 10 out of 10 every week, standards weren't allowed to slip. I believe the way I was helped along put me in good stead for later in my career when I was captain and gave advice to Ian Rush, Steve Nicol and Ronnie Whelan when they came into the side'.[100]

Of the strongest starting eleven, only Peter Cormack and Emlyn Hughes had been signed from First Division clubs and both had been relegated in the seasons that they signed. Ray Clemence, Kevin Keegan, Alec Lindsay, Larry Lloyd and John Toshack had come from the lower divisions, Steve Heighway from amateur football and Ian Callaghan, Chris Lawler and Tommy Smith through the ranks. Of those who didn't start as regularly, Phil Boersma and Phil Thompson had been youth players at the club and Brian Hall had joined from university.It was a policy that was to pay dividends throughout the next ten years, with Joey Jones, Phil Neal and Ian Rush being plucked from the English lower divisions by Shankly's successor, Bob Paisley, and going on to great success. Also there was Alan Hansen and Steve Nicol from lesser-known Scottish clubs and Ronnie Whelan from amateur football in Ireland. There were occasions, of course, when Liverpool did spend big, such as when Kenny Dalglish arrived for £440,000 from Celtic in 1977, but even then the Reds were up on the deal as Kevin Keegan had been sold to Hamburg for £500,000.

The glories that followed and the passage of time have meant that the achievements of 1972-73 have been forgotten by many Liverpool fans. However, it is debatable that had Liverpool not achieved what they did that season, the success of later years may not have happened.

Appendix 1. The Players

During the course of 1972-73 Liverpool used just sixteen players in the league, two of whom only played five games between them. Of the fourteen players who featured prominently ten of them were effectively automatic choices when they were fit, three being ever-presents and three more missing just one league game. Phil Boersma and John Toshack were more or less in direct competition for a place while Brian Hall was very much a spare man, filling in across the midfield or up front when somebody was unavailable after he lost his place early in the season to Peter Cormack. Phil Thompson, who played fourteen league games, was initially in the side when Tommy Smith was unavailable, although he would play in midfield with Emlyn Hughes dropping back into defence. He performed so well, though, that in some games towards the end of the season, he was able to command a place of his own and it was other midfielders who were making way for him.

The three ever-presents in the league – Ian Callaghan, Chris Lawler and Larry Lloyd – also played in every cup game during the campaign, with the UEFA Cup appearance statistics mirroring those of the league. Only one player, Jack Whitham, didn't feature in a league game but he did play in a cup tie and in his case it was limited to just sixteen minutes of action. In addition to the seventeen players who appeared on the pitch, another six were unused substitutes during the campaign.

Ian Callaghan (66 games)

By 1972-73 Callaghan was Liverpool's longest serving player and during the course of the season he overtook Billy Liddell's club appearance record. He may have only scored three league goals during the campaign but that does not tell the story of his contribution, which was one of quiet efficiency in the middle of the park, breaking up opposition play and using his vision to begin attacks for the Reds. Callaghan continued playing at Liverpool until 1977-78, finishing his Reds career with a total of 857 games, a figure that it is hard to see being overtaken. After leaving Liverpool he joined and played for John Toshack at Swansea City where he remained for three seasons and finally hung up his boots shortly before his 40th birthday in 1981-82 after a brief stint with Crewe Alexandra. Now living in Lydiate, after finishing playing Callaghan moved into pubs and the insurance business and is still a regular visitor to Anfield.

Chris Lawler (66 games)

Another player who surpassed Billy Liddell's appearance total during 1972-73, Lawler was one of three survivors from the 1966 title-winning side. He had first appeared in 1962-63 and played six games in 1963-64, but not enough to earn a championship medal. After ousting Ronnie Moran from the side in 1964-65, he was a solid defender who had an incredible habit of ghosting unnoticed into the box and weighing in with several important goals. His four goals in 1972-73, still a respectable total for a full back, was his lowest total since 1967-68. An injury sustained in December 1973 meant he lost his place in the side to Phil Thompson, although he was an unused substitute for the 1974 FA Cup final. After making just ten appearances in 1974-75, Lawler joined Portsmouth and later played for Stockport County. He returned to Anfield in 1983 and managed the Reds reserve side for three seasons, before moving to North Wales where he managed Cemaes Bay. He is still involved in the game in a scouting and youth coaching capacity.

Larry Lloyd (66 games)

Lloyd was one of the players who made the breakthrough after Liverpool's FA Cup defeat to Watford in February 1970, establishing himself in the side as a centre back in place of Ron Yeats, who moved to left back. Lloyd had signed from Bristol Rovers in April 1969 but made just three appearances prior to the Watford game. In 1972-73 he was an ever present and put in several impressive displays at the heart of the Reds defence, while also lending his height and weight to attack, scoring two league goals as well as the crucial third in the first leg of the UEFA Cup final. Lloyd looked set for a long career at Anfield. However, towards the end of 1973-74 a defensive reshuffle saw Tommy Smith move to right back, with Phil Thompson and Emlyn Hughes playing in the middle as Shankly looked to build-up attacks from the back. Lloyd was sold to Coventry in the summer of 1974 but he later went on to greater glory with Nottingham Forest, winning the First Division Championship and two European Cups. In the early to mid-1980s he had spells as manager of Wigan Athletic and Notts County before drifting out of active involvement in the game, instead focusing on pubs and media work in the Nottingham area and working for a property development company in Spain.

Emlyn Hughes (65 games)

The son of a professional rugby league player, Hughes signed from Blackpool for £65,000 in February 1967 and immediately established himself in the side at left half. During the 1972-73 season he surpassed the 300 game mark and his marauding runs from midfield and crucial goals, none more so than his double at Goodison Park in March, made him a contender for player of the season. The following season Hughes moved into central defence where he formed an effective partnership with Phil Thompson and was also appointed club captain. Hughes moved to left back following the emergence of Alan Hansen in 1977-78 and in the summer of 1979 joined Wolverhampton Wanderers, captaining them to League Cup success in 1980. After a brief managerial stint with Rotherham United, he wound down his playing career with Swansea City, Hull City and Mansfield before concentrating on his business interests and media work. Hughes died on 9th November 2004 aged 57 after a long battle against a brain tumour. He has been honoured with a statue and office building named after him in his home town of Barrow-in-Furness.

Kevin Keegan (64 games)

Signed from Scunthorpe United a few days before the 1971 FA Cup final, Keegan impressed enough in a few reserve friendlies to claim a place in the first team for the opening day of the 1971-72 season, scoring against Nottingham Forest. In 1972-73 he was Liverpool's leading scorer with 22 goals in all competitions, double his tally from the previous season. His boundless enthusiasm and energy and ability to do the unexpected made him a key player for the Reds and his performances were rewarded with his first England caps. Keegan remained at Anfield until 1977 when he joined Hamburg for £500,000, where he won the Bundesliga and played against Nottingham Forest in the 1980 European Cup final. In 1980 he returned to England to play for Southampton and later Newcastle, winning promotion to the First Division with them in 1983-84 before retiring from playing. After seemingly being happy out of the game he answered a managerial SOS from Newcastle in 1992 as they faced relegation to the Third Division. After securing their status he led them to the Premiership where they looked set to win the title in 1996, only to lose a twelve-point lead on Manchester United. After resigning in 1997, Keegan later managed Fulham, England, Manchester City and Newcastle again but has been out of the game since 2008 and concentrating on media work and his own business interests.

Ray Clemence (64 games)

Like Keegan, Clemence had joined Liverpool from Scunthorpe United, although he had to wait nearly three seasons before establishing himself in the side, being another player to benefit from the shake-up that followed the FA Cup defeat to Watford in February 1970. In his first full season Clemence was the last line of the meanest defence the First Division had ever seen as he conceded just 22 goals in 41 appearances, the other two being conceded by Tommy Lawrence. Clemence went on to break this record again, in 1978-

79 when the Reds let in just sixteen goals. In 1972-73 Clemence missed two games due to a thigh injury but was otherwise a crucial player for the Reds, making a number of key saves and earning his first England cap. His best moment came in the second half of the first leg of the UEFA Cup final when he guessed right and saved a Jupp Heynckes penalty, which proved pivotal given the Reds lost the second leg 2-0. After 665 appearances and 335 clean sheets for the Reds, Clemence left for Tottenham Hotspur in 1981, winning the FA Cup and playing until he was 40. After retiring in 1988 he went into a coaching role with Spurs before jointly managing them in 1992-93 with another former Red, Doug Livermore. After managing Barnet from 1994 to 1996 he joined the England set-up and is now overseeing the Under 16 to Under 20 sides.

Steve Heighway (62 games)

Signed from Skelmersdale United in May 1970, Heighway had initially been considering going into teaching after gaining a degree from Warwick University. He burst onto the scene the following November, inspiring a memorable comeback against Everton when he scored one and made one for John Toshack as the Reds came from 2-0 down to win 3-2. He also established himself in the Republic of Ireland side that season and scored the opening goal of the FA Cup final, which the Reds lost 2-1 to Arsenal. In 1972-73 he continued to terrorise defenders leaving them trailing in his wake and as well as creating goals, managed to score ten in all competitions himself, including the vital away goal in the UEFA Cup semi-final against Tottenham. Heighway remained at Anfield until 1981 when he moved to the USA to play for Minnesota Kicks. He remained in America coaching until 1989 when he returned to Liverpool to take on a role in the club's youth development side. He oversaw the progress of Steve McManaman, Robbie Fowler, Steven Gerrard and Jamie Carragher to the first team and left the club in 2007 after a second successive FA Youth Cup triumph.

Alec Lindsay (59 games)

Initially signed from Bury as a left half in March 1969, Lindsay seized his chance at left back towards the end of 1970-71 after Ian Ross and Roy Evans had failed to make the position their own. During 1972-73 his ability to make overlapping runs, strong left foot and eye for a set-piece meant he scored five goals in addition to his impressive contribution in defence. Midway through 1974-75 Lindsay lost his place to Phil Neal but stayed with the Reds until the summer of 1977, making just twelve appearances in his final two seasons. After a season with Stoke City he went to the North American Soccer League, playing for Oakland Stompers and Toronto Blizzard before returning to the North West where he became a publican in Leigh.

Peter Cormack (52 games)

Liverpool's one major signing prior to the beginning of the season, Scottish international Cormack had already been in England two years with Nottingham Forest after moving there from Hibernian in 1970. An injury sustained in the pre-season friendly at Bochum postponed his competitive debut and he also missed some matches during the campaign. However, when he played, his ability to get forward and find goalscoring positions was invaluable, as he endeared himself to the Kop with the winning goal in the first derby of the season. His tally of ten goals in all competitions was a telling contribution to the season's success. Cormack enjoyed another two seasons as a regular but in 1975-76 lost his place as Ray Kennedy made the successful conversion to midfield. After moving to Bristol City at the end of that season he spent four years there before returning to Scotland to finish his career with Hibernian and Partick Thistle. He spent four years managing Partick in the early 1980s and has also managed Anorthosis, Botswana and Greenock Morton. He now works on the after-dinner speaking circuit.

Tommy Smith (49 games)

Liverpool's captain in 1972-73, Smith had joined Liverpool as an apprentice during the Second Division days and established himself in the side during the 1964-65 season. His season was twice interrupted, first by a calf injury and then by cracking four ribs in a car crash. He was also unfortunate to miss four penalties during the season as well as to get sent off for the only time in his career. However, his solid tackling and leadership qualities were a key part of Liverpool's success. Smith stayed with Liverpool for five more years as his versatility allowed him to command a place anywhere across the back four while his greatest moment came in the 1977 European Cup final when he headed Liverpool's second goal. Smith spent a season with Swansea City before retiring as a player and re-joining Liverpool for a brief stint as a youth coach. He now works as an after-dinner speaker and newspaper columnist. In February 2012 Smith's 1973 UEFA Cup-winning medal was bought by Liverpool FC for display in the club museum.

John Toshack (40 games)

Signed from Cardiff City in November 1970 for a club record £110,000, Toshack endeared himself immediately by scoring against Everton on only his second appearance. He started 1972-73 in blistering form but as the season went on was sacrificed as Bill Shankly opted for the speed and counter-attacking qualities of Brian Hall or Phil Boersma. His campaign was also upset by niggling leg injuries that saw him play through the pain barrier for four months. Despite these problems he was still the club's second highest scorer with seventeen goals from forty appearances, ending the season on a high when he was recalled to the side for the re-arranged UEFA Cup final first leg and set up two goals for Kevin Keegan. Toshack left Liverpool in February 1978 to become player-manager of Swansea City, taking them from the Fourth to the First Division. He has since gone on to enjoy a successful managerial career abroad, mainly in Spain where he has taken charge of Real Madrid, Real Sociedad, Real Murcia and Deportivo La Coruna. After six years in charge of Wales, in August 2011 he was appointed manager of the Macedonian national side and also works as a television pundit.

Brian Hall (31 games)

Hall signed for Liverpool as an amateur in 1966 while he was still studying for a mathematics degree at university. He broke into the team in 1970-71 when Ian Callaghan was injured, making such an impact that when Callaghan returned it was in central midfield. Hall's most memorable moment came when he scored the winning goal against Everton in the 1971 FA Cup semi-final, but when Peter Cormack arrived it was his place that was most under threat. With Cormack being injured at the start of the season, Hall stated his intention not to let his place go with a goal in the opening game of the season against Manchester City, although ultimately it would be him who made way. However, he did fight his way back into the side in the second half of the season to make a telling contribution, scoring the opening goal of the UEFA Cup quarter final against Dynamo Dresden. However, there would be subsequent heartbreak in the final, when he was dropped to make way for John Toshack in the re-arranged game, having started the one that was abandoned. In 1976 Hall moved to Plymouth Argyle and later played for Burnley. After retiring from playing he was a teacher before returning to Anfield in 1991 as the club's community liaison officer, a post he held until his retirement on health grounds in 2011.

Phil Boersma (31 games)

Although he had made his Liverpool debut in 1969-70 after progressing through the youth ranks, Boersma's appearances before 1972-73 had been limited due to the presence of Alun Evans, Kevin Keegan and John Toshack. However, this was the season in which he finally established himself as a First Division player, initially replacing an injured Toshack and then holding his place in the team as Bill Shankly preferred to move the ball quickly along the ground. He scored a respectable thirteen goals from thirty-one appearances, including an important matchwinner at Leeds and two at Coventry in April that took the Reds to the brink of the title. He also managed to find the net in four rounds of the UEFA Cup. However, at the end of the season he found himself back out of the side as Brian Hall re-established himself, and during the next two seasons Boersma found himself unable to match his games tally of 1972-73. In 1975 he left the club to join Middlesbrough, where he established a friendship with Graeme Souness that would lead to him returning to Anfield in a backroom role between 1991 and 1994 when Souness was manager. His most recent involvement in football was in 2008 when he was assistant manager at Welsh side Llangefni Town.

Phil Thompson (20 games)

Like Boersma, Thompson was from Kirkby and came through the youth ranks at Anfield, making his first team debut as a substitute at Old Trafford in April 1972 and being a member of the side that reached that year's FA Youth Cup final. He would likely have figured in more games in 1972-73 had he not been injured in pre-season, having to wait until October for his first appearance at Norwich as a replacement for Alec Lindsay. In December he got a brief run in the side after Tommy Smith was injured in a car crash and then forced his way back in in March for the title run-in, completing the fourteen games needed for a medal. However, he had to make do with a place on the bench for both legs of the UEFA Cup final. All his appearances were in midfield, but in 1973-74 he was moved back into defence where he formed an effective partnership with Emlyn Hughes and then Alan Hansen until 1982. Injury and the emergence of Mark Lawrenson saw him lose his place towards the end of 1982-83 and after nearly two seasons in the reserves he joined Sheffield United in 1985. His spell at Bramall Lane was brief and in 1986 he was back at Anfield as reserve team coach, a position he held until he was dismissed by Graeme Souness in 1992. Six years later he was back at the club as assistant to Gerard Houllier and spent six months as caretaker manager in 2001-02 after the Frenchman had heart surgery. Houllier and Thompson left the club in 2004 and since then he has worked as a television pundit, his passion for Liverpool FC never wavering.

Trevor Storton (10 games)

Storton had played over 100 games for Tranmere Rovers as a striker, although when he joined Liverpool in the summer of 1972 it was as a defender. Injuries to Tommy Smith allowed him to make ten appearances in the first half of the season but he was dropped following the League Cup defeat at Tottenham and didn't feature again as Phil Thompson emerged, although he was an unused substitute in both legs of the UEFA Cup final. After just two appearances in 1973-74, he was sold to Chester, where he played 468 games in the next ten years. He later returned to his native Yorkshire, setting up a window cleaning business and managing Bradford Park Avenue in the Northern Premier League for seven years. After working as a coach with Harrogate Town he was appointed assistant manager of FC Halifax Town in 2009, but after being diagnosed with cancer he died on 23rd March 2011 aged 61.

Frank Lane (2 games)

A former train driver, keeper Lane had joined in 1971 as cover for Ray Clemence. He made two appearances in 1972-73 as Ray Clemence rested a thigh injury, but was unfortunate to score an own goal away to Derby County when he caught a cross and stepped back over the line. He was on the bench for eleven of Liverpool's twelve UEFA Cup games, including both legs of the final. He never played any more games for the Reds, moving to Notts County in 1975 where he was also second choice. He later played in non-league for Kettering Town and Bedford Town and died on 19th May 1911 aged 62.

Jack Whitham (1 game)

Signed in 1970 from Sheffield Wednesday for £57,000, Whitham was a striker whose opportunities were limited by injury and the form of others. After recovering from almost a year out with knee and back problems he was given a sixteen-minute run-out in the UEFA Cup against Dynamo Berlin in December, but his injury jinx struck again and he made no more appearances for the club. In the summer of 1974 he left to join Cardiff City and, after a season there and one with Reading, he drifted into the non-league scene. He remains actively involved in the game today having scouted for Sunderland, Wolverhampton Wanderers, Luton Town and Sheffield United, and away from football he has been a publican and also achieved acclaim as an acoustic singer/songwriter in the Sheffield area.

John Webb (6 unused substitute)

A twenty-year-old defender who had fought back from a broken leg, Webb came on as a substitute in the pre-season game at Bochum but he didn't make it onto the pitch again during the season. He was on the bench for five UEFA Cup games and once in the league, away to West Bromwich Albion in December. After a loan spell with Plymouth Argyle in 1973-74, he left at the end of the season to join Tranmere Rovers and later played in the United States, Canada, Belgium and Holland, eventually settling in Maastricht where he met his Dutch wife and set up a painting business.

John McLaughlin (5 unused substitute)

A local youngster, McLaughlin had made his debut in 1969-70 and played thirty league matches in midfield in 1970-71 before losing his place to Brian Hall. By 1972-73 he had slipped down the pecking order and was an unused substitute in the league games at Crystal Palace and Norwich, as well as for both legs of the UEFA Cup tie with AEK Athens and home leg against Dynamo Berlin. After a spell on loan with Portsmouth in 1975-76 he was forced to quit full time playing due to a knee injury but did go on to play part time with South Liverpool and Barrow.

Derek Brownbill (3 unused substitute)

A youth system product, attacking midfielder Brownbill was on the bench for both legs of the UEFA Cup semi-final against Tottenham as well as the home leg of the quarter-final against Dynamo Dresden. The following season he made his only appearance for the club, away to Birmingham City before being transferred to Port Vale in February 1975. He later played in the United States before returning to England to play non-league football and he has most recently been director of football at Warrington Town, a position he left in 2009.

Peter Spiring (2 unused substitute)

A forward signed the day before deadline day from Bristol City for £60,000, an impressive reserve team debut earned him a place on the bench for the home game with Tottenham on 31st March. He was unable to be on the bench for UEFA Cup games, having signed after the European deadline and made the bench for just one more First Division game, away to Coventry on 17th April. He never made the grade at Anfield, being an unused substitute on just two more occasions, the second of which was at Wembley in the 1974 Charity Shield. Soon after this he signed for Luton town and later played for Hereford United. His son Reuben went on to play professional cricket for Worcestershire.

Grahame Lloyd (1 unused substitute)

Keeper Lloyd deputised on the bench for the injured Frank Lane in the away leg of the UEFA Cup with Dynamo Berlin. He never made a first team appearance for the Reds and in 1974 was signed by Ian St John for Motherwell as their back-up keeper. He followed St John to Portsmouth, playing 73 games in the Second and Third Divisions between 1975 and 1977.

Hughie McAuley (1 unused substitute)

Signed as a professional in 1970, McAuley was a reserves regular but failed to make the breakthrough at Anfield, the closest he came to action being when he was an unused substitute in the home leg of the UEFA Cup second-round tie against AEK Athens. He later played for Tranmere Rovers, Plymouth Argyle, Carlisle United, Charlton Athletic and Formby before returning to Anfield in 1990 working in youth development, winning the FA Youth Cup in 1996. After six years as reserve manager, he left in 2009 and now runs a football academy.

Appendix 2. The Manager and Backroom Staff

Bill Shankly

After playing for Carlisle United and Preston North End, Shankly went back to Carlisle to begin his management career in 1949. For the next ten years he enjoyed steady but not spectacular progress at Brunton Park, Grimsby Town, Workington and Huddersfield Town, always maintaining that he would achieve great things at a big club. Liverpool, he believed, matched his ambitions but after joining in December 1959 he had a tough battle to convince the directors to fund the purchases that would take Liverpool out of the Second Division. After winning that battle he brought Liverpool two titles in three years, as well as the club's first FA Cup triumph. The 1972-73 season saw the coming together of his second great side that he had been building since February 1970, but there would be disappointment in the following season's European Cup when the Reds were beaten home and away by Red Star Belgrade. After guiding the club to a second FA Cup triumph he sensationally quit as manager in July 1974, the reasons for which have never been fully discovered. During the next seven years he continued to follow Liverpool, being a guest at all the European finals, but he was also often to be seen at Everton and Tranmere. At the age of just 67, he died in Broadgreen Hospital on 29th September 1981 after suffering a second heart attack within a week.

Bob Paisley

After retiring from playing in 1954, following fifteen years with the club, Paisley became a physio and reserve team trainer. In 1957 he became first team coach after Phil Taylor's appointment as manager, and when Bill Shankly arrived two years later, Paisley retained the role. After being Shankly's trusted lieutenant for over a decade, he was formally appointed assistant manager in 1971 and, when Shankly retired in 1974, he became manager, taking the club on to even greater glory, winning six titles, three European Cups, three League Cups and a UEFA Cup in six years. After retiring in 1983 he remained on the board until 1992, as well as acting in an advisory role to Kenny Dalglish in 1985-86. On 14th February 1996, Paisley died after a long battle with Alzheimer's Disease.

Joe Fagan

Originally from Kirkdale but a player with Manchester City, Fagan went into management with Lancashire Combination side Nelson in 1951, later becoming assistant to Harry Catterick at Rochdale. In 1958 he came to Liverpool as a coach, taking over as reserve team trainer in the 1960s and becoming first team trainer in 1971. In 1972-73 he was effectively third in command, acting as a go-between for players and manager, the one they could turn to if they had a problem for a friendly arm-around-the-shoulder. Fagan stepped up to assistant manager after Shankly retired and took over the managerial reins in 1983, leading the club to an unprecedented Treble in his first season. In 1985, what should have been a glorious end to his career was overshadowed by Heysel. He continued to live in the Anfield area until his death in 2001.

Reuben Bennett

A former goalkeeper with Hull City, Queen of the South, Dundee and Elgin City, Bennett managed Ayr United and was trainer at Motherwell and Third Lanark before being brought to Anfield by Phil Taylor in the late 1950s. Like Paisley and Fagan, he was retained by Shankly after his arrival in 1959 and, as a fitness fanatic, was responsible for maintaining the players' physical condition. Time and time again during 1972-73, this was to prove vital as the Reds played 66 games and rarely tired, scoring several late goals. By 1972-73, with Ronnie Moran also involved in the fitness side, Bennett was further entrusted with the role of spying on Liverpool's European opponents along with Bob Paisley, although red tape and weather stopped them checking out the East German opposition. Bennett remained at Anfield as one of the groundstaff until his death in 1989.

Ronnie Moran

A no-nonsense left back when Shankly arrived as manager, Moran overcame injuries to remain in the side for the 1961-62 promotion campaign and 1963-64 title success. Chris Lawler's promotion to the first team meant he spent the whole of 1964-65 in the reserves but he did come into the side for both legs of the European Cup semi-final against Inter Milan after Gerry Byrne had broken his collarbone in the FA Cup final. Moran's total commitment no matter what the game led to Shankly offering him a place on the coaching staff, and in 1972-73 he was trainer of the reserve side, leading them to Central League success. After Shankly retired, he moved up to a coaching role with the first team where he remained until 1998, twice filling in as caretaker-manager in the early 1990s when Kenny Dalglish resigned and Graeme Souness had heart surgery. He had a testimonial in 2000 against Celtic and has lived in retirement in Crosby since, making occasional local media appearances. His grandson Ian Johnson played two games for Wigan Athletic in the Football League Trophy in 2001-02 before moving into the local non-league scene, playing for Marine, Burscough, AFC Liverpool and Bootle.

Tom Saunders

Liverpool's youth development officer, former headmaster Tom had joined the club in 1968 and took on a full-time role in 1970. Such was his success in the position that at the end of 1972-73, Bill Shankly said: 'The flow of youth talent is becoming a torrent now'.[101] Saunders went on to become Liverpool's chief European spy, compiling dossiers on opponents, and remained in his youth development role until 1986. He returned to the club as a director in 1993, remaining on the board until his death in 2001.

Endnotes

1   Daily Post 26th March 1971
2   Daily Post 12th July 1972
3   Liverpool Echo 11th July 1972
4   Liverpool Echo 18th July 1972
5   Liverpool Echo 22nd July 1972.
6   Liverpool Echo 3rd August 1972
7   Liverpool Echo 5th August 1972
8   Liverpool Echo pre-season special 12th August 1972
9   Liverpool Echo 7th August 1972
10   Daily Post 13th July 1972
11   Tommy Smith column, Liverpool Echo 9th September 1972.
12   Daily Post 5th September 1972
13   Daily Post 9th September 1972
14   Liverpool Echo 11th September 1972
15   Liverpool Echo 16th September 1972
16   Liverpool Echo 16th September 1972
17   Liverpool Echo 25th September 1972
18   Liverpool Echo 27th September 1972
19   Liverpool Echo 16th October 1972
20   Daily Post 6th October 1972
21   League Football 2nd December 1972
22   Tommy Smith column, Liverpool Echo 7th October 1972
23   Daily Post 24th October 1972
24   League Football 30th December 1972
25   Tommy Smith: Anfield Iron p285
26   League Football 30th December 1972
27   Daily Post 18th September 1972
28   Daily Post 28th September 1972
29   Tommy Smith Column, Liverpool Echo 7th October 1972
30   Tommy Smith Column, Liverpool Echo 14th October 1972
31   Interview with author 5th April 2012
32   Interview with author 5th April 2012
33   Phil Thompson: Stand Up Pinnochio, Trinity Mirror 2005
34   Daily Post 10th November 1972
35   Liverpool Echo 10th November 1972
36   Daily Post 13th November 1972
37   Daily Post 18th November 1972
38   Tommy Smith column Liverpool Echo 9th December 1972
39   Liverpool Echo 9th December 1972
40   Daily Post 4th November 1972
41   Derek Dougan column Liverpool Echo 5th January 1972
42   Liverpool Echo 1st January 1972
43   Liverpool Echo 6th January 1973
44   Interview with author 5th April 2012
45   Liverpool Echo 6th January 1973
46   Match Programme, West Ham United v Liverpool 6th January 1973.

47 Liverpool Echo 20th January 1973
48 Liverpool Echo, 20th January 1973
49 Daily Post 22nd January 1973
50 Liverpool Echo 3rd February 1973
51 Tommy Smith column Liverpool Echo 10th February 1973
52 Interview with author 5th April 1973
53 Daily Post 26th February 1973
54 Interview with author 5th April 2012
55 Liverpool Echo 9th December 1972
56 Liverpool Echo 12th December 1972
57 Daily Post 27th October 1972
58 Tommy Smith column Liverpool Echo 31st March 1973
59 Daily Post 6th March 1973
60 Daily Post 8th March 1973
61 Liverpool Echo 10th March 1973
62 Liverpool Echo 10th March 1973
63 Daily Post 20th March 1973
64 Tommy Smith Anfield Iron p290
65 Liverpool Echo 2nd April 1973
66 Liverpool Echo 24th March 1973
67 Liverpool Echo 3rd April 1973
68 Daily Post 17th April 1973
69 Daily Post 17th April 1973
70 Daily Post 19th April 1973
71 Daily Post 21st April 1973
72 Tommy Smith column, Liverpool Echo 28th April 1973
73 Daily Post 26th April 1973
74 Daily Post 26th April 1973
75 Tommy Smith column Liverpool Echo 7th April 1973
76 Liverpool Echo 11th April 1973
77 Liverpool Echo 25th April 1978
78 Tommy Smith Anfield Iron p286
79 Derek Dohren Ghost on the Wall The Authorised Biography of Roy Evans Mainstream Publishing 2004
80 Interview with author 5th April 1973
81 Interview with author 5th April 2012
82 Daily Post 30th April 1973
83 Rogan Taylor & Andre Ward: Three Sides of the Mersey. Robson Books 1993
84 Liverpool Echo 3rd May 1973
85 Liverpool Echo special 5th May 1973
86 Match Programme Liverpool v Leeds 23rd April 1973
87 Daily Post 1st May 1973
88 Personal conversation between Peter Etherington and the author 23rd March 2012
89 Daily Post 4th May 1973
90 Liverpool Echo 5th May 1973
91 Email to author 20th March 1973
92 Tommy Smith Anfield Iron p294
93 Tommy Smith My Anfield Secrets p143
94 Liverpool Echo 23rd May1973
95 Daily Post 23rd May 1973
96 Interview with author 5th April 2012
97 Liverpool Echo 24th May 1973
98 Liverpool Echo 24th May 1973
99 Daily Post 24th April 1973
100 Interview with author 5th April 1973
101 Daily Post 27th May 1973

About the Author

Born in 1971, Steven Horton's first Liverpool game was Tommy Smith's testimonial in 1977 and he has been a Kop season ticket holder since 1986, also attending most away matches at home and abroad.

He started writing in the early 1990s by contributing to Liverpool fanzines and since the internet revolution has regularly written match reports, historical narratives and opinion pieces for both fanzines and websites. He has also been a member of the *Liverpool Echo's* 'fans jury' and written for *The Times*.

Although he has written four local history books to date, this is his first Liverpool FC related book to be published and more are in the pipeline, the next one being a book about the club's foreign tours to be published by Vertical Editions in 2013.